The Mary Magdalene Cover-Up

The Mary Magdalene Cover-Up

The Sources Behind the Myth

ESTHER DE BOER

TRANSLATED BY JOHN BOWDEN

t&t clark

Published by T&T Clark
A Continuum imprint
The Tower Building, 11 York Road, London SE1 7NX
80 Maiden Lane, Suite 704, New York, NY 10038

www.continuumbooks.com

Translated by John Bowden from the Dutch *De geliefde discipel. Vroegchristelijke teksten over Maria Magdalena* by Esther de Boer, published 2006 by Uitgeverij Meinema, Zoetermeer (slightly revised).

Copyright © 2006 Uitgeverij Meinema, Zoetermeer

First published in English by T&T Clark 2007
Translation copyright © 2007 John Bowden

British Library Cataloguing-in-Publication Data
A catalogue record for this book is available from the British Library

ISBN-10: 0-567-03223-X (hardback)
ISBN-10: 0-567-03182-9 (paperback)
ISBN-13: 978-0-567-03223-2 (hardback)
ISBN-13: 978-0-567-03182-2 (paperback)

Typeset by Kenneth Burnley, Wirral, Cheshire.
Printed on acid-free paper in Great Britain by MPG Books Ltd, Bodmin, Cornwall

Contents

What This Book is About

This book has been written in response to the many portraits of Mary Magdalene which have been circulating recently. It contains an anthology of early Christian texts about Mary Magdalene and on the basis of these texts it sketches a historically reliable portrait of her. If Mary Magdalene is seen within the historical context of early Christianity, she proves to be surprisingly relevant to a new form of Christian faith.

I referred to a number of the texts presented here in my book *Mary Magdalene: Beyond the Myth* (London: SCM Press 1997) in which I described my first quest for Mary. In a sense this anthology is a sequel. My second book, *The Gospel of Mary. Listening to the Beloved Disciple* (London and New York: Continuum International 2005), contained a detailed investigation of Mary Magdalene in five of these texts: the Gospel of Mary and the four New Testament Gospels. In the present book the explanations of these Gospels are a summary of the conclusions drawn there. For the sake of readability I have not always referred to the other studies that I have used for this book: they are listed in the Bibliography. Full publication details of all works quoted and mentioned are also to be found in the Bibliography.

The translations from the early Christian texts are from the languages in which the texts have been preserved: Latin, Greek and Coptic. The translations of the biblical texts have been taken, with some minor revisions, from the New Revised Standard Version (NRSV); I have provided them with notes. For biblical names and places I have kept to the renderings of the NRSV. When church fathers or other authors quote from the scripture of their time I do not follow the NRSV translation. The translations of several other texts are by distinguished scholars. I have gratefully made use of their work. When no reference has been made the translations are mine.

My father-in-law Jan Spoelstra proved a great support in reading Greek and Latin texts of which there is as yet no translation and in discussing difficult passages. Dr R. Roukema read some chapters of the book and made valuable comments on them; I could also turn to him with questions about the church fathers. The final text of this book was read through critically by Margreet Spoelstra and Anneke Havermans. I am grateful to all these for their help.

I hope that this book will help to clarify the various ideas about Mary Magdalene.

Esther de Boer
Berg en Terblijt, 8 March 2006

Chapter 1

The Mary Magdalene Cover-Up

'Has he chosen her above us?' Peter asks his fellow-disciples in despair. Levi replies in the affirmative: 'He loved her more than us.' Jesus' two disciples are talking about Jesus and Mary Magdalene. These words do not occur in the New Testament but in the Gospel of Mary (Magdalene). Part of the Gospel of Mary was first found in 1896; until then no one knew of such a Gospel. Gospels were always attributed to men: to Mark, Matthew, Luke, John, Philip, Peter and Judas. Now suddenly a Gospel is attributed to a woman. What kind of woman could she be?

Novels

The Gospel of Mary aroused interest world-wide in Mary Magdalene and her role in the origin of Christianity. The internationally known Swedish writer Marianne Fredriksson writes in the preface to her novel *According to Mary Magdalene*:

> Supposing there had been a free, clear-thinking person among his disciples, someone who was open, unprejudiced, and acquainted with both Jewish and Greek thinking. Briefly, someone who had 'ears to listen'. One day I was looking for something in the *Nag Hammadi Library* and happened to come upon the fragment that remains of the gospel of Mary Magdalene. In it she accounts for what Jesus said in personal conversations with her – among them: 'Make no rules of life on this which I have revealed to you. Write no laws as the law-makers do.' And it struck me: here is perhaps someone with ears to listen, eyes to see, and a mind to understand. The disciple whom Jesus loved the most. And a woman with no power to influence. That was how my Mary Magdalene was born. (p. viii)

Marianne Fredriksson describes how years after the death of Jesus, Mary Magdalene, Peter and Paul had great difficulty in expressing precisely what Jesus meant for them. They proved to have very different views. In this way Fredriksson wants to object, on the basis of her view of the diversity of early Christianity, to what in her eyes is the terrible claim by the later churches to possess the only truth. Jesus' warning against rules and laws in the Gospel of Mary are central to her description of Mary Magdalene's recollections, but other aspects of that Gospel are also woven into her novel. Thus Mary Magdalene's testimony to her encounter with the risen Lord and Peter's anger at her words come straight out of the Gospel of Mary.

In his novel *The Da Vinci Code*, the American author Dan Brown also bases himself on the Gospel of Mary. When the main characters, Professor Langdon and Sophie Neveu, are in Sir Leigh Teabing's library, Teabing shows them his collection of Gnostic writings and especially points to a passage from the Gospel of Mary in which Peter and Levi are discussing the question whether or not one has to listen to a woman. Teabing and Sophie have a discussion:

'The woman they are speaking of,' Teabing explained, 'is Mary Magdalene. Peter is jealous of her.'

'Because Jesus preferred Mary?'

'Not only that. The stakes were far greater than mere affection. At this point in the gospels, Jesus suspects He will soon be captured and crucified. So He gives Mary Magdalene instructions on how to carry on His Church after He is gone. As a result, Peter expresses his discontent over playing second fiddle to a woman. I daresay Peter was something of a sexist.'

Sophie was trying to keep up. 'This is Saint Peter. The rock on which Jesus built His Church.'

'The same, except for one catch. According to these unaltered gospels, it was not *Peter* to whom Christ gave directions with which to establish the Christian Church. It was *Mary Magdalene*.'

Sophie looked at him. 'You're saying the Christian Church was to be carried on by a *woman*?'

'That was the plan. Jesus was the original feminist. He intended for the future of His Church to be in the hands of Mary Magdalene.' (pp. 333–34)

Although Dan Brown refers explicitly to the Gospel of Mary in this passage and to the teaching of Mary that it contains, he does not allow her to say anything in his book. In Dan Brown's plot Mary Magdalene is important only as a female body. She is the sexual partner of Jesus and the one who bears his child. That is said to be her most important contribution to Christian faith, because according to Brown in this way she shows Jesus' humanity. Moreover, a sexual relationship on the part of Jesus would break the rule of obligatory celibacy laid down by the church and above all damage the proclamation that Jesus is divine. That is why in Brown's plot the truth about Jesus and Mary Magdalene has been deliberately covered up by the church:

> 'Behold,' Teabing proclaimed, 'the greatest cover-up in human history. Not only was Jesus married, but He was a father. My dear, Mary Magdalene was the Holy Vessel. She was the chalice that bore the royal bloodline of Jesus Christ. She was the womb that bore the true lineage, and the vine from which the sacred fruit sprang forth!' (p. 336)

By contrast, in the Gospel of Mary Jesus is the saviour who comes from God and Mary is explicitly valued for her teaching. The Gospel of Mary is also extremely critical of Peter's attempt to reduce Mary's role to that of the silent woman in the background who is said to have been loved more by Jesus than his other women followers.

In recent years countless publications on Mary Magdalene have appeared which contain very different pictures of her. The classical, legendary picture of Mary Magdalene portrays her above all as a reformed prostitute and a penitent sinner. Alongside this there is a more esoteric tendency which sees Mary Magdalene as an initiate. Moreover, an increasing amount of literature has appeared in which Mary Magdalene appears as the wife of Jesus and a symbol of the feminine. This last view has recently attracted a great deal of attention through the description of Mary Magdalene in *The Da Vinci Code*. Mary Magdalene has again become topical above all because of this international best-seller.

What is fact and what is fiction in all these views of her? That is the question that people keep asking. How do the various views about Mary Magdalene relate to what the early sources say about her? And what do the sources show about her role in the origin of Christianity?

Myth and esotericism

The mythical current by which Dan Brown was inspired in *The Da Vinci Code* explicitly refers to historical sources. But it is presupposed that these sources present the truth in a veiled way and that the true significance of Mary Magdalene has deliberately been forced into the background. It is said that for centuries these texts and the imagery of Mary Magdalene have been interpreted wrongly and assimilated to the teaching of the church. It is necessary to search behind the texts and the imagery for the hidden meaning that authors and artists wanted consciously or unconsciously to pass on. The myths about the gods and goddesses which were driven out of Western culture by the emphasis on the one God in Jewish and Christian doctrine are said to be an important help here. On the basis of this quest, Margaret Starbird in particular says that Mary Magdalene was not a common prostitute but a prostitute priestess and as such involved in the worship of fertility gods. She says that Mary Magdalene entered into a sacred marriage with Jesus and supported him in his work as a partner on an equal footing. Starbird calls her the lost goddess of Christian belief. She gives her an important place in Christian doctrine as the bride of Christ. In Starbird's eyes, Western culture has been too long dominated by the male principle. This dominance has produced violence and devastation. The re-evaluation of the feminine principle of love and bonding can bring wholeness again.

The more esoteric current values Mary Magdalene specifically for her knowledge. According to this view, Mary is an initiate of the highest, seventh, degree. Like John, she has gone through the first six stages of initiation in many lives. However, in contrast to John she attained the seventh initiation, which is given from above, during her lifetime with Jesus. In my country, the Netherlands, authors like Jakob Slavenburg, Hans Stolp and Paul van Oyen write about her in these terms. Comparable to their views on Mary Magdalene are those of Jean-Yves Leloup, who is more internationally known. In this current Mary Magdalene is the symbol of the new Christianity which stands on a spiritually higher level than the Christianity of Peter and Paul. The self-knowledge and personal growth of the believer, the initiate, occupy a central role. This current also makes use of historical sources, but they are not valued for their historical contribution. The ancient writings are above all sources for one's own spiritual development, and the interpretation of the texts is true if it promotes inner growth.

Legend

The classic image of Mary Magdalene as prostitute and converted sinner is based above all on legends. Mary Magdalene is said to be the sinner who anointed Jesus' feet, was forgiven by him, converted and changed into one of his most ardent followers. In France, Mary Magdalene is a national heroine because this penitent sinner is said to have brought the Christian faith to France. She is also said to have done penance for her life as a prostitute for thirty years in a cave in St Baume in Provence which can still be visited.

This image of Mary Magdalene is not based on historical sources, because according to this view the sources have little or nothing to say about her. It is said that the classical image of Mary Magdalene may not be historical, but it is the most valuable image of her, because the image of the penitent prostitute shows that however low sinners may have fallen, they can climb up and become believers with an ardent love of the Lord. This image of Mary Magdalene has long been venerated in the Roman Catholic tradition. The penitent sinner has still regularly been defended above all in France, as recently by Régis Burnet, who discusses present-day views of Mary Magdalene and concludes that they have little to offer for the faith.

According to Burnet, the images of Mary Magdalene down the centuries are a reflection of the society in which they were formed. Present-day images show above all the leaning towards perfection in our society. Mary Magdalene is perfect in her love for Jesus, perfect in her spiritual initiation. Over against this the message of Mary Magdalene as sinner is meant to emphasize the great value of grace. Burnet concludes his book with these memorable words about the penitent Mary Magdalene:

> The story of her life proclaims that 'all is grace'; individuals cannot be the sum of their faults and weaknesses, they are not trapped in their past, their future accords with their hope. Why should we reduce this Mary Magdalene to the suppression of the feminine when she is also an image of human liberation? (p. 118)

Attractive though this may sound, here Burnet is forgetting one aspect that is central in the classical tradition about Mary Magdalene. In this tradition she is not just a penitent sinner but a penitent prostitute.

This image has strengthened the double morality which was already present in our culture and the antipathy to autonomous female sexuality.

That this image can lead to disastrous behaviour is evident from the film *The Magdalene Sisters*, which is based on fact. The film shows how in the twentieth century unmarried mothers and extremely attractive girls were shut up in convents to do penance for the rest of their lives in the name of Mary Magdalene. They had to wash liturgical garments from morning till night. Testimonies about this show they were also subjected to sexual abuse in these convents.

This book

What, then, can be an inspiring image of Mary Magdalene? Anyone who is looking for the significance of a historical figure first of all looks at the historical sources and tries to understand them in their own context. From the survey I have just given it proves that the early Christian sources about Mary Magdalene were used and evaluated in very different ways. Focused on the Gospel of Mary, the differences emerge as follows:

For the mythical current around Margaret Starbird, which sees Mary Magdalene as the bride of Jesus, the discovery of the Gospel of Mary is of great importance because it mentions the exclusive love of Jesus for Mary Magdalene.

The esoteric current is above all interested in the knowledge that the Gospel of Mary communicates. This is not interpreted against the background of the second century, the century from which it comes, but against that of present-day esoteric tradition.

For the legendary current, the Gospel of Mary is an untrustworthy source because it is said to belong to the Gnostic movement which was fought against by the early church.

This book sets out to offer a historical survey of the early sources about Mary Magdalene. It contains an anthology of all kinds of early Christian texts, some of which appear in English for the first time. The texts are both biblical and non-biblical, and are by known and unknown early Christian writers. From them it becomes clear how Mary Magdalene was described and evaluated in the early centuries of our era, from the first century, the time when she lived, to the sixth century, when the image of her became fixed. This is also the time when 'the church tradition' came into being out of great diversity. The book also looks at the forces which determined the formation of the image of Mary Magdalene and the discussion of the position of women at that time. The texts have been arranged thematically and provided with a brief explanation of their historical context.

On the basis of which early sources was Mary Magdalene seen as a converted prostitute, as Jesus' beloved and as a perfect initiate, and is that right? The next chapter is about that. In the following chapters, Mary Magdalene appears as a disciple of Jesus, a witness and an apostle. Then come the reactions of the early church fathers to these images. Finally there are two sermons, each from the sixth century and each written by a Gregory. For centuries one view dominated the history of Western culture at the expense of the other, with all the consequences. The last chapter offers a retrospect. What was at issue in the formation of the early Christian images of Mary? What does a historically reliable portrait of her look like? And what does that mean for Christian belief?

Chapter 2

Who was Mary Magdalene?

In her novel *According to Mary Magdalene*, Marianne Fredriksson describes the meeting between Mary the mother of Jesus and her namesake Mary of Magdala. Jesus' mother greets her with the words, 'Are you the whore my son lives with?' (p. 138). The whole popular image of Mary Magdalene is contained in this one sentence. For centuries the image of Mary Magdalene as a prostitute has been commonplace. Clearly she would have been a former prostitute, since she is said to have changed her way of life under the impact of Jesus. In addition, the image of Mary Magdalene as a friend and beloved of Jesus is already centuries old.

At present both these images are being vigorously defended and vigorously disputed. For example, in Dan Brown's thriller *The Da Vinci Code* the main female character asks about the figure next to Jesus in Leonardo Da Vinci's painting of the Last Supper: 'Who is she?'

'That, my dear,' Teabing replied, 'is Mary Magdalene.'
Sophie turned. 'The prostitute?'
Teabing drew a short breath, as if the word had injured him personally. 'Magdalene was no such thing. That unfortunate misconception is the legacy of a smear campaign launched by the early Church. The Church needed to defame Mary Magdalene in order to cover up her dangerous secret – her role as the Holy Grail'. (p. 328)

The important secret in *The Da Vinci Code* is the marriage between Jesus and Mary Magdalene and the blood-line that they produce. A daughter is born from their relationship. That is a shocking notion for believers who see sexuality as a sin. The thought of a married Jesus is also unacceptable for a church which requires its priests and religious to go through life unmarried. The image of Jesus as a married man is through it.' 5 Accordingly, though Jesus loved Martha and her sister and Lazarus, after having heard that Lazarus was ill, he stayed two days longer in the place where he was. *[The story of the death and resurrection of Lazarus follows here.]*

55 Now the Passover of the Jews was near, and many went up from the country to Jerusalem before the Passover to purify themselves. 56 They were looking for Jesus and were asking one another as they stood in the temple, 'What do you think? Surely he will not come to the festival, will he?' 57 Now the chief priests and the Pharisees had given orders that anyone who knew where Jesus was should let them know, so that they might arrest him.

12.1 Six days before the Passover Jesus came to Bethany, the home of Lazarus, whom he had raised from the dead. 2 There they gave a dinner for him. Martha served, and Lazarus was one of those at the table with him. 3 Mary took a pound of costly ointment made of pure nard, anointed Jesus' feet, and wiped them with her hair. The house was filled with the fragrance of the ointment. 4 But Judas Iscariot, one of his disciples (the one who was about to betray him), said, 5 'Why was this ointment not sold for three hundred denarii and the money given to the poor?' (6 He said this not because he cared about the poor, but because he was a thief; he kept the common purse and used to steal what was put into it.) 7 Jesus said, 'Leave her alone. She bought it so that she might keep it for the day of my burial. 8 You always have the poor with you, but you do not always have me.'

9 When the great crowd of the Jews learned that he was there, they came not only because of Jesus but also to see Lazarus, whom he had raised from the dead. 10 So the chief priests planned to put Lazarus to death as well, 11 since it was on account of him that many of the Jews were deserting and were believing in Jesus.

Explanation

Nothing is known from the first-century sources about the life of Mary Magdalene before she met Jesus. Not that much is known about the other disciples. Still, we are told, for example, that Peter was a fisherman from Capernaum, that he had a father and a brother. It also appears that he was married and had a mother-in-law. From the early sources all we know about the background of Mary Magdalene is her name: Mary the Magdalene. In addition, Luke says that she had seven demons driven out of her (Luke 8.2). This sparse information greatly stimulated people's imagination. Thus a past for Mary Magdalene came into being, constructed of elements of biblical narratives about her namesake Mary from Bethany, close to Jerusalem. Stories about anonymous women also formed a source of inspiration for the formation of a picture of Mary Magdalene's past. However, those who do not want to be guided by the imagination must maintain that the early sources tell us virtually nothing about Mary Magdalene's background.

The most probable significance of the addition 'the Magdalene' is that Mary came from Magdala. In the New Testament she is called 'the Magdalene' to distinguish her from the many other Maries who appear in the stories about Jesus. It is striking that these other Maries are often called by their family names, like Mary the mother of Jesus, Mary the sister of Martha and Lazarus and Mary the mother of James. Perhaps none of the members of Mary Magdalene's family were known to Jesus' followers. Perhaps it was not her family which determined who she was, but her town. Magdala was a market town and later also a fortified town on the west shore of the Sea of Galilee, about six miles from Capernaum, where Jesus lived. The town lay on a well-known trade route, and people from all kinds of different backgrounds could meet there. Magdala was known for its salted fish, abundant fruit and the fabric dyed there. Anyone going from Nazareth, where Jesus grew up, to Capernaum, where he lived, almost certainly went through Magdala. So we can assume that Jesus must have been there.

In addition to this literal interpretation of the addition 'the Magdalene' there is also a figurative one. Just as Jesus gave Simon the nickname Peter (rock), so he is said to have given Mary the nickname 'the Magdalene'. The church father Jerome relates this in the fourth century. 'Migdal' means 'tower', so Mary's nickname 'the Magdalene' would mean 'strengthened with towers'. She is said to have received this name 'because of her earnestness and the power of her faith'.[12] This meaning has been almost completely lost. If you look up 'Magdalene' in a modern English dictionary you will find quite a different interpretation. 'Magdalene' means 'prostitute'. Over the centuries this image of Mary has become so established that it is almost impossible not to think of it.

In the Western church, the conviction arose that the anonymous sinner of Luke 7.36-50 was none other than Mary Magdalene. John relates that the woman who anointed Jesus' feet was called Mary (John 11.2), and in direct connection with the story of the sinner who anointed Jesus Luke names Mary Magdalene as the one from whom seven demons were driven out (Luke 8.2). The demons have been seen as sins. On the basis of the two stories the notion has been defended that the woman who did the anointing was Mary, indeed Mary Magdalene. Luke's story is said to indicate that to betray him to them. 11 When they heard it, they were greatly pleased, and promised to give him money. So he began to look for an opportunity to betray him.

Fragments from the Gospel of Philip[13]

58.25–59.19 All who are begotten in the world are begotten in a natural way, and the others [are nourished] from [the place] whence they have been born. It is from being promised to the heavenly place that man [receives] nourishment.

[. . .] him from the mouth. [And had] the word gone out from that place it would be nourished from the mouth and it would become perfect. For it is by a kiss that the perfect conceive and give birth. For this reason we also kiss one another. We receive conception from the grace which is in one another.

There were three who always walked with the Lord: Mary his mother and her sister and the Magdalene, the one who was called his companion. His sister and his mother and his companion were each a Mary.

'The Father' and 'the Son' are single names, 'the holy spirit' is a double name. For they are everywhere: they are above, they are below; as they are in the concealed, they are in the revealed. The holy spirit is in the revealed: it is below. It is in the concealed: it is above.

63.32–64.9 As for the Wisdom who is called 'the barren', she is the mother [of the] angels. And the companion of the [. . .] Mary Magdalene. [. . . loved] her more than [all] the disciples and [used to] kiss her [often] on her [. . .]. The rest of [the disciples . . .]. They said to him, 'Why do you love her more than all of us?' The saviour answered and said to them, 'Why do I not love you like her?' When a blind man and one who sees are both together in darkness, they are no different from one another. When the light comes, then he who sees will see the light, and he who is blind will remain in darkness.

64.31–66.6 Great is the mystery of marriage! For [without] it the world would [not exist]. Now the existence of [the world . . .], and the existence [. . . marriage]. Think of the [. . . relationship], for it possesses [. . .] power. Its image consists of a [defilement].

The forms of evil spirit include male ones and female ones. The males are they that unite with the souls which inhabit a female form, but the females are they which are mingled with those in a male form, through one who was disobedient. And none shall be able to escape them since they detain him if he does not receive a male power or a female power, the bridegroom and the bride. One receives them from the mirrored bridal chamber.

When the wanton women see a male sitting alone, they leap down on him and play with him and defile him. So also the lecherous men, when they see a beautiful woman sitting alone, they persuade her and compel her, wishing to defile her. But if they see the man and his wife sitting beside one another, the female cannot come in to the man, nor can the male come in to the woman. So if the image and the angel are united with one another, neither can any venture to go in to the man or the woman.

He who comes out of the world and (so) can no longer be detained on the grounds that he was in the world evidently is above the desire of the [. . .] and fear. He is master over . . .]. He is superior to envy. If [. . .] comes, they seize him and throttle [him]. And how will [this one] be able to escape the [great . . .] powers? How will he be able to [. . .] There are some [who say], 'We are faithful,' in order that [. . . the unclean spirits] and the demons. For if they had the holy spirit, no unclean spirit would cleave to them. Fear not the flesh nor love it. If you (sg.) fear it, it will gain mastery over you. If you love it, it will swallow and paralyze you.

Explanation

There is nothing in the first-century sources about a possible marriage of Jesus. Nor is there any mention of his wife or his in-laws. On the basis of this it seems probable that he was unmarried. One could also say that it was so logical that he was married and so unimportant that his marriage is not mentioned. Some think that the sources do not mention his wife and his in-laws for security reasons. The marriage in Cana in John 2 is said to be a concealed allusion to Jesus' marriage. The supposition that Jesus and Mary were married is based above all on the Jewish religious obligation to produce offspring. It is said that as a Jewish man, Jesus could not have avoided this. The question immediately arises what the arguments are for assuming that this wife was Mary Magdalene. Couldn't it have been a woman of whom we know nothing? Moreover there are examples of Jewish men of this time who remained unmarried for religious reasons, for example prophets, or men who devoted themselves wholly to the study of scripture.

Reference is made to the story in John 20.1-18 about the moving quest of Mary Magdalene for the dead body of Jesus and her recognition of the living Lord as an argument for a relationship of love between Jesus and Mary Magdalene. An erotic tension between the two is said to arise from this story, and hidden references are seen in it, particularly to the biblical love song *par excellence*, the Song of Songs. John's story is indeed about the relationship between Jesus and Mary Magdalene; it is also about love, but not of love between lovers. It is about the love between disciple and teacher.

The anointing of Jesus by a woman above all also plays a role in the present-day supposition of a love relationship between Jesus and Mary Magdalene. Just as the two stories about the anointing of Jesus' feet are important for the image of Mary Magdalene as a reformed prostitute, so the two stories about the anointing of his head are important for the conviction that Mary Magdalene was Jesus' wife. However, this happens in an unexpected context.

In her book *The Woman with the Alabaster Jar*, Margaret Starbird writes about the rite of the *hieros gamos* (sacred marriage), an old fertility rite:

> The anointing of the head had erotic significance, the head being symbolic of the phallus 'anointed' by the woman for penetration during the physical consummation of marriage. The chosen bridegroom was anointed by the royal priestess, the surrogate of the Goddess. (p. 36)

With this rite the bridegroom took on the status of king and was called the 'anointed'. In some traditions this 'anointed' then gave his life in the course of the fertility ritual so that the harvest and prosperity should be abundant. Starbird writes: 'If Judas was a fundamentalist Zealot "zealous for the Law", he would have been appalled to see Jesus willingly assume the role of the sacrificed pagan fertility/sun god' (p. 45).

Starbird's book and others are certainly attractive literature. They too provide a great stimulus for the imagination. However, if we read the New Testament Gospels there is nothing to indicate Jesus' involvement in a fertility religion. According to these Gospels, Jesus is not dedicated to a God who gives well-being and prosperity through particular rites. On the contrary, with an appeal to God Jesus represents a lifestyle in which that does not seem appropriate. Think, for example, of these words:

> You have heard that it was said, 'You shall love your neighbour and hate your enemy.' But I say to you, 'Love your enemies and pray for those who persecute you, so that you may be children of your Father in heaven; for he makes his sun rise on the evil and on the good, and sends rain on the righteous and on the unrighteous'. (Matthew 5.43-45; cf. Luke 6.35)

In connection with the anointing of Jesus' head it is much more probable that we should think of the anointing of the heads of prophets and kings in the Old Testament. This showed that they were in the service of

God, the God who in the Old Testament, too, does not want to have anything to do with sacrifices in the sphere of fertility religion. There are countless examples of this; here I shall quote the prophet Micah:

'With what shall I come before the LORD,
and bow myself before God on high?
Shall I come before him with burnt-offerings,
with calves a year old?
Will the LORD be pleased with thousands of rams,
with tens of thousands of rivers of oil?
Shall I give my firstborn for my transgression,
the fruit of my body for the sin of my soul?'
He has told you, O mortal, what is good;
and what does the LORD require of you
but to do justice, and to love kindness,
and to walk humbly with your God? (Micah 6.6-8)

Jesus indeed faithfully went the way of the righteous, to the death which followed. The anonymous woman who anoints Jesus' head reminds him that his way is like that of kings and prophets in the service of God. The words from Psalm 23 can movingly be applied to Jesus at that moment in Bethany, at the table, shortly before Judas was to betray him.

Even though I walk through the darkest valley,
I fear no evil;
for you are with me;
your rod and your staff –
they comfort me.

You prepare a table before me
in the presence of my enemies;
you anoint my head with oil;
my cup overflows.
Surely goodness and mercy shall follow me
all the days of my life,
and I shall dwell in the house of the LORD
my whole life long. (Psalm 23.4-6)

With his own interpretation of the anointing of his head (Mark 14.8, 'She has done what she could; she has anointed my body beforehand for its burial'), Jesus indicates that he will die a violent death and will not be able to be buried with the usual ritual. But 'goodness and mercy shall follow me all the days of my life, and I shall dwell in the house of the LORD my whole life long' (Psalm 23.6).

The special feature of the stories of the anointing of Jesus' head is not the supposed reference to a fertility ritual but the notion that it is a woman who performs the act. The most important names of Jesus are Jesus Christ and Jesus Messiah. Messiah is the Hebrew word and Christos the Greek word for 'anointed'. In the Old Testament stories it is always a male prophet who anoints someone's head. In contrast, according to Mark and Matthew Jesus has himself anointed Messiah and Christ by a woman. That says something about the important role that Jesus attributes to women according to these stories. The later Gospels Luke and John change this prophetic gesture of 'a' woman (it can be any woman) into a feminine gesture of hospitality and love by someone who is known (this specific woman has done it). In Luke the unknown woman of Mark and Matthew has become a well-known sinner from the city and in John Mary is the sister of Jesus' friend Lazarus. It is no longer Jesus' head that is anointed but his feet. We shall see that this is typical of Luke and John, who have difficulty with a 'male' role for women. However, the stories about Jesus' anointing do not say anything about his relationship with Mary Magdalene. She simply does not occur in them.

Those who conjecture a sexual relationship between Jesus and Mary often point to the Gospel of Philip, and are preoccupied above all with one particular sentence:

And the companion of the [. . .] Mary Magdalene. [. . . loved] her more than [all] the disciples and [used to] kiss her [often] on her [. . .]. (GosPhil 63.33-36)

Mostly, in view of the direct context, this sentence is rendered as:

And the companion of the [Lord] is Mary Magdalene. [Christ loved] her more than [all] the disciples and used to kiss her [often] on her [mouth]. (GosPhil 63.33 36)

Indeed this is at any rate clearly about Mary Magdalene. She is Jesus' companion and he often kisses her on the mouth. This certainly must indicate a loving relationship, but what this sentence is about in the context of the Gospel of Philip as a whole is questionable. Many sayings in this Gospel have a deeper meaning. It might perhaps be that the community to which the Gospel of Philip was important in the third century supposed that Jesus and Mary were married. Marriage seems to be given a positive significance in the Gospel of Philip. At the same time, however, marriage is only an earthly reflection of the so-called 'undefiled marriage', which is given a higher value.

The Gospel of Philip begins by assuming that there are male and female demons which manifest themselves, for example, in fear, desire and envy. No one can escape their power except by a male or female force from above which is received in the 'bridal chamber'. It is not clear precisely what this process is. It is like a sacrament or an initiation in which men and women are united with their female or male angels. Later we get the impression that this bridal chamber is the moment when one receives the Holy Spirit. According to the Gospel, the Holy Spirit is a double name, probably the Holy Spirit and Sophia together. Sophia means wisdom and, according to the Gospel of Philip, is the mother of the angels. It seems that as the companion of the Lord Mary Magdalene is his female angel: perhaps Sophia, Wisdom herself, the mother of the angels.

The word 'mouth' is in square brackets because it is somewhat illegible. It is suggested that it can also stand for 'feet', 'cheek' or 'forehead'. It is clear that the power of kisses is of great importance for the Gospel of Philip.

> [...] him from the mouth. [And had] the word gone out from that place it would be nourished from the mouth and it would become perfect. For it is by a kiss that the perfect conceive and give birth. For this reason we also kiss one another. We receive conception from the grace which is in one another. (GosPhil 58.3–59.6)

Here too there is mention of 'mouth' and 'kissing', but whether this is kissing on the mouth is an open question. Kissing each other proves to be an important custom. Through a kiss people pass on grace to one another; it is perhaps comparable to the kiss of peace in the letters of Paul. Perhaps according to the Gospel of Philip through kissing Mary Magdalene the Lord received the power of Lady Wisdom and became pregnant by wisdom? At all events there is a clear distinction between Mary Magdalene and the other disciples. When they ask why Jesus loves Mary Magdalene more than them, his answer seems to be that she sees, whereas the others are (still) blind.

The perfect initiate

Those who see Mary Magdalene as the perfect initiate base themselves above all on writings from the second and third century in which mention is made of Mary Magdalene's great knowledge, as in the Gospel of Philip. The champions of the image of Mary Magdalene as the perfect initiate presuppose that she underwent an initiation of the kind that occurred in the Eastern culture of Jesus' time. Seven transformations are central to this initiation. There is one text from the first century to which appeal is made for this image of Mary Magdalene, namely Luke 8.2. This says that seven demons were driven out of Mary Magdalene. This text is printed below together with other texts from Luke in which Jesus is described as someone who drives out demons. In Luke is the driving out of demons a way of initiation?

Luke 8.1-3

1 Soon afterwards he went on through cities and villages, proclaiming and bringing the good news of the kingdom of God. The twelve were with him, 2 as well as some women who had been cured of evil spirits and infirmities: Mary, called Magdalene, from whom seven demons had gone out, 3 and Joanna, the wife of Herod's steward Chuza, and Susanna, and many other women,[14] who provided for them out of their resources.

Luke 8.26-39

26 Then they arrived at the country of the Gerasenes, which is opposite Galilee. 27 As he stepped out on land, a man of the city who had demons met him. For a long time he had worn no clothes, and he did not live in a house but in the tombs. 28 When he saw Jesus, he fell down before him and shouted at the top of his voice, 'What have you to do with me, Jesus, Son of the Most High God? I beg you, do not torment me' — 29 for Jesus had commanded the unclean spirit to come out of the man. (For many times it had seized him; he was kept under guard and bound with chains and shackles, but he would break the bonds and be driven by the demon into the wilds.) 30 Jesus then asked him, 'What is your name?' He said, 'Legion'; for many demons had entered him. 13 They begged him not to order them to go back into the abyss. 32 Now there on the hill-

ıe herd of swine was feeding; and the demons begged Jesus to let them enter ...ᴗᴄ. So he gave them permission. 33 Then the demons came out of the man and entered the swine, and the herd rushed down the steep bank into the lake and was drowned. 34 When the swineherds saw what had happened, they ran off and told it in the city and in the country. 35 Then people came out to see what had happened, and when they came to Jesus, they found the man from whom the demons had gone sitting at the feet of Jesus, clothed and in his right mind. And they were afraid. 36 Those who had seen it told them how the one who had been possessed by demons had been healed. 37 Then all the people of the surrounding country of the Gerasenes asked Jesus to leave them; for they were seized with great fear. So he got into the boat and returned. 38 The man from whom the demons had gone begged that he might be with him; but Jesus sent him away, saying, 39 'Return to your home, and declare how much God has done for you.' So he went away, proclaiming throughout the city how much Jesus had done for him.

Luke 11.14-26

14 Now he was casting out a demon that was mute; when the demon had gone out, the one who had been mute spoke, and the crowds were amazed. 15 But some of them said, 'He casts out demons by Beelzebul, the ruler of the demons.' 16 Others, to test him, kept demanding from him a sign from heaven. 17 But he knew what they were thinking and said to them, 'Every kingdom divided against itself becomes a desert, and house falls on house. 18 If Satan also is divided against himself, how will his kingdom stand? — for you say that I cast out the demons by Beelzebul. 19 Now if I cast out the demons by Beelzebul, by whom do your exorcists cast them out? Therefore they will be your judges. 20 But if it is by the finger of God that I cast out the demons, then the kingdom of God has come to you. 21 When a strong man, fully armed, guards his castle, his property is safe. 22 But when one stronger than he attacks him and overpowers him, he takes away his armour in which he trusted and divides his plunder. 23 Whoever is not with me is against me, and whoever does not gather with me scatters.

24 When the unclean spirit has gone out of a person, it wanders through waterless regions looking for a resting-place, but not finding any, it says, 'I will return to my house from which I came.' 25 When it comes, it finds it swept and put in order. 26 Then it goes and brings seven other spirits more evil than itself, and they enter and live there; and the last state of that person is worse than the first.'

Explanation

Luke is the only first-century source to mention that seven demons were driven out of Mary Magdalene. No narrative of this expulsion has been preserved in this Gospel or elsewhere. There is only Luke's brief mention. The conclusion to Mark which was added later and also mentions the seven demons comes from the second century (Mark 16.9).

In the Western church Mary Magdalene's seven demons are interpreted as the seven deadly sins: pride, avarice, gluttony, lust, sloth, jealousy and anger. An esoteric interpretation often heard nowadays is that Luke had heard that Mary Magdalene underwent a sevenfold way of initiation. Ways of initiation from Eastern culture were known in Jesus' time. Reference is made to the cult of Mithras or the Vedanta system of Yoga. There are also references to Gnostic, Hermetic and Jewish writings which describe a heavenly journey of the soul in which the soul pays a toll or pronounces passwords in order to be able to pass the seven heavenly guards. According to this view the expulsion of seven demons means that Mary Magdalene got through all her karma, transformed her astral possibilities or overcame her inner blockages.

However, those who read Luke's stories about the expulsions of demons must come to other conclusions. In Luke, demons have nothing to do with a way of initiation but with sickness. In Luke 8.1 it is said that women were *healed* of evil spirits and infirmities. Sadly, Luke does not narrate the liberation of Mary Magdalene from her seven demons. So we have to guess at the state in which Luke thinks her to have been. In the context of the Gospel of Luke it is most probable that the 'seven demons' refers to a spiritual or physical sickness. Luke describes the man who is possessed by a legion of spirits as spiritually sick, under great psychological pressure (Luke 8.26-30). He also sees the man who cannot speak as someone who is possessed by a demon (Luke 11.14).

But why seven demons in particular? The only time that Luke speaks of seven evil spirits is in connection with the man who is freed from an evil spirit and now has a tidy soul, but is not guarded by the Spirit of God (Luke 11.21-25). This man is in a bad way. Seven evil spirits will enter him because they do not encounter any resistance from the soul (Luke 11.26). The number seven is the full count of perfection. From this perspective a physical or psychological illness had Mary Magdalene completely in its grip. So according to Luke, Mary Magdalene as Jesus' disciple not only saw Jesus' healing power in others but also experienced it herself.

We do not know how Luke arrived at the addition of the seven demons. Does the supposed possession go back to the historical Mary Magdalene or is it his invention? Some exegetes think that Luke himself added the healings of Mary Magdalene and the other women who followed Jesus to show that the women followed Jesus on their own initiative and out of gratitude. They were not chosen and called specially by Jesus like the twelve apostles. As we shall see in the next chapter, there is a tendency in Luke to belittle the role of Mary Magdalene and the female followers of Jesus in comparison to that of Peter and the other apostles.

Chapter 3

Disciple and Witness

For centuries, church tradition regarded Mary Magdalene as a converted sinner. But Mary Magdalene was also held in veneration within the walls of the church in another way, namely as the first witness to the resurrection. Although according to church tradition women could not be apostles, in the Middle Ages Mary Magdalene was increasingly given the title *apostola apostolorum*, 'apostle of the apostles'. This was because she brought the apostles the great news of the resurrection. Indeed, the early sources narrate that as a follower of Jesus, Mary Magdalene was a witness to his crucifixion, his empty tomb and a revelation about his resurrection. However, in this chapter it will emerge that in the first centuries of early Christianity the stories and the evaluation of Mary Magdalene's role as witness are very different.

An invented figure

The oldest report of Jesus' crucifixion and resurrection to have been preserved comes from Paul's first letter to the Corinthians, probably written in AD 53.

In 1 Corinthians 15.3-7 Paul hands down what he has received. Thus the testimony is probably older than the letter itself. Mary Magdalene is nowhere mentioned here, in the oldest teaching about the crucifixion and resurrection to have been handed down. The Gospel of Mark, from around AD 70, forty years after Jesus' crucifixion, is the oldest writing to have been preserved which tells of Mary Magdalene. Has Mark invented her? The Gospels of Matthew (*c.* AD 80) and Luke (*c.* AD 80–90) retell Mark's narrative, but each in its own way. How are we to explain the differences?

1 Corinthians 15.1-11

1 Now I would remind you, brothers and sisters, of the good news that I proclaimed to you, which you in turn received, in which also you stand, 2 through which also you are being saved, if you hold firmly to the message that I proclaimed to you — unless you have come to believe in vain. 3 For I handed on to you as of first importance what I in turn had received: that Christ died for our sins in accordance with the scriptures, 4 and that he was buried, and that he was raised on the third day in accordance with the scriptures, 5 and that he appeared to Cephas, then to the twelve. 6 Then he appeared to more than five hundred brothers and sisters at one time, most of whom are still alive, though some have died. 7 Then he appeared to James, then to all the apostles. 8 Last of all, as to someone untimely born, he appeared also to me. 9 For I am the least of the apostles, unfit to be called an apostle, because I persecuted the church of God. 10 But by the grace of God I am what I am, and his grace towards me has not been in vain. On the contrary, I worked harder than any of them — though it was not I, but the grace of God that is with me. Whether then it was I or they, so we proclaim and so you have come to believe.

Mark 15.33–16.8

33 When it was noon, darkness came over the whole land until three in the afternoon. 34 At three o'clock Jesus cried out with a loud voice, 'Eloi, Eloi, lema sabachthani?' which means, 'My God, my God, why have you forsaken me?' 35 When some of the bystanders heard it, they said, 'Listen, he is calling for Elijah.' 36 And someone ran, filled a sponge with sour wine, put it on a stick, and gave it to him to drink, saying, 'Wait, let us see whether Elijah will come to take him down.' 37 Then Jesus gave a loud cry and breathed his last. 38 And the curtain of the temple was torn in two, from top to bottom. 39 Now when the centurion, who stood facing him, saw that in this way he breathed his last, he said, 'Truly this man was God's Son!'

40 There were also women looking on from a distance; among them were Mary Magdalene, and Mary of James the younger, and (Mary) the mother of Joses, and Salome.[1] 41 These used to follow and serve him when he was in Galilee;[2] and there were many other women who had come up with him to Jerusalem. 42 When evening had come, and since it was the day of Preparation, that is, the day before the sabbath, 43 Joseph of Arimathea, a respected member of the council, who was also himself waiting expectantly for the kingdom of God, went boldly to Pilate and asked for the body of Jesus. 44 Then Pilate wondered if he were already dead; and summoning the centurion, he asked him whether he had been dead for some time. 45 When he learned from the centurion that he was dead, he granted the body to Joseph. 46 Then

Joseph bought a linen cloth, and taking down the body, wrapped it in the linen cloth, and laid it in a tomb that had been hewn out of the rock. He then rolled a stone against the door of the tomb. 47 Mary Magdalene and Mary of Joses[3] saw where the body was laid.

16.1 When the sabbath was over, Mary Magdalene, and Mary of James,[4] and Salome bought spices, so that they might go and anoint him. 2 And very early on the first day of the week, when the sun had risen, they went to the tomb. 3 They had been saying to one another, 'Who will roll away the stone for us from the entrance to the tomb?' 4 When they looked up, they saw that the stone, which was very large, had already been rolled back. 5 As they entered the tomb, they saw a young man, dressed in a white robe, sitting on the right side; and they were alarmed. 6 But he said to them, 'Do not be alarmed; you are looking for Jesus of Nazareth, who was crucified. He has been raised; he is not here. Look, there is the place they laid him. 7 But go, tell his disciples and Peter that he is going ahead of you to Galilee; there you will see him, just as he told you.' 8 So they went out and fled from the tomb, for terror and amazement had seized them; and they said nothing to anyone, for they were afraid.

Matthew 27.45–28.20

45 From noon on, darkness came over the whole land until three in the afternoon. 46 And about three o'clock Jesus cried with a loud voice, 'Eli, Eli, lema sabachthani?' that is, 'My God, my God, why have you forsaken me?' 47 When some of the bystanders heard it, they said, 'This man is calling for Elijah.' 48 At once one of them ran and got a sponge, filled it with sour wine, put it on a stick, and gave it to him to drink. 49 But the others said, 'Wait, let us see whether Elijah will come to save him.' 50 Then Jesus cried again with a loud voice and breathed his last. 51 At that moment the curtain of the temple was torn in two, from top to bottom. The earth shook, and the rocks were split. 52 The tombs also were opened, and many bodies of the saints who had fallen asleep were raised. 53 After his resurrection they came out of the tombs and entered the holy city and appeared to many. 54 Now when the centurion and those with him, who were keeping watch over Jesus, saw the earthquake and what took place, they were terrified and said, 'Truly this man was God's Son!'

55 Many women, who had followed Jesus from Galilee to serve him, were looking on from a distance.[5] 56 Among them were Mary Magdalene, and Mary the mother of James and Joseph, and the mother of the sons of Zebedee.

57 When it was evening, there came a rich man from Arimathea, named Joseph, who was also a disciple of Jesus. 58 He went to Pilate and asked for the body of Jesus; then Pilate ordered it to be given to him. 59 So Joseph took the body and wrapped it in a clean linen cloth 60 and laid it in his own new tomb, which he had hewn in the rock.

He then rolled a great stone to the door of the tomb and went away. 61 Mary Magdalene and the other Mary were there, sitting opposite the tomb.

62 The next day, that is, after the day of Preparation, the chief priests and the Pharisees gathered before Pilate 63 and said, 'Sir, we remember what that impostor said while he was still alive, "After three days I will rise again." 64 Therefore command that the tomb be made secure until the third day; otherwise his disciples may go and steal him away, and tell the people, "He has been raised from the dead", and the last deception would be worse than the first.' 65 Pilate said to them, 'You have a guard of soldiers; go, make it as secure as you can.' 66 So they went with the guard and made the tomb secure by sealing the stone.

28.1 After the sabbath, as the first day of the week was dawning, Mary Magdalene and the other Mary went to see the tomb. 2 And suddenly there was a great earthquake; for an angel of the Lord, descending from heaven, came and rolled back the stone and sat on it. 3 His appearance was like lightning, and his clothing white as snow. 4 For fear of him the guards shook and became like dead men. 5 But the angel said to the women, 'Do not be afraid; I know that you are looking for Jesus who was crucified. 6 He is not here; for he has been raised, as he said. Come, see the place where he lay. 7 Then go quickly and tell his disciples, "He has been raised from the dead, and indeed he is going ahead of you to Galilee; there you will see him." This is my message for you.' 8 So they left the tomb quickly with fear and great joy, and ran to tell his disciples. 9 Suddenly Jesus met them and said, 'Rejoice!'[6] And they came to him, took hold of his feet, and worshipped him. 10 Then Jesus said to them, 'Do not be afraid; go and tell my brothers to go to Galilee; there they will see me.'

11 While they were going, some of the guard went into the city and told the chief priests everything that had happened. 12 After the priests had assembled with the elders, they devised a plan to give a large sum of money to the soldiers, 13 telling them, 'You must say, "His disciples came by night and stole him away while we were asleep." 14 If this comes to the governor's ears, we will satisfy him and keep you out of trouble.' 15 So they took the money and did as they were directed. And this story is still told among the Jews to this day.

16 Now the eleven disciples went to Galilee, to the mountain to which Jesus had directed them. 17 When they saw him, they worshipped him; but some doubted. 18 And Jesus came and said to them, 'All authority in heaven and on earth has been given to me. 19 Go therefore and make disciples of all nations, baptizing them in the name of the Father and of the Son and of the Holy Spirit, 20 and teaching them to obey everything that I have commanded you. And remember, I am with you always, to the end of the age.'

Luke 23.44–24.35

44 It was now about noon, and darkness came over the whole land until three in the afternoon, 45 while the sun's light failed; and the curtain of the temple was torn in two. 46 Then Jesus, crying with a loud voice, said, 'Father, into your hands I commend my spirit.' Having said this, he breathed his last. 47 When the centurion saw what had taken place, he praised God and said, 'Certainly this man was righteous.'[7] 48 And when all the crowds who had gathered there for this spectacle saw what had taken place, they returned home, beating their breasts. 49 But all his acquaintances, including the women who had followed him from Galilee, stood at a distance, watching these things.

50 Now there was a good and righteous man named Joseph, who, though a member of the council, 51 had not agreed to their plan and action. He came from the Jewish town of Arimathea, and he was waiting expectantly for the kingdom of God. 52 This man went to Pilate and asked for the body of Jesus. 53 Then he took it down, wrapped it in a linen cloth, and laid it in a rock-hewn tomb where no one had ever been laid. 54 It was the day of Preparation, and the sabbath was beginning. 55 The women who had come with him from Galilee followed, and they saw the tomb and how his body was laid. 56 Then they returned, and prepared spices and ointments. On the sabbath they rested according to the commandment.

24.1 But on the first day of the week, at early dawn, they came to the tomb, taking the spices that they had prepared. 2 They found the stone rolled away from the tomb, 3 but when they went in, they did not find the body. 4 While they were perplexed about this, suddenly two men in dazzling clothes stood beside them. 5 The women were terrified and bowed their faces to the ground, but the men said to them, 'Why do you look for the living among the dead? He is not here, but has risen. 6 Remember how he told you, while he was still in Galilee, 7 that the Son of Man must be handed over to sinners, and be crucified, and on the third day rise again.' 8 Then they remembered his words, 9 and returning from the tomb, they told all this to the eleven and to all the rest. 10 Now it was Mary Magdalene, Joanna, Mary of James,[8] and the other women with them who told this to the apostles. 11 But these words seemed to them an idle tale, and they did not believe them. 12 But Peter got up and ran to the tomb; stooping and looking in, he saw the linen cloths by themselves; then he went home, amazed at what had happened.

13 Now on that same day two of them were going to a village called Emmaus, about seven miles from Jerusalem, 14 and talking with each other about all these things that had happened. While they were talking and discussing, Jesus himself came near and went with them, but their eyes were kept from recognizing him. 17 And he said to them, 'What are you discussing with each other while you walk along?' They stood still, looking sad. 18 Then one of them, whose name was Cleopas, answered him, 'Are you

the only stranger in Jerusalem who does not know the things that have taken place there in these days?' 19 He asked them, 'What things?' They replied, 'The things about Jesus of Nazareth, who was a prophet mighty in deed and word before God and all the people, 20 and how our chief priests and leaders handed him over to be condemned to death and crucified him. 21 But we had hoped that he was the one to redeem Israel. Yes, and besides all this, it is now the third day since these things took place. 22 Moreover, some women of our group astounded us. They were at the tomb early this morning, 23 and when they did not find his body there, they came back and told us that they had indeed seen a vision of angels who said that he was alive. 24 Some of those who were with us went to the tomb and found it just as the women had said; but they did not see him.' 25 Then he said to them, 'Oh, how foolish you are, and how slow of heart to believe all that the prophets have declared! 26 Was it not necessary that the Messiah should suffer these things and then enter into his glory?' 27 Then beginning with Moses and all the prophets, he interpreted to them the things about himself in all the scriptures.

28 As they came near the village to which they were going, he walked ahead as if he were going on. 29 But they urged him strongly, saying, 'Stay with us, because it is almost evening and the day is now nearly over.' So he went in to stay with them. 30 When he was at the table with them, he took bread, blessed and broke it, and gave it to them. 31 Then their eyes were opened, and they recognized him; and he vanished from their sight. 32 They said to each other, 'Were not our hearts burning within us while he was talking to us on the road, while he was opening the scriptures to us?' 33 That same hour they got up and returned to Jerusalem; and they found the eleven and their companions gathered together. 34 They were saying, 'The Lord has risen indeed, and he has appeared to Simon!' 35 Then they told what had happened on the road, and how he had been made known to them in the breaking of the bread.

Explanation

In contrast to the later church tradition, Paul does not mention Mary Magdalene first among the witnesses to the resurrection, but Cephas. Cephas is Aramaic for Peter. This is the oldest report to have been preserved. Paul says that it is not his own but that he has received it from others. Among other things, on the basis of this earliest-preserved report it is assumed that the author of Mark invented the story of the women at the empty tomb. According to this view, Mark mentions the women at the crucifixion as followers of Jesus in order to introduce them for the later narrative (Mark 15.40-41). The women are said to have related nothing in the (first) conclusion to Mark (Mark 16.8) because there was simply no tradition of a Mary Magdalene and other women as witnesses to the resurrection. Thus before Mark there are said to have been no narratives about Mary Magdalene who followed Jesus and received a revelation at the empty tomb. All the later stories about the role of Mary Magdalene as witness to the crucifixion and the resurrection are said to be based on this one writing, the Gospel of Mark. The extreme consequence of this argument is that Mary Magdalene as a witness is a figure who never existed and has been invented by Mark.

The presupposition for this view is that Paul provides the only summary testimony that there was in the first period after Jesus and that at that point there were no stories about Mary Magdalene as witness. Today the starting point is rather a broad stream of oral tradition from which Paul in his letters took what he needed for his preaching. Thus the fact that Paul says so little about the earthly life of Jesus does not mean that no stories about Jesus were doing the rounds in his day, for that would mean that Mark had invented a very great deal.

In 1 Corinthians 15.1-11 Paul indicates the great importance of the scriptures and wants to show that the appearance of the risen Lord stopped at a given moment. So in his view the Corinthians cannot appeal to their own appearances but must keep to the scriptures and the most important figures to whom the risen Christ appeared. For the tradition which Paul follows, the most important names are Cephas (Peter) and the twelve, James and all the apostles, and finally Paul himself. He sums up the fact that there had been more appearances in the past to 'more than five hundred brothers and sisters at one time'. By the way, no stories have been preserved about an appearance to Peter alone (cf. Luke 24.34), to James alone and to 500 people at the same time.

Another argument for Mary Magdalene as an invented figure is that the stories about the empty tomb cannot be historically reliable unless the body of Jesus was indeed stolen. A dead body does not move by itself. The stories about the empty tomb must be literary inventions which symbolize belief in a bodily resurrection. The fact that the stories about an appearance of the risen Lord to Mary Magdalene are each time interwoven with the empty tomb is said to make these stories historically untrustworthy. Thus the figure of Mary Magdalene as a witness is a literary invention.

Why should Mark invent a story about Mary Magdalene if there was a story about an appearance to Peter, as Paul suggests? Perhaps this is the case because Peter and the twelve disciples are criticized in Mark. But in Matthew Peter is held in high regard. Why should Matthew embroider Mark's invented story and moreover still make the risen Lord appear to

Mary Magdalene and the other Mary when a comparable story about Peter was doing the rounds? Later in this book we shall see how hard the first Christians wrestled with the question why Jesus first appeared to a woman. It is unacceptable that Matthew should have invented such a story. It is far more probable that what applies to Paul also applies to the Gospels of Mark and Matthew: they are drawing on a broad stream of oral tradition and mention by name people who are important figures in the environment and tradition from which the Gospels originated.

That Mary Magdalene was an important figure for the community for which the Gospel of Mark was written is evident from her role in this Gospel. When talking about the women, Mark always puts her first. According to Mark, in a changing company of women Mary Magdalene is the only witness who has a part both in the crucifixion and burial and in the revelation at the empty tomb (Mark 15.47 and 16.1). Moreover she is no chance witness but a witness who belonged to Jesus' disciples from the very beginning of his work. The introduction says that Mary Magdalene, Mary of James, Mary the mother of Joses and Salome already used to follow and serve Jesus in Galilee. In Mark, 'follow' and 'serve' are words which denote discipleship. Time and again people are called to follow Jesus, and Mark emphasizes that service is central.[9] In Jewish sources outside Mark the words 'follow' and 'serve' are also used for the occupations of the pupils of a rabbi. The pupils of a rabbi were expected not only to learn from the instruction of their teacher but also to share in his daily life and to be there to serve him. The disciples also do that in Mark: on various occasions they get hold of a boat and form its crew. They distribute food among the multitude, find a donkey for Jesus to ride on and prepare the Passover meal.[10]

Following and serving: the women mentioned by name are already occupied with this in Galilee, where Jesus begins his work. Thus Mark 15.40-41 invites readers to turn back and see Mary Magdalene, Mary of James, Mary the mother of Joses and Salome present whenever the word 'disciples' is used.[11] That from a very early stage Mark uses the term 'disciples' in his Gospel in an inclusive sense is evident from the splitting of the word 'brothers' into 'brothers and sisters' when Jesus points to those sitting around him (Mark 3.31-35). That this refers to disciples and that the number of disciples comprises more than just the twelve is later evident when Jesus calls them and those 'around him' 'his own disciples', to whom the mystery of the Kingdom of God is given directly. This contrasts with people who stand outside and who hear everything in parables (Mark 14.10-12 and 33-34).

At the end of the Gospel Mark finally mentions four of the women disciples by name because of the special role they go on to play in the story. They continue to follow and serve Jesus, in contrast to the Twelve, hitherto the central figures, of whom Peter has denied Jesus and Judas has betrayed him. At the end of Mark, Mary Magdalene, Mary of James, Mary the mother of Joses and Salome function as counterparts to the first four of the Twelve at the beginning of Mark, namely Simon (Peter), Andrew, James and John. First these four follow Jesus without hesitation in order to learn from him how to become 'fishers of men' (Mark 1.16-20). They also receive special teaching from Jesus about suffering in the future (Mark 13.3-37). In this teaching situation these four men in particular are called on to be watchful but prove to be incapable of that: three of them fall asleep (Mark 13.35-37 and 14.32-40). All the disciples flee when Jesus is arrested (Mark 14.50). Peter returns to Jesus, but when he risks being recognized as a follower of Jesus he denies that he is. By contrast, Mary Magdalene, Mary of James, Mary the mother of Joses and Salome return and follow and serve Jesus to the cross and tomb, though it is extremely dangerous for them to do.

However, the four women disciples fail like the men, and in a sense that is the reassuring thing about Mark's picture of discipleship. Mary the mother of Joses evidently drops out after the burial (Mark 15.47 and 16.1). The three other women, Mary Magdalene, Mary of James and Salome, who go to Jesus' tomb in the early morning and find it empty, are so upset that they keep quiet, although the young man clothed in white has called on them to talk about what they have seen and heard (Mark 16.1-8). It then emerges that to be a disciple is to follow and serve, with its ups and downs. It is evident from the later conclusion (Mark 16.10) that Mark's readers at an early stage supposed that the three women finally overcame their fear and began to speak, or at any rate that Mary Magdalene did, but that is also evident from the fact that the readers can read their story. Clearly it can be told only by the women themselves, and was handed down from mouth to mouth. The abrupt ending of Mark 16.8 is intended to shock readers and make them *not* keep silent, but overcome their fear as Mary Magdalene, Mary of James and Salome obviously did later. Those who keep silent allow the story of the risen Lord to be lost. So Mark urgently calls on its readers not only to be silently faithful as disciples, though even that is dangerous, but also to become apostles and preach the gospel in the footsteps of Mary Magdalene.

Compared with Mark, Matthew embellishes the role of Mary Magdalene as witness but at the same time also considerably diminishes its importance.

34   *The Mary Magdalene Cover-Up*

She no longer belongs to a small group of core women disciples but to the crowd which follows Jesus. She did not serve him in Galilee but from Galilee on, like many other women. She is no longer the only witness to all the events surrounding the cross and the tomb but shares this role with 'the other Mary', whoever that may be. Certainly she is courageous and full of faith. Matthew explicitly does not relate that the two Maries go to the tomb to anoint Jesus' dead body. Instead, after the burial they sit opposite the tomb for a long time. Through the story of the guards at the tomb Matthew suggests that the two Maries do not go to the tomb to anoint the dead body but watch it to see what will happen on the third day. They are not just upset like Mary Magdalene and the other two women in Mark, but are both upset and overjoyed. In contrast to Mark's account, they obey the command to the angel and go to 'the brothers'. On the way they meet the risen Lord and worship him, whereas the eleven later believe and also doubt. However, the progress of Jesus' work in no sense rests on the shoulders of Mary Magdalene (and the other Mary) as in Mark. In Matthew the eleven go to a mountain which the Lord has shown them. Evidently there has been a revelation to the eleven themselves. Clearly, the testimony of the two Maries alone is not sufficient. And only the eleven receive the missionary command.

For Matthew's readers, Mary Magdalene and the other Mary are models of service, courage, faith and stability, but that is all. Matthew does not call on its readers to become apostles like Mary Magdalene. By contrast, the Gospel invites its readers to be inspired by Mary Magdalene's faith, but to leave the apostleship to the eleven. Those who want to be instructed and baptized must turn to them. Whereas in Mark Mary Magdalene is the model of apostleship, in Matthew that role is played by Peter. These two emphases are to be found again in all the later views of the role of Mary Magdalene. Mary Magdalene either has an important leading role or she is an intermediary for the male disciples.

In contrast to Mark and Matthew, in Luke it is not only the women who are present at the crucifixion but 'all his acquaintances' (Luke 23.49). Thus in Luke the women are no longer an exception. Nor are they mentioned by name. In Luke they are called the women who had followed Jesus from Galilee and had seen everything happen. These women prepare fragrant oil and balsam, go to the tomb and find it empty. The (anonymous) women are not commanded to tell the others, as they are in Mark and Matthew, but are called to remember Jesus' words. They do so, and it emerges from this that these women are Jesus' disciples (see Luke 9.18-22 and compare Luke 24.22).

In Luke, on their own authority the women go to the eleven and all the rest to tell them what they have seen and heard. Only then do some names appear: Mary Magdalene, Joanna, Mary of James and 'the others who were with them'. They tell the apostles what has happened, but the apostles do not believe them. The two on the road to Emmaus express it to Jesus like this: 'some women of our group astounded us'. When they put it like this, Jesus does not correct them. In Luke Jesus does not emphasize the trustworthiness of the women but the trustworthiness of the scriptures.

Luke's message is clear: although everything shows the women to be trustworthy witnesses, they have no commission to bear witness actively. Their active witness only causes confusion and is superfluous. Even the Lord does not stand behind their words. According to Luke, as in Paul, the risen Lord appears to Peter.[12] In Luke, as in Paul, the scriptures are central. The risen Lord can be encountered in the breaking and sharing of the bread.

Matthew and Luke both use Mark as a source, but go very different ways. In Matthew, Mary Magdalene along with the other Mary is a special and inspirational model of faith. In Luke she is one of the many women disciples who have to learn their limitations.

But Matthew and Luke also show agreements. Each in its own particular way, both Matthew and Luke limit the role which Mark gives to Mary Magdalene, her role as witness. The fact that they both do this, in different ways, makes it all the more improbable that Mary Magdalene is a figure invented by Mark. If that were the case, Matthew and Luke would have been able to pass over her story instead of so explicitly weakening her importance as a witness. Evidently the oral and perhaps also written tradition about her in the time of Matthew and Luke was too strong to be denied. It is striking that, compared with Mark, both Gospels make the role of Mary Magdalene less important by adding male figures to the resurrection narrative. This suggests that the fact that Mary Magdalene was a woman played a part.

Important or not

I shall discuss the resurrection narrative from the Gospel of John, from around AD 90, in the next chapter. There are also sources from the second and third centuries in which Mary Magdalene appears as a witness. The conclusion added later to Mark (Mark 16.9-20) comes from the beginning of the second century and is the earliest report in which Mary Magdalene is mentioned outspokenly as the first witness to the resurrection.

The Letter of the Apostles comes from the second century, probably the first half, but the second half cannot be excluded. In this writing the apostles relate very briefly the earthly Jesus and his miracles. Then they mention the crucifixion and burial and deal more extensively with the role of the women, including Mary Magdalene, as witnesses. However, the greater part of the writing is devoted to a dialogue between the apostles and the risen Lord in which the women no longer appear.

The third fragment comes from the Gospel of Peter, parts of which have been discovered. In it Peter is the figure who relates the crucifixion and resurrection in the first person. The Gospel comes from the beginning or middle of the second century and is special, because it is the oldest account which introduces Mary Magdalene as a disciple of the Lord without any inhibitions.

Finally, I have included in this section a moving Psalm of Heraclides from the end of the third or beginning of the fourth century. The Psalm celebrates the command of the risen Lord to Mary and her readiness and steadfastness to bring her task to a good end.

The fragments which follow express in very different ways the importance of the role of Mary Magdalene as a witness to the resurrection.

Mark 16.9-20 (added to Mark later)

9 Now after he rose early on the first day of the week, he appeared first to Mary Magdalene, from whom he had cast out seven demons. 10 She went out and told those who had been with him, while they were mourning and weeping. 11 But when they heard that he was alive and had been seen by her, they would not believe it.

12 After this he appeared in another form to two of them, as they were walking into the country. 13 And they went back and told the rest, but they did not believe them.

14 Later he appeared to the eleven themselves as they were sitting at the table; and he upbraided them for their lack of faith and stubbornness, because they had not believed those who saw him after he had risen. 15 And he said to them, 'Go into all the world and proclaim the good news to the whole creation. 16 The one who believes and is baptized will be saved; but the one who does not believe will be condemned. 17 And these signs will accompany those who believe: by using my name they will cast out demons; they will speak in new tongues; 18 they will pick up snakes in their hands, and if they drink any deadly thing, it will not hurt them; they will lay their hands on the sick, and they will recover.'

19 So then the Lord Jesus, after he had spoken to them, was taken up into heaven and sat down at the right hand of God. 20 And they went out and proclaimed the good

news everywhere, while the Lord worked with them and confirmed the message by the signs that accompanied it.

Letter of the Apostles 7–12[13]

7 Cerinthus and Simon have come to go through the world. But they are enemies of our Lord Jesus Christ, for they pervert the words and the object, which is Jesus Christ. Now keep yourselves away from them, for death is in them and a great stain of corruption – these to whom shall be judgment and the end and eternal perdition. 8 Because of that we have not hesitated to write to you concerning the testimony of our Saviour Christ, what he did when we were behind him watching and yet again in thoughts and deeds. 9. He concerning whom we bear witness that this is the Lord who was crucified by Pontius Pilate and Archelaus between the two thieves and who was buried in a place called the place of the skull. There went to that place three women: Mary, and[14] Martha and Mary Magdalene. They took ointment to pour upon his body, weeping and mourning over what had happened. But when they had approached the tomb they looked inside and did not find the body. 10 But as they were mourning and weeping the Lord appeared and said to them, 'For whom are you weeping? Now do not weep. I am he whom you seek. But let one of you go to your brothers and say, Come, the Master has risen from the dead.' Martha came and told it to us. We said to her, 'What do you want with us, O woman? He who has died is buried, and could it be possible for him to live?' We did not believe her, that the Saviour had risen from the dead. Then she went back to the Lord and said to him, 'None of them believed me that you are alive.' He said, 'Let another one of you go to them saying this again to them.' Mary came and told us again, and we did not believe her. She returned to the Lord and she also told it to him. 11 Then the Lord said to Mary and also to her sisters, 'Let us go to them.' And he came and found us inside, veiled. He called us out. But we thought it was a ghost, and we did not believe it was the Lord. Then he said to us, 'Come, do not be afraid. I am your master whom you, Peter, denied three times; and now do you deny again?' But we went to him, doubting in our hearts whether it was possibly he. Then he said to us, 'Why do you still doubt and are you not believing? I am he who spoke to you concerning my flesh, my death, and my resurrection. That you may know that it is I, put your finger, Peter, in the nail prints of my hands; and you, Thomas, put your finger in the spear-wounds of my side; but you Andrew, look at my feet and see if they do not touch the ground.' For it is written in the prophet, The foot of a ghost or demon does not join to the ground. 12 But we touched him that we might truly know whether he had risen in the flesh, and we fell on our faces confessing our sin, that we had been unbelieving. Then the Lord our Saviour said, 'Rise up, and I will reveal to you what is above heaven and what is in heaven, and your rest that is in the kingdom of heaven. For my Father has given me the power to take up you and those who believe in me.'

Gospel of Peter 34–60[15]

34 But early when the Sabbath was dawning, a crowd came from Jerusalem and the surrounding area in order that they might see the sealed tomb.

35 But in the night in which the Lord's Day dawned, when the soldiers were safeguarding (it) two by two in every watch, there was a loud voice in heaven. 36 And they saw that the heavens were opened and that two males who had much radiance had come down from there and come near the sepulchre. 37 But that stone which had been thrust against the door, having rolled by itself, went a distance off to the side; and the sepulchre opened, and both the young men entered. 38 And so those soldiers, having seen, awakened the centurion and the elders (for they too were present, safeguarding). 39 And while they were relating what they had seen, again they see three males who have come out from the sepulchre, with the two supporting the other one, and a cross following them. 40 And the head of the two reaching unto heaven, but that of the one being led out by hand by them going beyond the heavens. 41 And they were hearing a voice from the heavens saying, 'Have you made proclamation to the fallen-asleep?'

42 And an obeisance was heard from the cross, 'Yes.'

43 And so those people were seeking a common perspective to go off and make these things clear to Pilate. 44 And while they were still considering it through, there appeared again the opened heavens and a certain man having come down and entered into the burial place.

45 Having seen these things, those around the centurion hastened at night before Pilate (having left the sepulchre which they were safeguarding) and described all the things that they indeed had seen, agonizing greatly and saying, 'Truly he was God's Son.' 46 In answer Pilate said, 'I am clean of the blood of the Son of God, but it was to you that this seemed (the thing to do).' 47 Then all, having come forward, were begging and exhorting him to command the centurion and the soldiers to say to no one what they had seen. 48 'For,' they said, 'it is better for us to owe the debt of the greatest sin in the sight of God than to fall into the hands of the Jewish people and be stoned. 49 And so Pilate ordered the centurion and the soldiers to say nothing.

50–51 Now at the dawn of the Lord's Day Mary Magdalene, a female disciple of the Lord (who, afraid because of the Jews since they were inflamed with anger, had not done at the tomb of the Lord what women were accustomed to do for the dead beloved by them), having taken women friends with her, came to the tomb where he had been placed. 52 And they were afraid lest the Jews should see them and were saying, 'If indeed on that day on which he was crucified we could not weep and beat ourselves, yet now at his tomb we may do these things. 53 But who will roll away for us even the stone placed against the door of the tomb in order that, having entered, we may sit beside him and do the expected things? 54 For the stone was large, and we are afraid lest anyone see us. And if we are unable, let us throw against the door what we bring in memory of him; let us weep and beat ourselves until we come to our homes.' 55 And having gone off, they found the sepulchre opened. And having come forward, they bent down there and saw there a certain young man seated in the middle of the sepulchre, comely and clothed with a splendid robe, who said to them, 56 'Why have you come? Whom do you seek? Not that one who was crucified? He is risen and gone away. But if you do not believe, bend down and see the place where he lay, because he is not here. For he is risen and gone away to there whence he was sent.' 57 Then the women fled frightened.

58 Now it was the final day of the Unleavened Bread; and many went out, returning to their homes since the feast was over. 59 But we twelve disciples of the Lord were weeping and sorrowful; and each one, sorrowful because of what had come to pass, departed to his home. 60 But I, Simon Peter, and my brother Andrew, having taken our nets, went off to the sea. And there was with us Levi of Alphaeus whom the Lord . . .
[Here the fragment of the Gospel of Peter which has been discovered breaks off.]

Psalm of Heraclides 187.2-36[16]

[Mary], Mary, know me, but do not touch [me].
[Dry] the tears of your eyes, and know that I am your master.
Only do not touch me, for I have not yet seen my Father's face.
Your God was not taken away, as you thought in your pettiness.
Your God did not die; rather, he mastered [death].
I am not the gardener.
I have given, I have received . . .
I did [not] appear to you, until I saw your tears and grief . . . for me.
Cast this sadness away and perform this service.
Be my messenger to these lost orphans.
Hurry, with joy, go to the eleven.
You will find them gathered on the bank of the Jordan.
The traitor convinced them to fish as they did earlier,
and to lay down the nets in which they caught people for life.
Say to them, 'Arise, let us go, Your brother calls you.'
If they disregard me as brother, say to them, 'It is your master.'
If they disregard me as master, say to them, 'It is your lord.'
Use all your skill and knowledge until you bring the sheep to the shepherd.
If you see that they do not respond, make Simon Peter come to you.
Say to him, 'Remember my words, between me and you.
Remember what I said, between me and you, on the Mount of Olives,

mething to say, I have no one to whom to say it.'

ıy master, I shall carry out your instructions with joy in my whole heart.

.ot let my heart rest,

I shall not let my eyes sleep,

I shall not let my feet relax until I bring the sheep to the fold.

Glory to Mary, because she has listened to her master,

she has carried out his instructions with joy in her whole heart.

Explanation

The conclusion later added to Mark resembles Luke's resurrection narrative. As in the Gospel of Luke, according to this conclusion to Mark seven demons are driven out of Mary. As in Luke, the message about the resurrection is not believed and the Lord also appears to two men outside the city. However, there are also great differences. In contrast to Luke, Mary Magdalene stands all alone in the spotlight and does not see any angels, but the Lord himself. This later conclusion to Mark is the earliest text in which Mary Magdalene is explicitly mentioned as the first witness to the resurrection: 'he appeared first to Mary Magdalene, from whom he had cast out seven demons' (Mark 16.9). In contrast to Luke, here the seven demons have a clear function. Mary Magdalene is more than the first witness to have seen the Lord and talked about this. She is also the living proof and the recollection of the power of Jesus to drive out demons. This force will live on in those who come to believe, as the risen Christ promises the eleven in Mark 16.17.

Another difference is that Mary Magdalene delivers her message to all who were with Jesus and are now mourning and grieving. Later it proves that the eleven are among their number. When the mourners do not believe her report or the other two witnesses, Jesus comes to the eleven and reproves their unbelief 'because they had not believed those who saw him after he had risen' (Mark 16.13). This too differs from Luke. The later conclusion to Mark makes Jesus himself confirm the trustworthiness of Mary Magdalene and the two other witnesses. The eleven should have believed them. So they should also have believed Mary Magdalene, whereas in Luke the witness of the women has no effect and only causes perplexity. But where Luke still has the mission charge given to the eleven and those who are with them (Luke 24.33-39), in the later conclusion to Mark, as in Matthew, the mission charge is meant for the eleven.

The Letter of the Apostles shows something comparable, with the difference that here the witnesses are exclusively women and not only their message is unbelievable. The first witness, Martha, is addressed as 'Woman'. 'What do you want with us, O woman?' In contrast to the later conclusion to Mark, in the Letter of the Apostles the apostles clearly emphasize that the witnesses are women. Another difference is that here the risen Christ goes with the women to the apostles to convince them that he is alive and in this way confirms their trustworthiness even more explicitly.

The Letter of the Apostles has been handed down in Ethiopic and Coptic. A translation from the Coptic version is printed above, because this is said to be closest to the original Greek version. However, in the Ethiopic version it is clear that Mary Magdalene plays the chief role, whereas that is not the case in the Coptic version. In neither version do the apostles relate precisely what the relation is between the Lord and the women, nor do they appear as witnesses to the crucifixion and burial. Speaking to the women, the Lord calls the apostles 'your brothers'. So the women are the sisters of the apostles. Moreover in the Ethiopic version the Lord presupposes that the women can speak of him as 'our Master'. So they are depicted as his disciples. The Coptic version has 'the Master' here, which is more ambiguous.

In the Ethiopic version the names of the women are Sarah, Martha and Mary Magdalene. Mary is the first to go to the apostles, and then Sarah. In the Coptic version the names are Mary, Martha and Mary Magdalene. Martha is the first to go to the apostles and then Mary. Because the Coptic version has two Maries and the Ethiopic version one, the sentence which the two versions have in common has very different meanings: 'Then the Lord said to Mary and also to her sisters, "Let us go to them."' In the Ethiopic version this Mary is clearly Mary Magdalene. After all, there is only one Mary in this version, namely Mary from Magdala. However, in the Coptic version this can be either Mary the sister of Martha or Mary Magdalene. The first possibility is more plausible for the reader, because there is no 'Magdalene' after Mary. Moreover it seems as if the risen Lord is addressing Mary, who has just brought the message of the resurrection to the apostles. That is the Mary without the addition 'the Magdalene'. That means that in the Coptic version there is no role for Mary Magdalene as a witness to the resurrection. In the later Ethiopic version she plays a main role as a witness. The reason for this could be that the Ethiopic narrator saw Mary Magdalene and the sister of Martha as one person, something that often happened. It is striking that the earlier Coptic version seems to make Mary Magdalene's role invisible in favour of Mary the sister of Martha. However, that is perhaps a hasty conclusion. Luke introduces Mary the sister of Martha as a silent and listening figure (Luke 10.28-38). Perhaps that is also the case here. But the two Maries at least confuse the reader over the role of Mary Magdalene.

The Gospel of Peter diminishes the role of Mary Magdalene as witness to the resurrection in an unmistakable way. There are no women as witnesses to the crucifixion and the burial. And in the night 'in which the Lord's day dawned' the soldiers, the centurion and the elders see the resurrection take place. It is a pity that the part of the Gospel that has been preserved breaks off with Simon Peter, his brother Andrew and Levi fishing. It seems that Peter is on the point of relating an appearance of the risen Lord to the three of them. All this means that the revelation to the women at the empty tomb is of no significance for the course of the resurrection narrative in this Gospel. Nor are they given any commission to go and tell what they have seen. They are simply witnesses to the tomb in which the dead body of Jesus no longer lies and hear the revelation that he has returned whence he had been sent. And they flee full of fear. This reaction of the women also occurs in Mark, but there it is shocking to the reader and of great importance. Here, however, the sentence is meaningless and simply meant to make the women vanish silently from the scene. As the omniscient narrator, Peter knows the story about Mary Magdalene and the other women as witnesses to the empty tomb; evidently it is so taken for granted as part of the tradition that it has to be told, but it has no function in the story as a whole.

However, the Gospel of Peter describes Mary Magdalene in a special way. She is (literally translated) 'the disciple of the Lord', 'disciple' being a female noun. This Gospel thus does not present Mary Magdalene with the addition 'from whom seven demons were cast out' or a version of the words 'follow' and 'serve', nor even as *a* disciple, but as '*the* disciple (female) of the Lord'. This is the earliest version to speak explicitly of the idea that Jesus had female disciples as well as male disciples, unless with the expression 'the female disciple' the Gospel wants to disparage her as the only female disciple. The formulation of the role of the other women could also point to this, as their relationship to Jesus is not described. They are described in relation to Mary Magdalene as 'her women friends', a clue which moreover sheds new light on Mary Magdalene as the leader of a group of women. However, this is not decisive, because as the first-person figure in the Gospel, after the burial of Jesus Peter also says 'I with the companions' (GosPet 26).

Then the Jews and the elders and the priests, having come to know how much wrong they had done to themselves, began to beat themselves and say, 'Woe to our sins. The judgment has approached and the end of Jerusalem.' But I with the companions was sorrowful; and having been wounded in spirit, we were in hiding, for we were sought after by them as wrongdoers and as wishing to set fire to the sanctuary. In addition to all these things we were fasting and we were sitting mourning and weeping night and day until the Sabbath. (GosPet 25–27)

Where questions are raised about the absence of Peter and the others by the presence of women at the cross and tomb in Mark and Matthew, the Gospel of Peter does not want to leave any misunderstandings about this. It is evident from this quotation that according to the author they have good reason: they are sought after as wrongdoers. Moreover, this Gospel had left out the women at the cross and tomb.

However, the Gospel of Peter also sheds positive light on Mary Magdalene and the other women by several times mentioning their fear and in the earlier part of the Gospel showing the fear of Peter and his friends. The men do not overcome this fear. Finally, they go home with great sadness and resume their old occupation. Mary Magdalene and her friends overcome their fear of the Jews because they want to do what is customary for a dead person. But they are again seized with fear when they receive the revelation about the empty tomb.

The Psalm of Heraclides about Mary Magdalene breathes a very different atmosphere. Here the role of Mary Magdalene is of great importance. The psalm is part of the Manichaean Psalm Book. This book was probably used in worship by the adherents of Manichaeism, a widespread form of Christian belief. Later this belief, central to which is the struggle between light and darkness in which the sparks of light have to be rescued from dark matter, was condemned as a heresy. The church father Augustine was an adherent of Manichaeism before he converted to the more orthodox variant of Christian faith. It may well be that at one time he sang this psalm, perhaps after a reading from John's resurrection narrative, to which the psalm refers. The psalm celebrates the readiness and resolve of Mary Magdalene to be of service to the risen Lord. Her role is not only to bring the message that the Lord is alive, as in the other texts, but also, in the words of the risen Lord, to bring 'the sheep to the shepherd' and 'the sheep to the fold', as Mary puts it. It is as though there are no other appearances of the Lord in which he himself instructs the disciples. In this psalm, it is Mary Magdalene who has to instruct the disciples who are fishing so that the eleven listen to the risen Lord as they did to the earthly Jesus in order once again to become fishers of men.

Two other Manichaean psalms give a summary of the qualities of all Jesus' disciples, men and women. Mary Magdalene is then called 'one who casts a net in order to catch the other eleven who were lost' (Psalm 192.21-23). And in the other psalm it is said of her election by Jesus: 'He chose Mary, the Spirit of Wisdom' (Psalm 194.19). Nowhere in the texts so far has it been said that Jesus chose Mary. In Mark, Matthew and Luke Jesus chooses only the twelve apostles.

The texts show that in early Christianity there were very different views of Mary Magdalene's importance as a witness to the resurrection. Only the Gospel of Mark and the Psalm of Heraclides single out her role as exceptional. The Gospel of Peter is the nadir as far as the limitation of the role of Mary Magdalene is concerned. Matthew, Luke and the Letter of the Apostles seem to suggest that the fact that Mary Magdalene is a woman is felt to be a problem. That comes out explicitly in the texts which follow.

An untrustworthy witness

First we hear Celsus, a Greek philosopher from the second century. He saw the Christian faith as a danger to the stability of society and therefore challenged it. He did so, among other things, in his book *The True Doctrine*, which he wrote around AD 178. It has not been preserved, but a good deal of it is known through the quotations from it which the church father Origen made in his book *Against Celsus*. In it Origen provides a commentary on the quotations from Celsus in order to defend the Christian faith. In the quotation printed here Celsus talks about the credibility of the women as witnesses to the resurrection.

In the other texts, the Gospels of Mary and Thomas, Mary Magdalene is attacked by her fellow believers, above all Peter. The two Gospels come from the second century. Whether or not they belong to Gnostic circles is a much-discussed question. They show some of the problems experienced over Mary Magdalene as a woman.

Celsus, On the True Doctrine *(from Origen,* Against Celsus *2.54-55 and 70)*[17]

54 By what, then, were you induced (to become his followers)? Was it because he fore-told that after his death he would rise again?

55 Come now, let us believe your view that he actually said this. How many others produce wonders like this to convince simple hearers whom they exploit by deceit? They say that Zamolxis, the slave of Pythagoras, also did this among the Scythians, and Pythagoras himself in Italy, and Rhampsinitus in Egypt. The last-named played dice with Demeter in Hades and returned bearing a gift from her, a golden napkin. More-over, they say that Orpheus did this among the Odrysians, and Protesilaus in Thessaly, and Heracles at Taenarum, and Theseus.

But we must examine this question whether anyone who really died ever rose again with the same body. Or do you think that the stories of these others really are the legends they appear to be, and yet that the ending of your tragedy is to be regarded as noble and convincing – his cry from the cross when he expired, and the earthquake and the dark-ness? While he was alive he did not help himself, but after death he rose again and showed the marks of his punishment and how his hands had been pierced. But who saw this? A hysterical female, as you say, and perhaps some other one of those who were deluded by the same sorcery, who either dreamt in a certain state and through wishful thinking had a hallucination due to some mistaken notion (an experience which has happened to thou-sands), or, which is more likely, wanted to impress the others by telling this fantastic tale, and so by this cock-and-bull story to provide a chance for other beggars.

70 At the time when he was disbelieved when in the body, he preached without restraint to all; but when he would establish a strong faith after rising from the dead, he appeared secretly to just one woman and to those of his own confraternity.

Gospel of Mary 10.1-6 and 17.10–19.5[18]

10.1-6 Peter said to Mary, 'Sister, we know that the Saviour loved you more than the rest of women. Tell us the words of the Saviour which you remember, the things that you know and we do not, nor have we heard them.'

Mary answered and said, 'What is hidden from you I shall tell you.'
[Mary's teaching follows here, see Chapter 4.]

17.10 But Andrew answered and said to the brothers (and sisters), 'Tell me, what do you say about what she has spoken? I at least do not believe that the Saviour said this. For these teachings seem to be according to another train of thought.'

Peter answered and spoke about these same things, he reflected about the Saviour: 'After all, he did not speak with a woman apart from us and not openly. Are we to turn and all listen to her? Has he chosen her above us?'

18 Then Mary wept, she said to Peter, 'My brother Peter, what are you thinking? Do you suppose that I devised this, alone, in my heart, or that I am deceiving the Saviour?'

Levi answered, he said to Peter, 'Peter, you have always been hot-tempered. Now I see you arguing with the woman as these adversaries do. If the Saviour has made her worthy, who are you indeed to reject her? Surely, the Saviour knows her very well. That is why he loved her more than us. Rather let us be ashamed and clothe ourselves with the perfect Human Being. Let us bring him forth to us, as he commanded us. Let us preach the Gospel, without laying down any other rule or law than the one the Saviour said.'

19.1-5 When Levi had said this, they began to go forth to proclaim and to preach.

The Gospel according to Mary

Gospel of Thomas 21–22 and 114[19]

21 Mary said to Jesus. 'Whom are your disciples like?' He said, 'They are like children who have settled in a field which is not theirs. When the owners of the field come, they will say, "Let us have back our field." They (will) undress in their presence in order to let them have back their field and to give it back to them. Therefore I say, "If the owner of a house knows that the thief is coming, he will begin his vigil before he comes and will not let him dig through into his house of his domain to carry away his goods. You (pl.), then, be on your guard against the world. Arm yourselves with great strength lest the robbers find a way to come to you, for the difficulty which you expect will (surely) materialize. Let there be among you a man of understanding. When the grain ripened, he came quickly with his sickle in his hand and reaped it. Whoever has ears to hear, let him hear."'

22 Jesus saw infants being suckled. He said to his disciples, 'These infants being suckled are like those who enter the kingdom.' They said to him, 'Shall we then, as children, enter the kingdom?' Jesus said to them, 'When you make the two one, and when you make the inside like the outside and the outside like the inside, and the above like the below, and when you make the male and the female one and the same, so that the male not be male nor the female female; and you fashion eyes in place of an eye, and a hand in place of a hand, and a foot in place of a foot, and a likeness in place of a likeness; then will you enter [the kingdom].'

114 Simon Peter said to them, 'Let Mary leave us, for women are not worthy of life.' Jesus said, 'I myself shall lead her in order to make her male, so that she too may

become a living spirit resembling you males. For every woman who will make herself male will enter the kingdom of heaven.'

Explanation

The above texts show that as an important witness to the Christian faith Mary Magdalene poses a problem because she is a woman. Celsus expresses the view of women in his time. They are prone to religious excesses. They are easy to influence and to mislead. They want to make an impression and therefore tell fantastic stories. For Celsus, this image of women is enough to relegate Mary Magdalene's testimony to the realm of fable.

In the Gospel of Mary Peter wants to hear what Mary Magdalene has to say, even though she is a woman. In his eyes she is a special woman by comparison with other women. He not only addresses her as 'sister', as a fellow-believer, but thinks that the Saviour singled her out from women. According to him she is able to remember words which the others do not yet know. But in the Gospel of Mary, Peter's image of Mary Magdalene as a special woman is disturbed by the image of women he has generally. According to the current image, Mary is a sexual threat to men and moreover she is of less value than they are. That means that the Saviour, as a man, cannot have spoken to her alone, as a woman. Nor can the Saviour as a man have put Mary Magdalene as a woman above the male disciples, and as men Peter and the others cannot listen to her as a woman.

By comparison with Peter, Andrew does not react to Mary as a woman but to the content of her teaching. At least, so it seems. Andrew says that he cannot believe that her words come from the Saviour because they show a different way of thinking. And indeed, Mary's teaching is new, as Peter has asked. However, it is not completely new, as the reader of the Gospel soon discovers. For the words of the Saviour which Mary Magdalene hands on form an explanation of the words which the disciples in the Gospel of Mary already have heard from the Saviour and thus elaborate on them. It is striking that in his reaction Andrew does not address Mary but only his brothers. In addition he does not use her name but speaks of 'she'. This again recalls the ideas about women which Celsus uses in his assessment of the trustworthiness of the woman or women who have seen Jesus. Andrew suggests that like all other women, Mary tells fantastic stories in order to make an impression.

Mary does not react to Andrew, but to Peter, who is the first to recognize her as a sister. She tries to call him back again as a brother by mentioning the consequence of his reaction: 'My brother Peter, what are you thinking? Do you suppose that I devised this, alone, in my heart, or that I am deceiving the Saviour?'

Levi reprimands Peter. However, he too does not mention Mary by name, but speaks of her as 'the woman'. He reproves Peter for his thoughtless hot temper and emphasizes that the Saviour has made 'her' worthy. In Levi's view, too, Mary is clearly different as a woman, but he also corrects Peter. 'He loved her more than us,' says Levi, whereas Peter said: 'Sister, we know that the Saviour loved you more than the rest of women.'

But Levi, too, sketches quite a different picture of the situation from the one that Mary herself sketches earlier in the Gospel. She says: 'He has made us Human Being' (GosMar 9.20). Mary presupposes that the Saviour draws no distinction between men and women. Peter, Andrew and Levi are convinced that he does. With the structure and the title of the Gospel of Mary the author shows that the men are making a big mistake here. Mary's teaching about the Saviour is indeed trustworthy. He has spoken alone with her and wants the men to listen to her. Moreover her teaching is important, because it corrects the disciples' view of the identity of their adversaries and shows what trust in the greatness of the Son of Man can do. I shall discuss this further in the next chapter.

In the Gospel of Thomas, too, Peter is fascinated with the fact that Mary is a woman. Mary must go away, 'for women are not worthy of life'. What is meant here is not earthly and material life but heavenly and spiritual life. Women are associated with 'the female', with perception through the senses, whereas men stand for 'the male', for perception through the mind. It is striking that here Jesus is described as someone who also thinks in these terms. He too draws a distinction between men and women. Women are inferior to 'you men'. He promises to make Mary male and goes on to say that every woman must make herself male in order to enter the kingdom of heaven.

At first sight this is directly opposed to what Jesus said earlier in logion 21-22. To Mary Magdalene's question about discipleship Jesus replies that one can enter the kingdom as a baby or a small child and that the male and female must be combined in such a way that neither can be recognized any more. That perhaps refers to the Platonic idea that the first human being was a hermaphrodite. It can also point to the sexlessness of babies and small children in which the male and the female do not yet emerge clearly, or to ideas like those in the Gospel of Philip according to which a man has to be united with his female spirit and a woman with her male spirit. In all these cases, in logion 114 one would have expected Jesus to show Peter and the other men the feminine that *they* had to make their own. In Chapter 8, however, we shall see in Philo that the union of the female and the male produces a male result. That a woman makes herself male can mean that she presents herself outwardly as a man and thus is no longer an object of temptation for men. It can also mean that she deliberately rejects any bodily enjoyment, or in the spiritual sense that she puts the mind before the perception through the senses. It can also be a combination of these three.

Why is Peter the one who time and again gets entangled in the images of women customary at that time? In the Gospel of Mary Levi rebukes him for his hot temper. In the Gospel of Mary Peter gives jealousy as an explanation when he asks the other disciples: 'Has he chosen her above us?' In present-day exegesis Peter is also seen as a representative of orthodox teaching who attacks Mary Magdalene not so much as a woman but as a representative of Gnostic teaching. However, this is improbable, because in the second century there was still a great diversity of Christian ideas. Believers with more 'Gnostic' or more 'orthodox' views still belonged to the same communities. The most important difference between the two gradually became clear in their answer to the question of the origin of evil. According to Gnostic teaching, creation itself is a misfortune and derives from a lesser God. According to more orthodox thought, which maintains the link with Judaism, creation is magnificent in origin and comes from the one God who has made heaven and earth.

If it is right to see the Gospel of Mary and the Gospel of Thomas as Gnostic texts, then it is still the case that in them Peter is described as being as much a Gnostic as the other disciples. If Peter may already be known as 'orthodox' in the second century, that is above all in his view of women and men, Mary Magdalene is a natural target, not as a Gnostic but as a woman who breaks through conservative barriers. However, in the third century Mary Magdalene unmistakably turns out to be known as an authoritative interpreter of Gnostic teaching.

An eminent witness to Gnostic teaching

In a number of second-century writings, Mary Magdalene emerges as someone with great insight. In the Dialogue of the Saviour from the beginning of the second century, in a conversation with the risen Lord and his disciples, she repeats a saying of Jesus about which the author remarks: 'She spoke this word as a woman who understood completely.'[20] We saw in Chapter 2 that the Gospel of Philip assigns Mary a place apart as one who sees among the blind. Both writings are known to be Gnostic, but the clearest Gnostic writing is Pistis Sophia from the third century.

We can translate the Greek *Pistis Sophia* as 'believing Wisdom', but also as 'Belief/Wisdom'. The book is in two parts and begins with the twelve disciples who are witnesses to the ascension of Jesus to heaven and his return. Then he tells them about his experiences and above all about his encounter with Pistis Sophia. This is a heavenly female figure with a great propensity towards the Light of the highest God. The Lord tells of her quest for the Light and of her fall, as a result of which creation came into being. He tells of her penitence, his heavenly task to rescue her and bring her to the Light and of the rulers of the world. The story shows how human beings are in search of the Light and go wrong, and how they can be saved by Jesus and can escape the grip of the rulers of the world. In the second book the Lord relates the mystery of the forgiveness of sins, the mystery of Golgotha, the mystery of baptism and the punishments for particular sins. Mary Magdalene often speaks in both books as the one who puts questions and interprets Jesus' words.

In the first fragment the risen Lord tells the disciples about their task. The second fragment shows Peter's vexation about the role of Mary Magdalene. He may then explain the penitence of Sophia. The third fragment contains Sophia's hymn to the Light. Mary Magdalene expresses her fear of Peter before she interprets the song of the Light.

Pistis Sophia 7[21]

Rejoice and be glad, and rejoice still more, that it is given to you that I should speak with you first from the beginning of the truth until its completion. Because of this indeed I have chosen you from the beginning through the First Mystery. Rejoice now and be glad, because when I entered the world I brought the twelve powers with me, as I told you from the beginning, which I took from the twelve saviours of the Treasury of Light, according to the command of the First Mystery. These now I cast into the wombs of your mothers when I came into the world, and it is these which are in your bodies today. For these powers have been given to you above the whole world, for you are those who are able to save the whole world, so that you should be able to withstand the threat of the archons of the world, and the sufferings of the world and their dangers, and all their persecutions which the archons of the height will bring upon you.

Pistis Sophia 36[22]

When Jesus finished saying these things to his disciples, he asked, 'Do you understand how I am speaking with you?' Peter stepped forward and said to Jesus: 'My master, we cannot endure this woman who gets in our way, and does not let any of us speak, though she talks all the time.' Jesus answered and said to his disciples: 'Let anyone in whom the power of the Spirit has arisen, so that the person understands what I say, come forward and speak. Peter, I perceive that your power within you understands the interpretation of the mystery of repentance that Pistis Sophia mentioned. So now Peter, discuss among your brothers the thought of her repentance.'

Pistis Sophia 72[23]

. . . The First Mystery however continued again and said: 'The Pistis Sophia continued again in this song of praise. She said: "I will say that you are the light which is on high, for you have saved me, and you have brought me to yourself. And you did not allow the emanations of the Authades, which are my enemies, to take away my light. O Light of Lights, I have sung praises to you: you have saved me O Light. You have brought my power up from the Chaos; you have saved me from among those that go down to the darkness." The Pistis Sophia said these words also. Now at this time, he whose mind has become understanding, to understand the words which the Pistis Sophia spoke, let him come forward and give their interpretation.'

When the First Mystery finished saying these things to the disciples, Mary came forward and said, 'My master, I understand in my mind that I can come forward at any time to interpret what Pistis Sophia has said, but I am afraid of Peter, because he threatens me and hates our gender.' When she said this, the First Mystery replied to her, 'Any of those filled with the Spirit of light will come forward to interpret what I say: no one will be able to oppose them.'

Explanation

Generally the twelve disciples consist exclusively of men, not only in the New Testament and the church fathers but also in Gnostic circles. In Gnostic writings such as the Wisdom of Jesus Christ and the First Apocalypse of James, women disciples are mentioned, but they are seven female disciples alongside the twelve male disciples. However, in Pistis Sophia the twelve disciples consist of men and women: four women and eight men. They are Mary Magdalene, Martha, Salome, Mary the mother of Jesus, Philip, Peter, John, Andrew, Thomas, Matthew, James and Bartholomew.

Four of these play a special role. There are three men: Philip writes down everything that he is told, supported by Thomas and Matthew (Pistis Sophia 22) and one woman: Mary Magdalene is the one who speaks by far the most.

In contrast to Mark, Matthew and Luke, in which Mary Magdalene seems to be the leader of a specific group of female disciples, in Pistis Sophia she is the spokesperson of the twelve disciples, a role that Peter plays elsewhere. Mary Magdalene says, 'We are your disciples' (Pistis Sophia 45). She regularly speaks in the name of the other disciples. It is their common task to listen to the revelations of the Saviour, to understand them and later to hand them on. The first fragment shows how the twelve disciples are chosen from the beginning to do this. On coming into the world Jesus therefore brought twelve forces with him to give to them.

In a detailed study of Mary Magdalene, among other works Erika Mohri has examined Pistis Sophia.[24] She argues that Mary Magdalene does not appear in it only as a representative of the twelve disciples but also as a Gnostic filled with the spirit. She is a teacher and exegete. She quotes the scriptures and remembers sayings of Jesus. Moreover she is a disciple who supports the other disciples and who also works for others.

It is again Peter who is described in Pistis Sophia as the one who attacks Mary Magdalene. Mary says: 'I am afraid of Peter, because he threatens me and he hates our gender' (Pistis Sophia 72). And Peter says: 'My master, we cannot endure this woman who gets in our way and does not let any of us speak, though she talks all the time' (Pistis Sophia 36). Peter disputes Mary's right to come forward authoritatively as a woman. It is clear where the writing Pistis Sophia itself stands. Anyone who feels the Spirit welling up may come forward and speak, whether man or woman. In Pistis Sophia Mary Magdalene is 'pure Spirit' and 'more directed towards the Kingdom of the heavens than all your brothers and sisters'.[25] She knows that the 'Light person' dwells in her.[26]

This preference does not alter the fact that the emphasis in Pistis Sophia is on the election of the twelve disciples: the eight men and the four women. They all have the task of understanding and handing on the revelations, and thus bringing about the salvation of the world, but the special position of Mary Magdalene makes it clear that the handing down of the Gnostic tradition to which the two books of Pistis Sophia refer is attributed above all to her. This brings us to the question whether perhaps there are Christian sources from an earlier period than the third century in which some of the teaching of Mary Magdalene is to be found.

Chapter 4

Mary's Teaching

The early sources agree that Mary Magdalene was a follower of Jesus. The Gospel of Peter explicitly calls her a disciple. The other Gospels indicate this more implicitly. As a witness to Jesus' crucifixion and the empty tomb, with the accompanying revelation, she is of great importance above all to Mark. By contrast, Matthew and Luke seem to limit her role deliberately. However, the Gospel of Peter, the later conclusion to Mark and the Letter of the Apostles seem to find Mary Magdalene unimportant as a witness. The later Manichaean Psalm of Heraclides and the two Gnostic books of Pistis Sophia assign her a central role. Does that mean that in the course of time Mary Magdalene was valued above all in Gnostic circles? Is little known about her from 'orthodox' sources because she was claimed by 'heretical' circles? In order to answer this question, in this chapter we shall look for the teaching that the early sources connect with Mary Magdalene.

We have already seen that Mary Magdalene is repeatedly involved both with the suffering of Jesus and with overcoming it. The message 'He is alive' is central, but there are different emphases. In Luke the risen Christ brings liberation from sins. In Matthew the risen Christ is the Mighty One who will support the disciples to the end of time while they make new disciples.[1] In Mark the risen Christ is the one who goes before the disciples to Galilee.[2] As no appearance takes place in Galilee, this seems above all to have a metaphorical meaning. The disciples will see him if they follow Jesus' foot-steps and live by the teaching that he gave in Galilee.[3] It is striking that according to Mark, Matthew and Luke, the teaching that Mary Magdalene received earlier is given by Jesus to all the disciples.[4]

This chapter is about early sources which connect Mary Magdalene with teaching about Jesus that she alone knows. These are the Gospel of John and the Gospel of Mary.

The significance of Jesus' life and death

The Gospel of John was probably composed around AD 90. Whether the Gospel made use of Mark, Matthew and Luke is much discussed. At all events it is clear that John breathes an atmosphere all of its own. The narratives about Jesus' death and resurrection are also different. As in Chapter 3, I assume that there were oral as well as written traditions, not all of which have been preserved. So the Gospel of John may be drawing on sources which are unknown to us. The Gospel itself speaks of one important eye-witness, the disciple whom he (Jesus) loved. It is thought that this figure grew very old, told of Jesus, and reflected on his meaning with disciples. The Gospel of John would have been written bit by bit over a long period on the basis of this teaching.

The first fragment contains part of the introduction to the Gospel of John. In it the distinctive atmosphere of the Gospel can clearly be felt. In the second fragment 'the disciple whom he loved' appears for the first time (John 13.23) and Jesus teaches his disciples about his death. The third fragment tells of Jesus' crucifixion and burial and of Mary Magdalene who finds the tomb empty and seeks her dead Master. The last fragment speaks about the eye-witness to whom the Gospel of John refers. Who is this beloved disciple? What is the content of the teaching which Mary Magdalene alone gets from Jesus and which she has to pass on to the others?

John 1.1-13

1 In the beginning was the Word, and the Word was with God, and the Word was God. 2 He was in the beginning with God. 3 All things came into being through him, and without him not one thing came into being. 4 What has come into being in him was life, and the life was the light of all people. 5 The light shines in the darkness, and the darkness did not overcome it.

6 There was a man sent from God, whose name was John. 7 He came as a witness to testify to the light, so that all might believe through him. 8 He himself was not the light, but he came to testify to the light. 9 The true light, which enlightens everyone, was coming into the world. 10 He was in the world, and the world came into being through him; yet the world did not know him. 11 He came to what was his own, and his own people did not accept him. 12 But to all who received him, who believed in his name, he gave power to become children of God, 13 who were born, not of blood or of the will of the flesh or of the will of man, but of God.

John 13.1-5 and 14.1-31

1 Now before the festival of the Passover, Jesus knew that his hour had come to depart from this world and go to the Father. Having loved his own who were in the world, he loved them to the end. 2 The devil had already put it into the heart of Judas son of Simon Iscariot to betray him. And during supper 3 Jesus, knowing that the Father had given all things into his hands, and that he had come from God and was going to God, 4 got up from the table, took off his outer robe, and tied a towel around himself. 5 Then he poured water into a basin and began to wash the disciples' feet and to wipe them with the towel that was tied around him.

[This is followed by instruction during the meal which is concluded in John 17 with a prayer.]

14.1 'Do not let your hearts be troubled. Believe in God, believe also in me. 2 In my Father's house there are many dwelling-places. If it were not so, would I have told you that I go to prepare a place for you? 3 And if I go and prepare a place for you, I will come again and will take you to myself, so that where I am, there you may be also. 4 And you know the way to the place where I am going.' 5 Thomas said to him, 'Lord, we do not know where you are going. How can we know the way?' 6 Jesus said to him, 'I am the way, and the truth, and the life. No one comes to the Father except through me. 7 If you know me, you will know my Father also. From now on you do know him and have seen him.'

8 Philip said to him, 'Lord, show us the Father, and we will be satisfied.' 9 Jesus said to him, 'Have I been with you all this time, Philip, and you still do not know me? Whoever has seen me has seen the Father. How can you say, "Show us the Father"? 10 Do you not believe that I am in the Father and the Father is in me? The words that I say to you I do not speak on my own; but the Father who dwells in me does his works. 11 Believe me that I am in the Father and the Father is in me; but if you do not, then believe me because of the works themselves. 12 Very truly, I tell you, the one who believes in me will also do the works that I do and, in fact, will do greater works than these, because I am going to the Father. 13 I will do whatever you ask in my name, so that the Father may be glorified in the Son. 14 If in my name you ask me for anything, I will do it.

15 'If you love me, you will keep my commandments. 16 And I will ask the Father, and he will give you another Advocate, to be with you for ever. 17 This is the Spirit of truth, whom the world cannot receive, because it neither sees him nor knows him. You know him, because he abides with you, and he will be in you.

18 I will not leave you orphaned; I am coming to you. 19 In a little while the world will no longer see me, but you will see me; because I live, you also will live. 20 On that

day you will know that I am in my Father, and you in me, and I in you. 21 They who have my commandments and keep them are those who love me; and those who love me will be loved by my Father, and I will love them and reveal myself to them.' 22 Judas (not Iscariot) said to him, 'Lord, how is it that you will reveal yourself to us, and not to the world?' 23 Jesus answered him, 'Those who love me will keep my word, and my Father will love them, and we will come to them and make our home with them. 24 Whoever does not love me does not keep my words; and the word that you hear is not mine, but is from the Father who sent me.

25 I have said these things to you while I am still with you. 26 But the Advocate, the Holy Spirit, whom the Father will send in my name, will teach you everything, and remind you of all that I have said to you. 27 Peace I leave with you; my peace I give to you. I do not give to you as the world gives. Do not let your hearts be troubled, and do not let them be afraid. 28 You heard me say to you, "I am going away, and I am coming to you." If you loved me, you would rejoice that I am going to the Father, because the Father is greater than I. 29 And now I have told you this before it occurs, so that when it does occur, you may believe. 30 I will no longer talk much with you, for the ruler of this world is coming. He has no power over me; 31 but I do as the Father has commanded me, so that the world may know that I love the Father. Rise, let us be on our way.'

John 19.16–20.23

16 Then Pilate handed him over to them to be crucified. So they took Jesus; 17 and carrying the cross by himself, he went out to what is called The Place of the Skull, which in Hebrew is called Golgotha. 18 There they crucified him, and with him two others, one on either side, with Jesus between them. 19 Pilate also had an inscription written and put on the cross. It read, 'Jesus of Nazareth, the King of the Jews.' 21 Many of the Jews read this inscription, because the place where Jesus was crucified was near the city; and it was written in Hebrew, in Latin, and in Greek. 21 Then the chief priests of the Jews said to Pilate, 'Do not write, "The King of the Jews", but, "This man said, I am King of the Jews."' 22 Pilate answered, 'What I have written I have written.' 23 When the soldiers had crucified Jesus, they took his clothes and divided them into four parts, one for each soldier. They also took his tunic; now the tunic was seamless, woven in one piece from the top. 24 So they said to one another, 'Let us not tear it, but cast lots for it to see who will get it.' This was to fulfil what the scripture says,

'They divided my clothes among themselves,
and for my clothing they cast lots.'

And that is what the soldiers did.

25 Meanwhile, standing near the cross of Jesus were his mother and his mother's relative, Mary of Cleopas and Mary Magdalene.[5] 26 When Jesus saw his mother and the disciple whom he loved standing beside her, he said to his mother, 'Woman, here is your son.' 27 Then he said to the disciple, 'Here is your mother.' And from that hour the disciple took her into his own home.

28 After this, when Jesus knew that all was now finished, he said (in order to fulfil the scripture), 'I am thirsty.' 29 A jar full of sour wine was standing there. So they put a sponge full of the wine on a branch of hyssop and held it to his mouth. 30 When Jesus had received the wine, he said, 'It is finished.' Then he bowed his head and gave up his spirit.

31 Since it was the day of Preparation, the Jews did not want the bodies left on the cross during the sabbath, especially because that sabbath was a day of great solemnity. So they asked Pilate to have the legs of the crucified men broken and the bodies removed. 32 Then the soldiers came and broke the legs of the first and of the other who had been crucified with him. 33 But when they came to Jesus and saw that he was already dead, they did not break his legs. 34 Instead, one of the soldiers pierced his side with a spear, and at once blood and water came out. (35 He who saw this has testified so that you also may believe. His testimony is true, and he knows that he tells the truth.) 36 These things occurred so that the scripture might be fulfilled, 'None of his bones shall be broken.' 37 And again another passage of scripture says, 'They will look on the one whom they have pierced.'

38 After these things, Joseph of Arimathea, who was a disciple of Jesus, though a secret one because of his fear of the Jews, asked Pilate to let him take away the body of Jesus. Pilate gave him permission; so he came and removed his body. 39 Nicodemus, who had at first come to Jesus by night, also came, bringing a mixture of myrrh and aloes, weighing about a hundred pounds. 40 They took the body of Jesus and wrapped it with the spices in linen cloths, according to the burial custom of the Jews. 41 Now there was a garden in the place where he was crucified, and in the garden there was a new tomb in which no one had ever been laid. 42 And so, because it was the Jewish day of Preparation, and the tomb was nearby, they laid Jesus there.

20.1 Early on the first day of the week, while it was still dark, Mary Magdalene came to the tomb and saw that the stone had been removed from the tomb. 2 So she ran and went to Simon Peter and the other disciple whom Jesus befriended,[6] and said to them, 'They have taken the Lord out of the tomb, and we do not know where they have laid him.' 3 Then Peter and the other disciple set out and went towards the tomb. 4 The two were running together, but the other disciple outran Peter and reached the tomb first. 5 He bent down to look in and saw the linen wrappings lying there, but he did not go in. 6 Then Simon Peter came, following him, and went into the tomb. He saw the linen wrappings lying there, 7 and the cloth that had been on Jesus' head, not lying with the linen wrappings but rolled up in a place by itself. 8 Then the other disciple, who reached the tomb first, also went in, and he saw and believed; 9 for as yet they did not understand the scripture, that he must rise from the dead. 10 Then the disciples returned to their homes.

11 But Mary stood weeping outside the tomb. As she wept, she bent over to look into the tomb; 12 and she saw two angels in white, sitting where the body of Jesus had been lying, one at the head and the other at the feet. 13 They said to her, 'Woman, why are you weeping?' She said to them, 'They have taken away my Lord, and I do not know where they have laid him.' 14 When she had said this, she turned round and saw Jesus standing there, but she did not know that it was Jesus. 15 Jesus said to her, 'Woman, why are you weeping? For whom are you looking?' Supposing him to be the gardener, she said to him, 'Sir, if you have carried him away, tell me where you have laid him, and I will take him away.' 16 Jesus said to her, 'Mary!' She turned and said to him in Hebrew, 'Rabbouni!' (which means Teacher). 17 Jesus said to her, 'Do not hold on to me, because I have not yet ascended to the Father. But go to my brothers and sisters[7] and say to them, "I am ascending to my Father and your Father, to my God and your God."' 18 Mary Magdalene went and announced to the disciples, 'I have seen the Lord'; and she told them that he had said these things to her.

19 When it was evening on that day, the first day of the week, and the doors of the house where the disciples had met were locked for fear of the Jews, Jesus came and stood among them and said, 'Peace be with you.' 20 After he said this, he showed them his hands and his side. Then the disciples rejoiced when they saw the Lord. 21 Jesus said to them again, 'Peace be with you. As the Father has sent me, so I send you.' 22 When he had said this, he breathed on them and said to them, 'Receive the Holy Spirit. 23 If you forgive the sins of any, they are forgiven them; if you retain the sins of any, they are retained.'

John 21.20-25

20 Peter turned and saw the disciple whom Jesus loved following them; he was the one who had reclined next to Jesus at the supper and had said, 'Lord, who is it that is going to betray you?'[8] 21 When Peter saw him, he said to Jesus, 'Lord, what about him?' 22 Jesus said to him, 'If it is my will that he remain until I come, what is that to you? Follow me!' 23 So the rumour spread in the community that this disciple would not die. Yet Jesus did not say to him that he would not die, but, 'If it is my will that he remain until I come, what is that to you?'

24 This is the disciple who is testifying to these things and has written them, and we know that his testimony is true. 25 But there are also many other things that Jesus did; if every one of them were written down, I suppose that the world itself could not contain the books that would be written.

Explanation

We could ask many questions of the text in which John introduces Mary Magdalene (John 19.25-27). How many women were standing there under the cross? Are there four, three, or two? Why are they mentioned, whereas Jesus addresses only his mother? Who is the disciple whom Jesus loves who suddenly makes an appearance? And who does Jesus mean with that word 'son'? What does it mean that Jesus makes 'his' mother the mother of the disciple whom he loves? And what does all this mean for the view of Mary Magdalene?

First of all, the explanation often given is that three or four women are standing there. John mentions them because the tradition on which the Gospel leans mentions Mary Magdalene and other women at the cross. The anonymous disciple 'whom he loved' is the witness behind the Gospel (John 21.24): the tradition calls him John. According to Roman Catholic exegesis the important role that Jesus gives his mother for the church is evident from his words on the cross. In this interpretation the disciple whom he (Jesus) loved is a symbol of the believer and Mary is a symbol of the church. Indeed she is more than a symbol; she is the mother of all believers. Jesus wants to make that clear shortly before he dies. He says: 'She was my mother; now she is the mother of you all.' Protestant exegesis points out that Mary hardly appears in John again and that in the other Gospels she does not seem to understand much of Jesus' purpose. According to Protestant exegesis it emerges from John 19.25-27 that the church is not about blood relationship. These patterns have been broken. In the church people become a new family. No one is left alone; they have the care and love of and for one another. They belong together as a new family in the one house of the church.

However, two women can also be standing there: Mary the mother of Cleopas and Mary Magdalene. In that case John would be introducing the two women in detail, as also happens elsewhere in this Gospel. Jesus' mother is Mary (the daughter) of Cleopas and her relative is Mary Magdalene. These two women each play their role in the Gospel, whereas the other supposed female figures are lacking from John's narrative. A Mary of Cleopas and/or a relative of the mother of Jesus on their own do not occur again in the Gospel of John. Moreover Jesus sees only two people, his mother and the disciple whom he loved. Doesn't that mean that only two people are standing under the cross instead of several, as in the traditional interpretation?

Here, in Jesus' last hour, we have the names of the two people who were previously known only through their relationship with him. Their bond with Jesus was what characterized them. Mary was initially called 'the mother of Jesus' in the Gospel (John 2.1-5) and Mary Magdalene 'the disciple whom he loved' (John 13.23-26 and possibly 1.37-42 and 18.15-16), but under the cross they stand lost. The man who means everything to them is almost dead. The son, the teacher, has gone away. Each is left behind alone. They become what they used to be before they came to know him and before he filled their lives. Jesus' mother again becomes Mary (the daughter) of Cleopas and the disciple whom he loved again becomes Mary from the town of Magdala.

There they stand, desperate and vulnerable. Jesus notices their feelings and he addresses his mother, 'Woman, here is your son.' Where is his mother looking when he says this; to whom other than her dying son? Yes, she sees him; her gaze is fixed on him, while he is speaking with his last breath. However he does not say anything else to *her*. Instead he turns to the disciple whom he loved and says, 'Here is your mother.'

What happens to Jesus' mother with these words, to the woman who is on the point of losing her son? What does he want to say to her? She looks from her dying son to his beloved disciple and suddenly remembers the words that Jesus spoke to his followers at the meal shortly before he was arrested:

> I will not leave you orphaned;
> I am coming to you.
> In a little while the world will no longer see me, but you will see me;
> because I live, you also will live.
> On that day you will know
> that I am in my Father,
> and you in me,
> and I in you. (John 14.18-20)

'You are not orphans. I live and you will live.' How can that be, while they are standing like that by the cross? 'You will know that I am in my Father, and you in me, and I in you.'

'Not orphans' – 'I in you.' 'On that day you will know.' And all at once she sees: that day is today. All at once she sees the eyes of Jesus in the face of Jesus' beloved disciple. And from that hour the disciple takes care of her. That is the vulnerable way in which the church begins: in this first fragile bonding of two women there under the cross. Mary (the daughter) of Cleopas and Mary from Magdala feel robbed through Jesus' death, they feel the ground falling away under their lives. Each is left to herself, alone. But through these last words of Jesus they discover one another. 'Woman, here is your son.' And Jesus' mother looks at her dying son. And to his disciple, 'Here is your mother.' And Mary (the daughter) of Cleopas sees the living Lord in the beloved disciple whom John here, for anyone who wants to see it, shows to be Mary Magdalene. She takes Jesus' mother to herself as her own mother.

But can Mary Magdalene be John's beloved disciple, and what does that mean? John's beloved disciple is not Jesus' lover. According to John, Jesus loved his disciples to the end (John 13.1, 34), and he will also love his future disciples (John 17.20-23). He loved those 'who have my commandments and keep them' (John 14.21). In this way he also loved Martha, Mary and Lazarus (John 11.5). This is a pupil–teacher relationship in which the pupil is instructed and follows the instruction. So Jesus says to his disciples:

> As the Father has loved me, so I have loved you; abide in my love. If you keep my commandments, you will abide in my love, just as I have kept my Father's commandments and abide in his love. I have said these things to you so that my joy may be in you, and that your joy may be complete. This is my commandment, that you love one another as I have loved you. No one has greater love than this, to lay down one's life for one's friends. You are my friends if you do what I command you. I do not call you servants any longer, because the servant does not know what the master is doing; but I have called you friends, because I have made known to you everything that I have heard from my Father. (John 15.9-15)

'The disciple whom he loved' is an anonymous way of denoting a disciple instructed in this way, of indicating such a friend. Why anonymous? 'Out of modesty,' say some exegetes, for this is John himself. 'So that as readers we identify with this disciple,' say others. 'Because it is a woman,' we also hear today. To disguise that fact, the designation 'the disciple whom he loved' is also always masculine.

There is certainly something to be said for this last point, given that it becomes clear at the end of the Gospel that this beloved disciple is the one who 'is testifying to these things and has written them, and we know that his testimony is true' (John 21.24). In Chapters 8 and 9 we shall see that written or oral teaching by a woman was not regarded very highly and that women were not allowed to teach. By contrast, in the Gospel of John Jesus takes women seriously as conversation partners. But at the same time there is not a single verse that relates that women followed Jesus, as is the case in Mark, Matthew and Luke. It seems that in the Gospel of John dealings between men and women follow strict rules. In complete contrast to Mark, Matthew and Luke, in John there is only one story about contact between Jesus and a woman whom he does not know, the Samaritan woman whom he meets outside her home by a well (John 4). She is an exception. The women with whom Jesus speaks later are known by him and moreover are in their domestic environment and not outside it (Martha and Mary, John 11). Moreover John, in contrast to the other three New Testament Gospels, gives Martha and Mary a brother. So they are presented as the sisters of a friend of Jesus.

The Samaritan woman even begins a conversation (John 4.9). She does so, although according to conservative tradition Jesus addresses her very briefly ('Give me a drink', John 4.7), because she is a stranger to him. His conservative image is confirmed when he asks about her husband and when his disciples are perplexed that Jesus is speaking with a woman (John 4.16, 27). The Samaritan woman then of her own accord seems to assume the role of disciple and apostle and the disciples may reap from Jesus what she has sown. But in the Gospel she is not called disciple or apostle. It seems as if there are two levels where women are concerned. They play an important role for the community for which the Gospel is intended, but at the same time there is a movement which wants to restrict their role. This tendency can also be found in John's narrative about Mary Magdalene as a witness to the empty tomb and the risen Lord.

In contrast to what we are told in Mark and Luke, Mary Magdalene does not go to the tomb to anoint Jesus' body or, as Matthew has it, to see what is happening after three days. It emerges from the course of John's narrative that Mary Magdalene wants to be with Jesus' body. When that body proves to have disappeared, she is inconsolable. To my knowledge there is no other early source which has Mary Magdalene crying by the tomb. In addition, the two angels make no impression on her. Moreover she does not recognize Jesus when he appears to her. And when she does so later, she holds him tight as if she wants to keep him for herself, so that he has to reprove her. Although she can see, she is blind. That is one level of the story.

The narrative also gives space for reading it in another way. Through Mary Magdalene the readers can gradually move from sorrow over the fact of Jesus' death to joy that he is alive. Six times there are things to be seen: the stone that has been taken from the tomb (John 20.1), the linen cloths (John 20.5), the cloth that had covered Jesus' face (John 20.6-7), the inside of the tomb (John 20.8), two angels in white (John 20.12) and Jesus the gardener (John 20.14). Six times something is perceived by three different persons. It is becoming increasingly clear that there is something special to see here. Only the seventh time, at the end of the narrative, is it Mary Magdalene who really sees and exclaims to the disciples, 'I have seen the Lord' (John 20.18). She then tells what Jesus has charged her to say. 'Do not hold on to me'; do not cling to my earthly form. And 'go to my brothers and sisters'. In contrast to Mark, Matthew and Luke, only in John are Jesus' brothers and sisters really his family. And in John Jesus never speaks of God as 'our Father', as in the other biblical Gospels, but always as 'my Father'. Mary Magdalene interprets Jesus' words 'my brothers and sisters' in a way which is completely new for John by not going to his physical brothers and sisters but to his disciples. In her interpretation the disciples are now not only no longer servants but are also no longer simply his friends (cf. John 15.16). They are now his brothers and sisters.

The introduction to the Gospel of John shows that for this Gospel Mary Magdalene's interpretation has become the central point in the confession of faith. According to the prologue Jesus has come to earth to turn disciples into brothers and sisters: to those who believe in him he gives the power to become children of God, as he himself is a child of God (John 1.12-13). So he also says to Mary Magdalene: 'I am ascending to my Father who is now also your Father, to my God who is now also your God.' Compared with Mark, Matthew and Luke, Mary Magdalene here in John receives a message that is new for the disciples. Moreover, according to the prologue to John (above all John 1.12-13), her proclamation and interpretation belong at the centre of the faith of the community from which John is written.

This fact convinces me that the anonymous 'disciple whom he loved' should be seen as Mary Magdalene. The other anonymous figure in John 20.2, 'the other disciple whom Jesus befriended', confirms that. Mary Magdalene is *the* disciple whom Jesus loved. The other figure is 'the other disciple' and the Greek verb is different.[9] When later in John two anonymous disciples are introduced (again, I assume, two women),[10] the author feels called to explain which of them is 'the disciple whom he loved' (John

21.7, 20). It is evident from this that there are clearly more disciples whom John keeps anonymous. The beloved disciple is the one who had reclined on Jesus' bosom during supper (John 13.25 and 21.10). Here is another reference to the prologue: to Jesus who is on the bosom of the Father and thus as the only-begotten son also really knows God and has made him known (John 1.18). Just as Jesus knows God and has made him known, so the beloved disciple knows Jesus as risen Lord and makes him known (cf. John 21.7). It is the witness of Mary Magdalene that provides the basis for the proclamation of the Gospel of John.

In the Gospel of John, Mary Magdalene's testimony is not limited to having been the first to see the risen Christ. In the Gospel of John, Mary Magdalene is also not just the one who has seen the crucifixion and the empty tomb and received a revelation about it. Nor does she get any message about the place where the disciples have to go to in order to meet him. Her testimony is not about external things but about the *significance* of the cross and tomb and about the *significance* of the statement that the Lord is alive. The cross and the tomb are a going to the Father. All the disciples had already been told that in Jesus' teaching about his death. He is going to 'prepare a place' for them. But now what that means is made clear with the covenantal words 'my Father' – 'your Father', 'my God' – 'your God'. Jesus gives them the power to become children of God, and these words 'I in you' – 'You in me' go with that. With good reason, the resurrection narrative in John continues to describe how Jesus blows the Spirit on the disciples (John 20.19-23).

What does it mean to see Mary Magdalene as 'the disciple whom he loved'? Because here we have a man and a woman, the first thought to arise is, 'Indeed, so Mary Magdalene was Jesus' beloved!' It should be clear that in the Gospel of John we do not have erotic love, since the bond of love is a relationship which Jesus has with all his disciples, as emerges from the texts above. The word used for love is *agape*, comparable not to the love between lovers, but to the love between parent and child and between brothers and sisters. As the Father loves Jesus, so Jesus loves Mary Magdalene. As Jesus reclines on the bosom of the Father, so does Mary Magdalene remain on the bosom of Jesus. In the Jewish tradition this staying on the bosom of the teacher symbolizes the handing on of authoritative tradition. In the Gospel of John, the fact that Mary Magdalene is seen as 'the disciple whom he loved' means that she is the anonymous figure on whom the Gospel leans. She is the eye-witness who has told of Jesus. The Gospel of John is based on her story.

It is not known by whom the Gospels which are included in the New Testament were written. They were attributed to Mark, Matthew, Luke and John only later in church tradition. If Mary Magdalene really is 'the disciple whom Jesus loved', then the Gospel of John could better be called the Gospel of Mary Magdalene.

At the same time, it is clear that those who wrote the Gospel did not want this. The Gospel of John shows women who have something to say, but within conservative limits. There is no question of women being disciples of Jesus in as open a way as men, following Jesus, travelling with him and his male disciples, relating their experiences with Jesus – not only in their own circle but outside it – and being authoritative witnesses. Thus the witness on whom the Gospel leans is not Mary Magdalene in all openness, a woman, but an anonymous figure. Not, of course, a woman but a man.

Nevertheless this is also a figure whom writers do not want to sweep away completely. Those with eyes to see can discover that this is Mary Magdalene. Chapter 9 considers texts which indicate that all this follows the conservative rules. Women may not have authority, certainly not over men. Wearing a veil is a symbol of this. But for Mary Magdalene it is the case that: 'She has the evangelist as a cover (veil) because the Gospel is not written under her name' (Dialogue between a Montanist and an Orthodox).[11] Accordingly the Gospel of John has been accepted by the orthodox tradition. The Gospel which openly bears her name, the Gospel of Mary, had quite a different fate.

God, creation and evil

The Gospel of Mary, from the first half of the second century, is the only early text in which Mary Magdalene speaks at length. It is also the only Gospel whose title points to a woman. No church father mentions it. Given its dating, Mary Magdalene cannot be the author. Probably the author is one of her disciples, and the Gospel of Mary presents the teaching about Jesus that was attributed to Mary Magdalene in the circle around the author. The first six pages are missing. On page 7 a conversation is going on between the risen Lord and the disciples. They are putting their last questions before he says farewell for good. The topics which come to the fore in this teaching are nature and matter, something contrary to nature, the origin and effect of passion, the divine and human law, and the indwelling of the Son of Man. When Mary Magdalene speaks, she talks about being truly human and about the way upwards to the heavenly Rest and to inner stability. The subsequent discussion about the trustworthiness of Mary's teaching has already been examined in Chapter 3.

The teaching in the Gospel of Mary sounds strange. That is because Jesus is seen through the spectacles of the philosophical thought of the Stoa and Platonism. In the first centuries of our era that thought had permeated into wide circles of the population of the Roman Empire. The Gospel of Mary is related to what emerges in the works of the Jewish exegete Philo of Alexandria (*c.* BC 20 to AD 45), who uses the thought of both the Stoa and Platonism for his exposition of the Jewish scriptures.

In order for us to be able to understand the Gospel of Mary, first fragments have been included which illuminate the alien themes in the Gospel of Mary from Stoic philosophy. Aetius from the first century and Alexander of Aphrodisias from the late second century relate the Stoic view of God, matter, creation and nature. Joannes Stobaeus, who in the second half of the fifth century composed an anthology of texts of great thinkers for his son, explains what, according to the Stoa, is the meaning of the passions of lust, pleasure, fear and sorrow, which are opposite to nature. Passion makes one prone to sickness. Also the passion for women and loathing for them are caused by living opposite to nature and letting passion take its course.

The text of Claudius Galen (*c.* AD 130–200) is about the view of the Stoic Poseidonius of Apamea from the first century BC on the underlying cause of passion and the inner power of the spirit that can overcome passion. Epictetus of Hierapolis (*c.* AD 55–135) then explains the difference between the human and the divine law and exhorts us to believe that we come from God and that God dwells in human beings. The next three fragments are from Philo of Alexandria. He relates the meaning of the expression 'human being' and explains the origin of evil. The last fragment comes from the Gospel of Matthew. Only after that do we turn to the Gospel of Mary. The central question is: where does evil come from, and what must we do about it?

Aetius, Teachings *I 7.33*[12]

The Stoics made God out to be intelligent, a designing fire which methodically proceeds towards creation of the world, and encompasses all the seminal principles according to which everything comes about according to fate, and a breath pervading the whole world, which takes on different names owing to the alterations of the matter through which it passes.

Alexander of Aphrodisias, On mixing and multiplying *225.1-2*[13]

They [the Stoics] say that god is mixed with matter, pervading all of it and so shaping it, structuring it, and making it into the world.

Joannes Stobaeus, Anthology II *90.19–91.9*[14]

[About how the four primary passions should be understood.]
… under appetite: anger and its species … intense sexual desires, cravings and yearnings, love of pleasures and riches and honours, and the like. Under pleasure: rejoicing at others' misfortunes, self-gratification, trickery, and the like. Under fear: hesitancy, anguish, astonishment, shame, confusion, superstition, dread and terror. Under distress: malice, envy, jealousy, pity, grief, worry, sorrow, annoyance, mental pain, vexation.

Joannes Stobaeus, Anthology II *93.1-13*[15]

Proneness to sickness is a tendency towards passion, towards one of the functions contrary to nature, such as depression, irascibility, malevolence, quick temper and the like. Proneness to sickness also occurs in reference to other functions which are contrary to nature, such as theft, adultery and violence; hence people are called thieves, violators and adulterers. Sickness is an appetitive opinion which has flowed into a tenor and hardened, signifying a belief that what should not be pursued is intensely worth pursuing, such as the passion for women, wine and money. By antipathy the opposites of the sicknesses occur, such as loathing for women and wine, and misanthropy.

Claudius Galen, On the teaching of Hippocrates and Plato *448, 11-12*[16]

The cause of the passions, that is a lack of harmony, and of the life of misery, lies in not following in everything the spirit within, which is kin to the one who rules the whole world, but rather living in subjection to the worse and the brutish.

Epictetus, Discourses I *13, 4-5*[17]

[When someone complained to Epictetus about the indifference of his slave he gives the following reply.]
Will you not endure your brother, who has Zeus as his forefather, who is as it were a son born of the same seed as you and begotten like you from above? Do you not remember what you are and to whom you give orders? Your kin, your brothers in nature, the offspring of Zeus. 'But I have bought them, they have not bought me!' You

see where you are looking – to the earth, to the pit, to these miserable laws made by corpses for corpses; you have no eyes for the divine law.

Epictetus, Discourses II 8, 11-14[18]

Why do you refuse to know whence you have come? When you eat will you not remember who it is that is eating and whom you are feeding? When you go to bed with a woman, who is doing that? When you mix in company, when you take exercise, when you engage in conversation? Don't you know that you are feeding God, exercising God? You carry God around with you, miserable creature, and do not know it. Do you think I mean some god outside you, a god made of silver or gold? No; you carry him within you, and do not perceive that you are defiling him with your unclean thoughts and filthy actions. In the presence of an image of God you would not dare to do any of those things you now do, but in the presence of God himself within you, who watches and hears all, are you not ashamed to entertain these thoughts and do these actions, insensible of your own nature and earning wrath of God?

Epictetus, Discourses I 16[19]

If, indeed, I were a nightingale, I would be singing as a nightingale; if a swan, as a swan. But as it is I am a rational being, therefore I must be singing hymns of praise to God. This is my task; I do it, and will not desert this post, as long as it may be given me to fill it, and I exhort you join me in this same song.

Philo, On Abraham 32[20]

[On the meaning of the words 'Noah was a righteous man' in Genesis 6.9.]
We must not fail to note that in this passage he (Moses) gives the name of 'human being'[21] not according to the common form of speech, to the mortal animal endowed with reason, but to the one who pre-eminently verifies[22] the name by having expelled from the soul the untamed and frantic passions and the truly beast-like vices. Here is a proof. After 'human being' he adds 'just', implying by the combination that the unjust is no human being, or more properly speaking a beast in human form, and that the follower after righteousness alone is human being.

Philo, That the Worse is Wont to Attack the Better *22-23*[23]

The name which most correctly describes the real human being[24] and most thoroughly belongs to him is simply 'human being', the most proper title of a mind endowed with reason and articulate utterance. This 'human being', dwelling in the soul of each of us, is discovered at one time as king and governor, at another as judge and umpire of life's contests. Sometimes he assumes the part of witness or accuser, and, all unseen, convicts us from within.

Philo, Questions and Answers on Exodus *1.23*[25]

(Why) does (Scripture) say that He will not let the destroyer enter your houses to strike (Exodus 12.23c)?

It weaves into the whole legislation the faithful and worthy sentiment that we are not to make the Deity the cause of any evil. For when it says that He will not suffer the destroyer, it makes plain that corruption and destruction are brought about through certain others as ministers but not through the sovereign King. There you have the literal meaning.

But as for the deeper meaning, this must be said. Into every soul at its very birth there enter two powers, the salutary and the destructive. If the salutary one is victorious and prevails, the opposite one is too weak to see. And if the latter prevails, no profit at all or little is obtained from the salutary one.

Through these powers the world too was created. People call them by other names: the salutary (power) they call powerful and beneficent, and the opposite one (they call) unbounded and destructive. Thus, the sun and moon and the appropriate positions of the other stars and their ordered functions and the whole heaven together come into being and exist through the two (powers). And they are created in accordance with the better part of these, namely when the salutary and beneficent (power) brings to an end the unbounded and destructive nature. Wherefore also to those who have attained such a state and a nature similar to this is immortality given.

But the nation is a mixture of both these (powers), from which the heavens and the entire world as a whole have received this mixture. Now, sometimes the evil becomes greater in this mixture, and hence (all creatures) live in torment, harm, ignominy, contention, battle and bodily illness together with all the other things in human life, as in the whole world, so in man.

And this mixture is in both the wicked and the wise but not in the same way.[26] For the souls of the foolish[27] have the unbounded and destructive rather than the powerful and salutary (power), and it is full of misery when it dwells with earthly creatures. But the prudent and noble (soul) rather receives the powerful and salutary power and, on the contrary, possesses in itself good fortune and happiness, being carried around with the heaven because of kinship with it.

   Most excellently, therefore, does (Scripture) say that He will not let the destroyer enter your houses to strike, and this is what (actually) happens, for the force which is the cause of destruction strives, as it were, to enter the soul, but is prevented by the divine beneficences from striking (it), for these are salutary. But those from whom the favours and gifts of God are separated and cut off suffer the experience of desertion and widowhood. The meaning is somewhat as follows. Into this soul there extend and enter visible appearances which are mixed in accordance with various kinds of involuntary traits of character, sometimes naked and unarmed, and sometimes armed and in a certain manner threatening death, and they inflict mighty blows upon the thoughts. Now, these blows are the admission of appearances. But perfect good is not obtained from any of these.

Matthew 13. 24-30[28]

24 He (Jesus) put before them another parable: 'The kingdom of heaven may be compared to someone who sowed good seed in his field; 25 but while everybody was asleep, an enemy came and sowed weeds among the wheat, and then went away. 26 So when the plants came up and bore grain, then the weeds appeared as well. 27 And the slaves of the householder came and said to him, "Master, did you not sow good seed in your field? Where, then, did these weeds come from?" 28 He answered, "An enemy has done this." The slaves said to him, "Then do you want us to go and gather them?" 29 But he replied, "No; for in gathering the weeds you would uproot the wheat along with them. 30 Let both of them grow together until the harvest; and at harvest time I will tell the reapers, Collect the weeds first and bind them in bundles to be burned, but gather the wheat into my barn."'

Explanation

Where does evil come from? What has evil to do with God and the creation? Gnostic thinking about this is radical: the creation in which we live and which we ourselves are, body and soul, is intrinsically an evil product. The whole cosmos did not need to be, but it is the consequence of a misfortune within the Divine and the creation of a lower deity. The aim is to undo that misfortune and this creation. Only in the human spirit is there a core which binds it to the Divine. This core must be liberated. It should be the task of human beings to awaken from the stupor of the material world and return to the highest God. In Christian Gnosticism this highest God is the Father of Jesus and Jesus points the way back upwards.

The topic of creation as a misfortune cannot be found in the Gospel of Mary, which has only partially been preserved. On the contrary, in the Gospel of Mary nature even seems to be a positive concept. Perhaps the missing first six pages speak about the lower deity and his unfortunate creation of the cosmos, but I do not think so, since in the surviving part of the Gospel of Mary quite a different view of evil can be found.

In the Jewish view creation is originally good. The one God is the Creator of heaven and earth. 'And behold he saw that it was good.'[29] But somewhere something went wrong. The serpent was able to mislead the woman and arouse her desire to be just like God. The man allowed himself to be seduced by the woman and together they ate of the tree of the knowledge of good and evil. God expelled them from paradise so that they should not also eat from the tree of life (Genesis 3.1-24). The creation is good in origin, but something produced evil in it.

Jesus' parable in the Gospel of Matthew takes this up. The kingdom of heaven is like a man who sows good seed, but in the night his enemy comes and sows weeds in it. And those weeds can be got out only at harvest. The same parable occurs in the Gospel of Thomas (57).

Such stories do not occur in the Gospel of Mary. The conversation between Jesus and his disciples is about philosophical concepts such as nature and anti-nature, passion that is against nature and the mixing of nature and matter. These concepts are also important within Stoic philosophy. According to the Stoa, creation comes from God. The four basic elements of the cosmos are earth, water, air and fire. Fire can be seen above all in the seven planets. However, God does not stand above nature, as in Jewish thought, but is himself nature. The vitality of nature is divine, and not just in the biological significance of the word. The Stoa sees nature as the divine force which creates the cosmos, breathes through it and supports it, which brings stability and growth and organizes everything in such a way that is best for the whole. According to Stoic philosophy the world, the whole cosmos, forms a harmonious unity which is held together by this divine power of growth. Matter, the material, has no independent existence but exists only in our thought. Matter is constantly permeated by and mixed with the divine nature.

In the Stoic view, evil does not exist. There is no place for it in this holistic thinking. According to the Stoa, God is the designing force of nature from which the cosmos has emerged, which creates, forms and sustains the cosmos. It is the task of human beings to live in accordance with this power of nature and to insert themselves into the harmony that is there. Everything that happens to them has a purpose and is a cog in that great whole, of which human beings may form a part. Human beings are happiest when they live in accordance with nature. But a person can also choose to act against nature and allow himself or herself to be led astray by their passion. That choice against nature emerges from a wrong insight into what is good for human beings. Human beings do experience suffering, but that is a consequence either of our limited view or of living against nature. Unnatural passion forms the basis of a life in which no harmony can be found. This is passion not in our present-day limited significance of above all sexual desire, but passion in the Stoic sense of appetite, pleasure, fear and distress and whatever else Stobaeus understands by these. As Poseidonius, according to Galen, puts it, passion causes a lack of harmony and a life in misery.

But where does passion come from? According to the general view of the Stoa it comes from a wrong pattern of thought. According to Ptolemy it comes from our bond with the animal kingdom. In his view, the cause of passion is life in subjection to the lower and animal in us. But there is a way out, since in human beings there is also the spirit which is bound up with the one who rules the cosmos. By following the spirit human beings take the way to harmony and happiness. Epictetus shows what that means in practice. All human beings are equal and are brothers and sisters, since we are born from the same seed, from God. And do not do in your life what you would not do in a temple in the presence of an image of God. The task in the life of a rational being is to praise God.

Philo is an exegete of the Jewish scriptures. At the same time he lives in a world in which Stoic thought is commonplace. What is his view of the creation and evil? He says that it is a good custom not to make God responsible for evil. But in Philo, too, evil certainly gets a place. Like Jesus according to the Gospel of Matthew, he begins from two forces. Philo takes up the Jewish notion that God's act of creation consists in ordering chaos (Genesis 1.1-5). Creation takes place where the wholesome and beneficent force calls a halt to the annihilating force. But throughout the cosmos there is a mixture of the two forces. When the annihilating force is sometimes greater, sickness, disputes and all kinds of torments arise. The two forces are also mixed in human beings, but not in the same way: noble and prudent people are more open to the healing force and foolish people are more open to the annihilating force. Human beings thus play an important role in the balance between the two forces. Here the noble soul receives the aid of divine benefits which help it to ward off the annihilating force from the soul. Moreover every man and woman has the help of the Human in themselves.

The Jewish–Christian notion that the creation is good yet that evil exists and has to do with two opposing forces, both of which are at work in the world and in human beings, can also be found in the Gospel of Mary. This notion is expressed with the philosophical concepts of the Stoa.

Seeking, finding and following the Son of Man

The Gospel of Mary comes from the beginning of the second century. Despite the missing pages we can still see clearly what is literally central to the Gospel. It is the reaction of the disciples to the departure of the Saviour and his missionary charge. They are afraid that, like him, they will have to pay for their mission with death. Before the reaction, the teaching of the Saviour is central, and after it the teaching of Mary Magdalene, who replaces him in the role of teacher. So we can as it were fold the Gospel of Mary in two. It contains a double portrait with the discussion about Mary's trustworthiness as the conclusion. Perhaps that also says something about the missing beginning. Perhaps the Gospel begins with Mary's testimony to the appearance of the risen Christ and the Lord himself appears, as in the Letter of the Apostles. Then follows the conversation with the disciples, where today's readers now pick up the thread on page 7.

Gospel of Mary 7.1–17.9

[1–6 are missing]

7 [. . .] will [matter) then be [destroyed] or not?'

The Saviour said, 'All natural phenomena, all that has been moulded, all that has been brought into being exist in and with each other, and will be unloosened again up to their own root, since the Nature of matter is unloosened up to what belongs to her Nature alone. He who has ears to hear, let him hear.'

Peter said to him, 'Since you have told us everything, tell us this also: What is the sin of the world?'

The Saviour said, 'Sin does not exist, but you are the ones who sin when you do things which are like the nature of adultery: that is called sin. Because of this the Good One came into your midst, to those who belong to all natural phenomena, in order to restore Nature up to her Root.' Then he continued and said, 'That is why you become sick and die, for [. . .]

8 [He who] understands, let him understand. Matter brought forth passion that, since it proceeded from an opposite nature, has no form. From then on confusion exists in the whole body. That is why I said to you, "Be fully assured and do not be persuaded (by what is opposite to Nature), since you are already persuaded (by the Good One) in the presence of the various forms of Nature." He who has ears to hear, let him hear.'

When the Blessed One had said this, he embraced them all, saying, 'Peace be with you. My peace bring her forth to you. Beware that no one leads you astray, saying, "Lo here!" or "Lo there!", for the Son of Man is within you. Follow him. Those who seek him will find him. Go then and preach the gospel of the kingdom.

9 Do not lay down any rule other than the one I appointed for you, and do not give a law like the lawgiver so that you are not imprisoned by it.'

When he had said this, he departed. But they were grieved and wept greatly, saying, 'How shall we go to the nations and preach the gospel of the kingdom of the Son of Man? If they did not spare him, how will they spare us?'

Then Mary stood up, embraced them all, and said to her brothers (and sisters), 'Do not weep and do not grieve and do not be in two minds, for his grace will be with you all and will shelter you. Rather let us praise his greatness, because he has prepared us. He has made us (true) Human Being'. When Mary had said this, she turned their hearts inward, to the Good One, and they began to discuss the words of the [Saviour].

10 Peter said to Mary, 'Sister, we know that the Saviour loved you more than the rest of women. Tell us the words of the Saviour which you remember, the things that you know and we do not, nor have we heard them.'

Mary answered and said, 'What is hidden from you I shall tell you.' And she began to say to them these words: 'I,' she said, 'I have seen the Lord in a vision and I said to him, "Lord, I have seen you today in a vision." He answered, he said to me, "Blessed are you, because you are not wavering when you see me. For where the mind is, there is the treasure." I said to him, "Lord, now, does he who sees the vision see it with the soul or with the spirit?" The Saviour answered, he said, "He does not see with the soul nor with the spirit, but with the mind which [is] between the two that is [what] sees the vision and that [. . .]"'

[pp. 11–14 are missing]

15 him and Desire said: "I did not see you, on your way downwards, but now I see you, on your way upwards. But how can you deceive me, when you belong to me?"

The Soul answered and said, "I have seen you. You did not see me nor recognize me. I was (like) a garment to you, and you did not know me." When she had said this, she went away rejoicing loudly.

Again she came to the third Power, which is called Ignorance. [She] questioned the Soul, saying, "Where are you going? In wickedness you were held prisoner. Yes, you were held prisoner. Do not judge then!" And the Soul said, "Why do you judge me when I do not judge you? I am taken prisoner although I did not take prisoners. I am not recognized, but I have recognized that the All is being unloosened, both the earthly 16 and the heavenly things."

When the Soul left the third Power powerless, she went upwards and saw the fourth Power. She took on seven appearances. The first appearance is Darkness, the second Desire, the third Ignorance, the fourth is the Jealousy of Death, the fifth is the Kingdom of the Flesh, the sixth is the Foolish Learning of the Flesh, the seventh is the Hot Tempered Wisdom. These are the seven powers of Wrath. They ask the Soul, "Where do you come from, you killer of people?", or, "Where are you going, you who leave places powerless?"

The Soul answered, she said, "What imprisons me is pierced. What turns me is left powerless and my Desire has been fulfilled, and Ignorance has died. From a world I am unloosened 17 through a world and from a model through a model which is from the side of Heaven. And the fetter of oblivion is temporal. From this hour on, at the time, of the decisive moment in the aeon, I shall receive the Rest in Silence.'"

When Mary had said this, she fell silent, since it was to this point that the Saviour had spoken to her.

Explanation

The Gospel of Mary is about the teaching of Jesus as he himself gives it and as Mary Magdalene puts it into words. According to the Gospel of Mary Jesus is the Saviour who comes from God. But what does he save from and how? What does the redeemed person look like? And how does this teaching, which is attributed by the title to Mary Magdalene, relate to what the other writings tell about her as a witness? They are similar in that here too Mary Magdalene plays a role in the suffering of Jesus and the transcending of it. The situation is like the one that the Manichaean psalm of Heraclides talks about. Jesus has gone away and Mary Magdalene tries to let the disciples listen to him nevertheless. But the language of the Gospel of Mary is quite different, just as the language of the prologue of the Gospel of John is different. It is more philosophical.

What does Jesus redeem from? Not from sin, since sin does not exist. What then is the wretched situation of which Jesus speaks? According to Jesus in the Gospel of Mary the cosmos is not in harmony, as it is in the Stoic view, but in great confusion. It is not the material world that is the evildoer which bears the evil within itself, as in Gnostic thought, but there is something that works against the divine force of nature, something opposite to nature. God's force of nature is indeed at work in the cosmos, as the Stoics think, but there is also an opposing force, as Philo indicates.

There are two forces at work on matter: nature and an anti-nature. The material on which the anti-nature works brings forth passion, whereas nature brings forth the various forms of nature. According to the Gospel of Mary the creative and formative force of the divine nature has made something splendid out of still unformed matter, the creation, but something against nature has brought confusion in this by producing passion.

The first question in the extant part of the Gospel of Mary is about matter. Will it be annihilated or not? It is not easy to understand the answer immediately, but the answer becomes clear if we keep at the back of our minds the two forces which appear in the course of the following answers. According to the Gospel of Mary, Jesus does not come in order to announce the annihilation of the material world, since matter, nature and anti-nature are mixed together (GosMar 7.1-9). Just as the weeds and the wheat in the parable in the Gospels of Matthew and Thomas cannot be separated while they are growing without destroying the wheat, so the fruits of anti-nature cannot be removed without damaging the fruits of nature.

According to the Gospel of Mary Jesus did not come to free the world from sin either (GosMar 7.10-20). 'What is the sin of the world?' Peter asks. 'Sin does not exist,' says Jesus. What is called 'sin' is none other than that people who originally belong to nature deliver themselves over to what anti-nature brings about: unbridled passions.

Redemption does not just consist of the right insight, as in Gnostic teaching. It also consists of an act of Jesus, an act of cosmic dimensions. Jesus puts it like this: 'the Good One came into your midst, to those who belong to all natural phenomena, in order to restore Nature up to her Root' (GosMar 7.17-20). Thus Jesus restores everything that was originally formed and created by the force of nature to the root from which the force of nature comes, God himself.

How does that come about? Some exegetes say that the specific feature of the Gospel of Mary is the rejection of the cross of Jesus as a way of redemption. I don't know whether that is the case. After all, we have only half of the Gospel of Mary. There is certainly talk of the suffering and death of Jesus, but whether that has anything to do with redemption remains unclear. We do not know what is perhaps said about the death and resurrection in the missing part of the Gospel of Mary.

When Mary Magdalene tells the disciples about the greatness of Jesus, at all events she does not mention his death and resurrection, but his recreation of human beings (GosMar 9.18-20). He has recreated the disciples of a human being with a lower case h and b into a Human Being with capital letters. Levi adds that you can put on the perfect Human Being: you can clothe yourself with it (GosMar 18.16).

A similar way of speaking also occurs in Paul.[30] According to Paul, God has recreated us to be new human beings and we can put on this new human being.[31] We are new persons by (the Spirit of) Christ dwelling in us. In the Gospel of Mary we are new persons by the Son of Man dwelling in us.

On the basis of these similarities in imagery it could perhaps be said that the Son of Man in the Gospel of Mary is the Crucified and Risen One, as Christ is in Paul. But that remains only a supposition. In the Gospel of Mary itself as we now have it there is no discussion of the meaning of Jesus' suffering and of belief in his resurrection.

However, there is this cosmic act: Jesus has come to restore all creation to the root from which it emerges, God himself. Among human beings that happens by the Son of Man coming to dwell in them, and they can put him on, the perfect Human Being.

So in the Gospel of Mary Jesus is not the Son of Man who returns on the clouds to judge the earth, as is for example the case in the Gospels of Mark, Matthew and Luke. The concept of the Son of Man is more like that in the Gospel of John. In John the Son of Man has come to earth to give his life and return to the Father with the promise to his disciples that he will live in them.

In the Gospel of John, just as in Paul and the Gospel of Mary, there are also two movements, 'I in you' – 'You in me' (John 14.18-20). In John Jesus explains this with the image of the vine (John 15.1-8). He is the vine and his disciples are the branches. Just as the branches are in the vine, so the disciples are in Jesus. Just as the sap of the vine is in the branches, so Jesus is in his disciples.

What does the redeemed person look like? What is the appearance of the person in whom the Son of Man can be sought and found? What is the appearance of the one who wants to follow the Son of Man? On his departure Jesus gives his last instructions about how his disciples can live (GosMar 8.12–9.4). At all events it is important to be steeped in the fact that one is created and formed by the force that comes from God, nature. We belong to God; we belong to the different forms of nature. But it is also important to know that the opposing force, anti-nature, time and again wants to confuse us and to convince us of its power over us, indeed over the whole cosmos (GosMar 8.6-11).

Jesus gives his disciples his peace and says to them as he embraces them, 'My peace, bring her forth to you' (GosMar 8.14-15). So instead of their being in confusion and bringing forth the untamed passion of anti-nature, he makes them bring forth the peace of the Son of Man.

Jesus impresses on his disciples that they are not to seek the Son of Man outside themselves (GosMar 8.15-20), not here or there, although there are people who say that. They must not be misled. Jesus assures his disciples that the Son of Man is in themselves. They can seek him there and find him. And he counsels them, 'Follow him!' The aim is not to follow an authority outside oneself but to follow the Son of Man who can be sought and found in one's innermost being.

It is evident from Jesus' farewell words that in any case, following the Son of Man means proclaiming to everyone who wants to hear it the good news of the Son of Man, about the sorting out of all confusion (GosMar 9.21-22). Here it is important not to be concerned for power, as is the opposing force. It is important not to want to make rules as earthly powers do, from above and compulsory. The one rule of Jesus is more important (GosMar 8.22–9.4). In the Gospel of Mary as we now have it, it does not become clear what the rule is, but probably it is the one rule with which Jesus is associated in most writings, the rule of love. That is especially credible because this rule also has a central place in Paul, Mark, Matthew, Luke and John, writings which we hear echoed in the Gospel of Mary.

After Jesus has related all this and has given his missionary charge, he goes away. There is no mention of ascension, but we get the impression that Jesus is making a final farewell (GosMar 9.5). When Jesus has gone, the disciples burst into tears. They begin from the fact that discipleship of the Son of Man means sharing in his suffering. They say: 'How shall we go to the nations and preach the gospel of the kingdom of the Son of Man? If they did not spare him, how will they spare us?' (GosMar 9.6-12). From that moment it is Mary Magdalene who speaks about what she knows and has understood about Jesus. To paraphrase her words, she says: 'You are letting yourselves be confused by the opposing force. Do not stop at Jesus' suffering, but concentrate on his greatness, which can be found in yourselves, since he has prepared you. You have become Human with a capital H. The Son of Man has not gone away but is in you and changes you' (GosMar 9.12-19). Under the impact of Mary Magdalene's words the disciples stop crying and begin to discuss Jesus' teaching.

At Peter's request, Mary Magdalene relates that she has seen the great-ness of Jesus. 'I have seen the Lord in a vision,' she says (GosMar 10.10-11). This reminds one of Mary Magdalene's words in the Gospel of John: 'I have seen the Lord' (John 20.18). There she is talking about the risen Lord. What is she talking about here? Perhaps also here she recalls her vision of the risen Lord. In any case, Mary Magdalene has seen Jesus as Lord. Probably this is an experience comparable to the vision in which Peter, James and John see Jesus in his glory. They may not tell anyone about this before the Son of Man has risen from the dead (Matthew 17.1-9; cf. 2 Peter 1.16-18). We can also think of Stephen, who shortly before being stoned sees the glory of God and Jesus and exclaims: 'Look, I see the heavens opened and the Son of Man standing at the right hand of God!' (Acts 7.55-56).

In the Gospel of Mary, Mary then reports a conversation between her and Jesus about where that vision comes from (10.11-23). Is it really a vision of God or is it a hallucination? Jesus replies that the vision comes from her mind. According to Mary's words about Jesus' teaching his or her mind enables the disciple first to see the greatness of the Lord, second, to reach inner stability and third, to experience bliss.

How can we understand the great importance of the mind? According to Philo, the mind is the seat of the true human being in a person. In his view the first human being became a living soul only when God had breathed his divine spirit into the human mind.[32] According to Philo those are really Human who through the thus renewed mind can banish unbridled pas-sions from their hearts.[33]

Paul speaks of the renewed mind through the indwelling of God's Spirit which has raised up Jesus (Romans 8.5-15). The renewed mind leads to a completely new lifestyle (Romans 12.1-2). The renewed mind comes about through teaching about Jesus, and Paul says that in accepting the teaching one puts off the old human being and puts on the new.[34] As we saw earlier, according to the Gospel of Mary one becomes a new human being by the indwelling of the Son of Man. At the same time one can put on the perfect human being.

The Gospel of Mary as we now have it says nothing about the origin of the renewed mind, but on the basis of Philo and the similarities in imagery with Paul we can assume that the renewed mind begins with the acceptance of teaching about Jesus and his role as Saviour. That in the Gospel of Mary, too, this leads to a new lifestyle is evident from what follows.

After a few pages which are missing, Mary Magdalene relates that Jesus has spoken about the soul which on its way upwards to the Rest in Silence

– to the experience of the divine and of inner stability – encounters four forces that seek to prevent it: darkness, desire, ignorance and wrath (GosMar 15.1–17.1). These four opposing forces try to hold back the soul on its journey upwards by means of false arguments which all have the same aim, namely to let the soul know that it is in their power. However, the soul can rob them of their power by answering the forces of darkness, desire, ignorance and wrath, in the conviction that it is freed from them already.

This notion also occurs in Philo. When he goes into the deeper significance of the story of the tower of Babel (Genesis 11), he explains that those who turn against God use arguments as it were to build fortresses of passions and vices, with the aim of destroying righteousness and virtue. They argue that the good is the slave of evil and that passions are stronger than the higher emotions, that orderliness and virtue are subject to folly and vice, and that obedience is therefore owed to these stronger powers. But the Father in his mercy will see that the cement of the fortresses does not harden so that the result is simply a formless mass. Real freedom from the slavery of the passions and vices, a freedom which is certain and steadfast, is gained through service of God. Thus it is possible to climb after Moses in thought to the heavenly height.[35] In Philo's deeper exegesis of Numbers 20.17, where Edom refuses to allow Israel into the land of milk and honey, Edom represents 'the earthly' that seeks to block the royal way upwards to the vision of God. But Philo assures his readers that the mind that comes from God blocks Edom's way. Thus Israel, 'the one who sees God', arrives at its destination and he or she can have the experience of the Rest that comes upon a human being who looks on the beauty of God.

Whereas according to the Stoa the divine force of nature has brought forth the four materials of the cosmos: air, water, light and fire, according to Jesus in the words of Mary Magdalene the force against nature has introduced four completely different elements, namely darkness, ignorance, lust and wrath. And just as in the Stoa the element of fire takes form in the seven planets, so in the teaching of Jesus as related by Mary Magdalene wrath also has seven forms. These seven forms are: darkness, desire, ignorance, the jealousy of death, the kingdom of the flesh, foolish knowledge of the flesh and hot-tempered wisdom (GosMar 16.4-13).

When these things are discussed we have the teaching of Jesus, which Mary is aware that only she knows. She says that herself. But in addition the ignorance of the disciples is evident from their fear of those who have not spared Jesus (GosMar 10.7-10 and 9.5-12). Mary's teaching makes it clear to the disciples that it is not the peoples who are to be feared but the powers which Mary describes (cf. Ephesians 6.12): darkness, desire, ignorance and wrath constitute the deeper motive behind the suffering that is inflicted on Jesus and that will perhaps also be inflicted on his followers. These powers can be overcome. This is a task not only for those who do not yet know the gospel but also for the followers of Jesus himself. This last is evident from what follows in the Gospel of Mary. Both Andrew and Peter try to convince the brothers that Mary's words cannot come from Jesus (GosMar 17.10-22, see Chapter 3). The Gospel of Mary then shows that in his attack on Mary, Andrew is motivated by ignorance and Peter by wrath.

Thus the Gospel of Mary makes it clear that it is not 'the peoples' who are the enemies of the disciples, by whom they will not be spared, but that things go far deeper. The enemies are not only outside oneself but also in oneself, in everyone, even in those who belong to God and seek to follow the Son of Man.

At the same time it is evident from what Mary Magdalene relates about the teaching of Jesus that the way to the Rest in Silence is not a hard one for those who are convinced of liberation through the Saviour. The soul is able to refute every power and can go its way upwards in joy. In order to make the experience of this joy possible for everyone, the gospel of the Kingdom of the Son of Man has to be preached to everyone who will hear it.

To sum up: according to the Gospel of Mary, from what does Jesus redeem? He redeems from the supremacy of anti-nature. How does he do that? He does it by separating anti-nature from nature and again rooting nature firmly in God. And he does that by making men and women Human Beings. The role that the crucifixion and resurrection play here is perhaps on the missing pages of the Gospel of Mary. What does the redeemed human being look like? This human being has allowed his or her mind to be redeemed by admitting the Son of Man to their thought-patterns. Time and again he or she seek the Son of Man in themselves, find him and follow him. On the basis of that process they bring peace into this confused world; they are not concerned with power but with love. They know that they are freed from the clutch of anti-nature, which expresses itself in darkness, desire, ignorance and wrath. They tell others about liberation by the Son of Man. They tell of the greatness of the Son of Man, who brings peace and harmony and protects against the influence of the opposing force.

What is the relationship between this teaching, which the title of the Gospel of Mary attributes to Mary Magdalene, and what is reported about her as a witness in the other writings? There are similarities above all with Paul, the Gospel of John and Philo. Paul and Philo do not mention Mary Magdalene. The Gospel of John does. This writing is the only Gospel to speak explicitly about Mary Magdalene's teaching.

> Mary Magdalene went and announced to the disciples, 'I have seen the Lord'; and she told them that he had said these things to her. (John 20.18)

At all events this 'all' includes the fact that Jesus says to her: 'I am ascending to my Father and your Father, to my God and your God' (John 20.17). But implicitly the Gospel of John gives a broader view of Mary Magdalene's teaching, since for those with eyes to see she is the eye-witness on whom the Gospel is based.

There are important agreements between the Gospel of Mary and the Gospel of John. Two forces are also central to the prologue of the Gospel of John, as to the Gospel of Mary. They are not nature and anti-nature but light and darkness. As in the Gospel of Mary, so in the Gospel of John Jesus is the Son of Man who comes from God, returns, and through this work can be found again in the disciples. In the Gospel of John, too, there is the double movement of 'I in you' – 'you in me' and joy is central. And in the Gospel of John Jesus' followers likewise take on a new identity. They are children of God, brothers and sisters of Jesus, whereas according to the Gospel of Mary they have become Human like the Son of Man. Both put this conviction in the mouth of Mary Magdalene. Both have her telling about the way upwards. And finally, in the Gospel of John, as in the Gospel of Mary, Mary Magdalene's teaching is of decisive importance.

Thus the Gospel of John and the Gospel of Mary seem to be shoots from the same stem. This stem does not show the kind of Gnostic teaching that can be found in Pistis Sophia. However, it is certainly conceivable that a third shoot developed from this same stem in which the two forces which influence matter, Jesus as the Saviour who comes from God, and the way upwards, have found a place within a Gnostic framework of thought. The Magdalene tradition on which Pistis Sophia is based could have arisen in this way.

Pistis Sophia, the Gospel of Mary and the Gospel of John all implicitly suggest that Mary Magdalene had disciples; that she gave teaching which was heard, passed on and written down. That leads to the question whether there are also early Christian sources which explicitly describe her as someone who indeed went out to preach the gospel.

Chapter 5

Apostle

According to the early Christians, did Mary Magdalene preach the gospel as, for example, Paul did? In their story about her did she begin to travel and tell of Jesus? In short, is she seen as an apostle? That is the impression that we had in the previous chapter. In this chapter we shall look for more explicit indications. There are two early definitions of apostleship. From them we get an answer to the question why Mary Magdalene does not appear in the first 'history' of the early church: the Acts of the Apostles. Other and much later Acts are known outside the New Testament, such as the Acts of Paul and Thecla, the Acts of Andrew, the Acts of John and the Acts of Peter. Mary Magdalene does not appear in them either. However, she does play a role in the fourth-century Acts of Philip in the company of Philip and Bartholomew. We shall see that her specific role is different from that of Philip and Bartholomew yet in a number of respects is the same.

Two views of apostleship

In his first letter to the Corinthians, written about AD 53, Paul defends his apostleship to people who evidently think that he is not an apostle.[1] The letter to the Galatians, written by Paul around 55, shows Paul's relationship to the twelve apostles. It is evident from the conclusion to the letter to the Romans, written by Paul between AD 55 and 57, that he worked with women and valued them as co-apostles. At the beginning of the Acts of the Apostles, written around 80–90, a twelfth apostle is chosen in place of Judas, who had betrayed Jesus. Here a quite different view of apostleship emerges from that which Paul clearly had.

1 Corinthians 9.1-19

1 Am I not free? Am I not an apostle? Have I not seen Jesus our Lord? Are you not my work in the Lord? 2 If I am not an apostle to others, at least I am to you; for you are the seal of my apostleship in the Lord.

3 This is my defence to those who would examine me. 4 Do we not have the right to our food and drink? 5 Do we not have the right to be accompanied by a woman as sister,² as do the other apostles and the brothers of the Lord and Cephas? 6 Or is it only Barnabas and I who have no right to refrain from working for a living? 7 Who at any time pays the expenses for doing military service? Who plants a vineyard and does not eat any of its fruit? Or who tends a flock and does not get any of its milk?

8 Do I say this on human authority? Does not the law also say the same? 9 For it is written in the law of Moses, 'You shall not muzzle an ox while it is treading out the grain.' Is it for oxen that God is concerned? 10 Or does he not speak entirely for our sake? It was indeed written for our sake, for whoever ploughs should plough in hope and whoever threshes should thresh in hope of a share in the crop. 11 If we have sown spiritual good among you, is it too much if we reap your material benefits? 12 If others share this rightful claim on you, do not we still more?

Nevertheless, we have not made use of this right, but we endure anything rather than put an obstacle in the way of the gospel of Christ. 13 Do you not know that those who are employed in the temple service get their food from the temple, and those who serve at the altar share in what is sacrificed on the altar? 14 In the same way, the Lord commanded that those who proclaim the gospel should get their living by the gospel.

15 But I have made no use of any of these rights, nor am I writing this so that they may be applied in my case. Indeed, I would rather die than that—no one will deprive me of my ground for boasting! 16 If I proclaim the gospel, this gives me no ground for boasting, for an obligation is laid on me, and woe betide me if I do not proclaim the gospel! 17 For if I do this of my own will, I have a reward; but if not of my own will, I am entrusted with a commission. 18 What then is my reward? Just this: that in my proclamation I may make the gospel free of charge, so as not to make full use of my rights in the gospel.

19 For though I am free with respect to all, I have made myself a slave to all, so that I might win more of them.

Galatians 1.11-20

11 For I want you to know, brothers and sisters, that the gospel that was proclaimed by me is not of human origin; 12 for I did not receive it from a human source, nor was I taught it, but I received it through a revelation of Jesus Christ.

13 You have heard, no doubt, of my earlier life in Judaism. I was violently persecuting the church of God and was trying to destroy it. 14 I advanced in Judaism beyond many among my people of the same age, for I was far more zealous for the traditions of my ancestors. 15 But when God, who had set me apart before I was born and called me through his grace, was pleased 16 to reveal his Son to me, so that I might proclaim him among the Gentiles, I did not confer with any human being, 17 nor did I go up to Jerusalem to those who were already apostles before me, but I went away at once into Arabia, and afterwards I returned to Damascus. 18 Then after three years I did go up to Jerusalem to visit Cephas and stayed with him for fifteen days; 19 but I did not see any other apostle except James the Lord's brother. 20 In what I am writing to you, before God, I do not lie!

Romans 16.1-16

I commend to you our sister Phoebe, a deacon of the church at Cenchreae, 2 so that you may welcome her in the Lord as is fitting for the saints, and help her in whatever she may require from you, for she has been a benefactor of many and of myself as well.

3 Greet Prisca and Aquila, who work with me in Christ Jesus, 4 and who risked their necks for my life, to whom not only I give thanks, but also all the churches of the Gentiles. 5 Greet also the church in their house. Greet my beloved Epaenetus, who was the first convert in Asia for Christ. 6 Greet Mary, who has worked very hard among you. 7 Greet Andronicus and Junia, my relatives who were in prison with me; they are prominent among the apostles, and they were in Christ before I was. 8 Greet Ampliatus, my beloved in the Lord. 9 Greet Urbanus, our co-worker in Christ, and my beloved Stachys. 10 Greet Apelles, who is approved in Christ. Greet those who belong to the family of Aristobulus.11 Greet my relative Herodion. Greet those in the Lord who belong to the family of Narcissus. 12 Greet those workers in the Lord, Tryphaena and Tryphosa. Greet the beloved Persis, who has worked hard in the Lord. 13 Greet Rufus, chosen in the Lord; and greet his mother—a mother to me also. 14 Greet Asyncritus, Phlegon, Hermes, Patrobas, Hermas, and the brothers and sisters who are with them. 15 Greet Philologus, Julia, Nereus and his sister, and Olympas, and all the saints who are with them. 16 Greet one another with a holy kiss. All the churches of Christ greet you.

Acts of the Apostles 1.1-26

In the first book,[3] Theophilus, I wrote about all that Jesus did and taught from the beginning 2 until the day when he was taken up to heaven, after giving instructions through the Holy Spirit to the apostles whom he had chosen. 3 After his suffering he presented himself alive to them by many convincing proofs, appearing to them over the course of forty days and speaking about the kingdom of God. 4 While staying with them, he ordered them not to leave Jerusalem, but to wait there for the promise of the Father. 'This,' he said, 'is what you have heard from me; 5 for John baptized with water, but you will be baptized with the Holy Spirit not many days from now.'

6 So when they had come together, they asked him, 'Lord, is this the time when you will restore the kingdom to Israel?' 7 He replied, 'It is not for you to know the times or periods that the Father has set by his own authority. 8 But you will receive power when the Holy Spirit has come upon you; and you will be my witnesses in Jerusalem, in all Judea and Samaria, and to the ends of the earth.'

9 When he had said this, as they were watching, he was lifted up, and a cloud took him out of their sight. 10 While he was going and they were gazing up towards heaven, suddenly two men in white robes stood by them. 11 They said, 'Men of Galilee, why do you stand looking up towards heaven? This Jesus, who has been taken up from you into heaven, will come in the same way as you saw him go into heaven.'

12 Then they returned to Jerusalem from the mount called Olivet, which is near Jerusalem, a sabbath day's journey away. 13 When they had entered the city, they went to the room upstairs where they were staying, Peter, and John, and James, and Andrew, Philip and Thomas, Bartholomew and Matthew, James son of Alphaeus, and Simon the Zealot, and Judas son of James. 14 All these were constantly devoting themselves to prayer, together with certain women, including Mary the mother of Jesus, as well as his brothers.

15 In those days Peter stood up among the believers (together the crowd numbered about one hundred and twenty people) and said, 16 'Friends, the scripture had to be fulfilled, which the Holy Spirit through David foretold concerning Judas, who became a guide for those who arrested Jesus — 17 for he was numbered among us and was allotted his share in this ministry.' (18 Now this man acquired a field with the reward of his wickedness; and falling headlong, he burst open in the middle and all his bowels gushed out. 19 This became known to all the residents of Jerusalem, so that the field was called in their language Hakeldama, that is, Field of Blood.) 20 'For it is written in the book of Psalms,

> "Let his homestead become desolate,
> and let there be no one to live in it";

and

> "Let another take his position of overseer,"

21 So one of the men who have accompanied us throughout the time that the Lord Jesus went in and out among us, 22 beginning from the baptism of John until the day when he was taken up from us—one of these must become a witness with us to his resurrection.' 23 So they proposed two, Joseph called Barsabbas, who was also known as Justus, and Matthias. 24 Then they prayed and said, 'Lord, you know everyone's heart. Show us which one of these two you have chosen 25 to take the place in this ministry and apostleship from which Judas turned aside to go to his own place.' 26 And they cast lots for them, and the lot fell on Matthias; and he was added to the eleven apostles.

Explanation

According to a long and impressive tradition an apostle is someone who belongs to the twelve apostles appointed by Jesus himself. The twelve could then nominate new apostles. Here the word 'apostolic' stands for the trustworthiness of a particular tradition. Anyone who can legitimately trace his consecration back to the twelve apostles is a legitimate bishop. At the beginning of the Acts of the Apostles it becomes clear who can be considered for appointment as one of the twelve. It must be someone who has been with the twelve from the baptism by John to the day on which Jesus is taken up into heaven. It also becomes clear what the task of an apostle is: to bear witness to the resurrection of the Lord (Acts 1.22).

The Acts of the Apostles is a sequel to the Gospel of Luke. In Luke, there are women with Jesus and the twelve from beginning to end. Mary Magdalene is explicitly mentioned as the first of these.[4] Luke also mentions Joanna at the beginning and the end of the Gospel.[5] Moreover Mary Magdalene and Joanna are among the women who discover the empty tomb and receive the revelation that Jesus has risen. However, Mary Magdalene and Joanna are not presented as possible candidates for the apostleship, but in their place two men who have not been mentioned earlier, Joseph Barsabbas and Matthias. Luke gives no reason for this. Peter's definition of discipleship simply excludes women. Apostles must be men (Acts 1.21). In the Acts of the Apostles Mary Magdalene and Joanna make no further appearance. They are not apostles, not men, but women.

Paul's definition of apostleship is different. According to him, an apostle is someone who has seen the risen Lord and then borne witness to him (1 Corinthians 9.1 and Galatians 1.11-12). In principle that process has nothing to do with the twelve apostles in Jerusalem. Only three years after the risen Lord has appeared to him, Paul goes to Jerusalem to meet Cephas (Peter). He also says that he has seen James, but no other apostles.

Mary Magdalene would fit this definition of apostleship well. According to various sources she has seen the risen Lord and borne witness to him. From the greeting at the end of Paul's letter to the Romans it emerges that Paul did not limit apostleship to himself or exclusively to men. In Romans 16.7 he mentions Junia who, together with Andronicus, 'are prominent among the apostles, and they were in Christ before I was'. Paul calls Prisca and Aquila those 'who work with me in Christ Jesus'. He also uses the word *kopiao* (work hard/take trouble) for the activities of Mary, Tryphoena and Tryphosa, and Persis. It is the verb that he also uses for his own apostolic work (e.g. 1 Corinthians 15.9-11).[6] By comparison, it is striking that Paul mentions so many women who are working for the faith: Phoebe, Priscilla, Mary, Junia, Tryphoena and Tryphosa, Persis, the mother of Rufus, Julia and the sister of Nereus. Of the twenty-six names, ten are women, on six of whom Paul sheds further light. Nothing in his further elucidation indicates that he makes a special distinction between the work of men and women.

In the Acts of the Apostles the author relates much about Paul, but of the women with whom Paul seems from the letter to the Romans to be in contact he mentions only Prisca (Acts 18.1-4, 18-24). With her husband Aquila she teaches Apollos 'the way of God'. What has happened to all these other women? Wasn't their contribution important enough? The Acts of the Apostles seems to contain the history of the early church, but nothing is less true. In terms of content, it would have been better had the book been called the Acts of Peter and Paul rather than the Acts of the Apostles.[7] In these Acts there is little room for other male apostles, let alone female apostles who proclaim the faith. In the Acts of Philip, however, it is the risen Lord himself who sends out Mary Magdalene.

The apostles Philip, Mary Magdalene and Bartholomew

The book of the Acts of Philip, probably composed in the second half of the fourth century or the first half of the fifth, describes the apostolate and martyrdom of Philip, Mary and Bartholomew. Together they are called 'the apostles' in the writing.[8] Sometimes a distinction is made between the three of them. Philip is then 'the apostle', Mary 'the sister of Philip' and Bartholomew 'one of the 72' who were sent out to proclaim the gospel.[9]

The first fragment is about the sending out of Philip and his two companions. The second relates how Philip heals a blind man, Stachys, with Mary's help. The following fragments come from the part of the Acts of

Philip which describe the martyrdom of Philip, Mary and Bartholomew. That is often also told separately and is included in more than fifty manuscripts, not all of which have yet been edited. Here we have two Greek manuscripts with an introduction to Philip's work in Hierapolis. There he will meet his death. A third manuscript is used more extensively.

Acts of Philip 8.1-5[10]

8 The Saviour distributed the apostles over cities and lands, so that each of them should go to the place that had been assigned to him by lot. It had fallen to Peter to go to Rome, Thomas received the charge to go to all the lands of the Parthians and India, it had fallen to Matthew to go to the hinterland of Pontus, to Bartholomew to go to Lycaonia, to Simon the Canaanite to go to Spain, Andrew to Achaea, John to Asia and Philip went to the land of the Hellenes.[11] That was the division determined by the Saviour.

2 When Philip heard the name of the land and the city that had been assigned to him, he found it hard and began to splutter and wail. The Saviour who saw his tears turned to him, and with him John and Mary, Philip's sister. She was the one who kept the register of lands and she was the one who prepared the bread and the salt, and made ready the breaking of the bread. Martha in her turn performed the ministry to the multitude and worked very hard.[12] Mary spoke with the Saviour about Philip, who was sorrowful at the choice of the city to which he had been sent.

3 And the Saviour said to her: 'I know that you are good and brave in your soul and blessed among women. Behold, the mentality of a woman has come over Philip whereas a manly and brave mentality dwells in you. So go with him to every place to which he goes and do not fail to support him with love and great compassion. For as I see it, he is a very turbulent man. If I leave him alone he will often seize the opportunity to recompense evil with evil wherever he goes.[13] But behold, Bartholomew is going with him.[14] Together with him he will endure persecutions and the inhabitants of those places will subject them to dishonour. In his turn I am also sending John, to support you in the pains of martyrdom and the redemption of the whole world.

4 As for you, Mary, change your clothing and appearance. Remove the summer clothing that you are wearing and everything that outwardly recalls a woman. Do not let the seam of your clothing trail over the earth, do not let it hang, but cut it off. Then go your way in company with your brother Philip to the city called Ophéorymos, which means 'the avenue of the snakes'.[15] The inhabitants of that city have a cult of the mother of the snakes, the viper.[16] When you enter the city, the snakes of this city must see you divested of the outward appearance of Eve and nothing in your appearance must betray a woman. For the woman is the manifestation of Eve and she embodies the

female form. Adam embodies the form of the man. And you know that from the beginning enmity arose between Adam and Eve. That was the beginning of the rebellion of
the snake against this man and his friendship with the woman, so much so that Adam
was misled by his wife Eve.[17] And the cast-off skin of the snake, that is, his poison, has
enveloped itself with Eve and by means of this cast-off animal skin the primal enemy
has found a lodging in Cain, Eve's son, so that he killed his brother Abel.[18] So, Mary,
escape the poverty of Eve to enrich you in yourself.

5 Behold, I send you as sheep, I who am the shepherd. I send you as disciples, I who
am your master. I send you as rays, I who am your sun. I send you as sons, I who am your
Father. I am with you wherever you go.[19] Lift up your eyes to the creation which is in
heaven and look at the sun, the moon and the stars, the air and the winds. Look how the
sun, when it gives its light, spreads its rays over the whole of creation. And conversely,
when it prepares to go down, see how it takes its rays back into itself before the darkness
of the night establishes itself. The moon does the same. It sends its wholesome dew over
the waters and the plants and distributes life and loveliness to all things. See how afterwards the moon changes to the season of winter. The moonlight spreads itself generously
in the winter light to increase the harvests so that they can give their nourishment to
human beings, to the animals, the birds of the air, the reptiles and the fish in the waters.[20]
All this happens through the promise of my Father who is also your Father.[21]

Acts of Philip 14.6-7[22]

6 Then after he (Philip) had grasped his right hand and Stachys had taken hold of his,
he said: 'Hold on to me firmly. For a long time ignorance has held you captive in your
need. For the truth has been revealed to you in your vision. Do not call it a dream, for
dreams are only projections, whereas your vision comes from the Holy Spirit. Indeed,
up to this day you were chained by Satan: he is the one who makes the whole of
humankind perish through the deadly anaesthetic means that he drips into souls so
that their thought grows dark. He prevents them from seeing the heavenly glory. By
means of oblivion he leads humankind to devastation and corruption. For as soon as
human beings are born they fall under the domination of ignorance. After they have
grown up they are overwhelmed by oblivion and succumb: first to the infatuation of
dissipation, then to idolatry, anger, passion, hatred and lies. Ignorance degenerates into
and leads to all kinds of evil works. Ignorance confuses people's mind and blinds them.
The darkness and the night are the crown of ignorance. Now recognize that the one
who calls you gives you the true light, so that through that light you recognize the devil
whom you have served hitherto. For he is the one who has made you blind all this time.'

7 After he (Philip) had drawn him to himself, he stretched out his hand and dipped
his finger in Mary's mouth . . .[23]

(A page of the manuscript has been torn out here.)

. . . and he offered them a great feast, roasted flesh of the animals of the field, and set wine before them.

Acts of Philip, The Martyrdom 1–2[24]

1 At that time, after the emperor Trajan had come to power over the Romans, the eighth year of his reign, and after Simon the son of Clopas, bishop of Jerusalem, the second after James, had suffered martyrdom, the apostle Philip went through the cities and villages of Lydia and Asia, preaching the gospel of Christ.

2 Having arrived in the city of Ophorymé, also called Hierapolis of Asia, he was received by a believer, Stachys by name. He was accompanied by Bartholomew, one of the 72 disciples of the Lord, and his sister Mary and the disciples who followed him. Philip baptized the men, Mary baptized the women. This was the custom in that city: all newborn children were taken to the sanctuary and delivered over to the viper. She licked them with her tongue, and through this mark they became tributary to the snakes. But during Philip's stay in their city they were baptized in the name of the Father, the Son and the Holy Spirit; they stopped visiting the viper and they joined the apostles. Baptism protected them against the bites of the snakes through the seal of the cross. Philip and Bartholomew remained in the city and went through it destroying the snakes, visiting the sick, caring for the widows, the orphans and the poor, providing them with grain, wine and oil from three large jars. All the people left their work and hastened to Stachys' house to learn of the works which had been performed by Philip.

3 This is what he taught them. . .

Acts of Philip, The Martyrdom 3[25]

3 Philip's sister had sat down at the entrance of Stachys' house. She inspected those who came there and convinced them to listen to the apostles, who said to them . . .

Acts of Philip, The Martyrdom 3, 8–10 and 19–20[26]

3 Blessed Mary, the sister of the holy apostle Philip, had sat down at the entrance of Stachys' house. She inspected those who came there and taught the women. Indeed numerous married women came to her in Stachys' house and many of them left their husbands because of the words that they heard from Mary's mouth. The girls cut the hairs of their head, gave up their jewellery and dressed themselves in holy garments. They remained in the neighbourhood where Mary, Philip and

Bartholomew were staying. In turn the blessed Philip and Bartholomew taught the men.

[What follows up to 8 describes the teaching of the men.]

8 Nicanora, the proconsul's wife,[27] who had been confined to bed by various sicknesses, above all of the eyes, had heard what people were saying about the apostle of Christ, Philip, and his preaching. She too found faith in our Lord Jesus Christ. When she had heard what people were telling about him for some time and had begun to call on his name, she was freed from the torments which overwhelmed her. Then, when she had risen from her bed, she sat in a golden sedan chair, left the house by a secret door borne by her own servants, and went to Stachys' residence, where the apostles were staying.

9 When she arrived at the entrance to Stachys' house, Mary, the sister of the apostle Philip, saw her and began to speak to her in Hebrew in the presence of Philip, Bartholomew and the whole crowd of those who had found the faith. She spoke these words: 'Be welcome, daughter of my Father and beloved child. You are my sister, my mistress. You were given as a pledge to the snake, but Jesus Christ our Saviour has come to free us from all torments and to destroy your fetters of suffering, to seize them by the roots and to pull them up. You are my sister and we are twin children of a single mother. You have forgotten your Father's house. You have forgotten the way that leads to your Mother's abode, you who were deceived and brought into confusion. From now on leave the temple of this life and this renown which mislead and are transitory and come to us, who avoid the enemy because that is the abode of death. Behold, your Liberator has come to redeem you from the bonds of sin and behold, he has made the sun of righteousness, Christ, rise over you to illuminate you with the light of grace and to establish you as an heir of eternal life.'

10 When Nicanora, who was in front of the gates, heard these words, full of confidence she raised her voice and said to all those present: 'I am a Jew and a daughter of Jews. Speak to me in the language of my fathers,[28] for as soon as I heard your preaching I was immediately cured of my sickness and of the pains that overwhelmed me. I worship and praise the goodness and benevolence of God who made you push through, because of his true and precious jewel,[29] to this distant land. He has slain the great dragon so that now that we have found faith in him we should live with you.'

[What follows up to 19 describes the great wrath of Nicanora's husband, the proconsul Tyrannographus, who addresses her in a very threatening way. Nicanora tries to convert him. She will return to him when he is ready to live in purity, in continence and in true fear of the one God. If not, she will leave his house for ever. Tyrannographus is beside himself with rage, pulls her around by the hair, kicks her, threatens her with a painful death and has Philip, Bartholomew and Mary Magdalene imprisoned and tortured 'in an inhuman and terrifying way'. After that he shuts them in the sanctuary with the viper.]

19 Then the unjust proconsul commanded them to be taken out of the sanctuary and to be led before the tribunal. He said to the executioners: 'First strip them and search them to discover their magical means.' So the soldiers went to the viper's sanctuary and stripped first Philip, then Bartholomew. Then they went to Mary and treated her roughly. They said: 'Let us display her naked, so that everyone can see how, although she is a woman, she follows men, for she above all is the one who misleads all the women.' When they arrived at the tribunal, the proconsul said to the priests: 'Have it proclaimed in the city that all men who are there or who are in the fields and all women must come here and see her shamelessness, because although she is a woman she has dealings with these magicians and certainly commits adultery with them.'[30] Afterwards, when a great crowd had assembled, he ordered that blessed Philip should be seized and his ankles pierced. Then he ordered that iron hooks should be brought and driven through his heels and that he should be hanged with his head down on the tree in front of the sanctuary which grew in the neighbourhood of the sanctuary. In the same way they laid hands on Bartholomew, quartering him and fixing his hands to the wall of the sanctuary gate.

20 After this Philip and Bartholomew smiled at each other while they looked at one another as if they did not have to endure martyrdom. And indeed their bodily tortures and trials were so many rewards and garlands. But when they wanted to strip Mary and display her naked, the nature of her body immediately changed before the eyes of all. And a cloud of fire surrounded her so that they were completely unable to approach her or to look at the place where the saint stood, but all fled from her countenance.[31]

Explanation

'Do we not have the right to be accompanied by a woman as sister, as do the other apostles and the brothers of the Lord and Cephas?' Paul asks in his first letter to the Corinthians (1 Corinthians 9.5). It is uncertain to what precise practice Paul is referring here. The following sentence, 'Or is it only Barnabas and I who have no right to refrain from working for a living?' seems to indicate that the sister above all had a task relating to their livelihood. It is also possible that men and women proclaimed the gospel together.

In the Acts of Philip, at least in the earlier version in Greek, we see that Jesus himself gives Philip a woman as companion. She has a specific task which has nothing to do with livelihood. She must support Philip with love and great compassion, for if he were to go by himself, as an impetuous man he would recompense evil for evil. This is Mary, Philip's sister. François Bovon, who has studied this work for years, is convinced that Mary

Magdalene is meant, because she is introduced in a context of resurrection and proclamation.[32] In addition, we also see agreements with the way in which Mary Magdalene comes to the fore in the Gospels of Mary and Philip. It would then be new that the Acts of Philip presents her as Philip's sister.

It is unlikely that the Acts of Philip wants to put Mary Magdalene forward as Philip's real sister. Further on in the text fellow-believers are repeatedly recognized as brothers and sisters. Probably Philip and Mary, too, are brother and sister in the faith, and more than that. Their bond is close, because Mary with her male mentality supplements Philip with his female mentality. This recalls the Gospel of Philip, in which Mary Magdalene, as an image of the divine Wisdom, is said to be the sister, mother and companion of the Lord. The possible relationship between the Gospel and the Acts is unclear. In the Acts of Philip, too, Mary seems to depict Wisdom when she welcomes people at the entrance to Stachys' house and teaches the women. In the book of Proverbs, Wisdom is the one who calls people to her at the gates of the city and teaches them (Proverbs 8.3). Moreover, the author of the Acts of Philip emphasizes Mary's union with Jesus when Philip heals Stachys' blind eyes with the spittle from Mary's mouth. In the Gospel of Mark Jesus heals a blind man with spittle from his own mouth (Mark 8.22-26).

We see that Martha is also mentioned in Mary's introduction in the Acts of Philip. This implicitly suggests that by Mary the author means not only Mary Magdalene but also Mary the sister of Martha. However, he does not state this explicitly. Moreover Mary in the Acts of Philip is not the Mary who as Martha's sister anointed Jesus' feet (John 11.2). On the contrary, she is the one who 'kept the register of lands and she was the one who prepared the bread and the salt, and made ready the breaking of the bread' (8.2). Here, too, the author emphasizes Mary's union with Jesus. He distributes the lands and cities, she keeps the register. He breaks and shares bread and salt; she prepares it. Those are evidently the activities by which one can recognize her. There is no mention of bread and wine here because wine does not fit the atmosphere of abstinence which the Acts of Philip presents. In Chapter 9 we shall see that some communities in Phrygia shared bread and cheese rather than bread and wine.

The situation over the mission charge also recalls the Gospel of Mary, where Mary addresses the crying disciples. Here only Philip is mentioned, and Mary addresses the Saviour about him. Another difference is that here male and female play a major role, which is not the case in the Gospel of

Mary, at least for the author. It is the case for Andrew and Peter. In the Acts of Philip the fact that Mary is a woman also plays a role for the author. The Saviour praises Mary for her masculinity, her goodness and bravery, and advises her to remove everything that betrays on the outside that she is a woman. The reason for this is theological. She is going to the city where serpents play a major role in the cult. The city is Hierapolis, where the originally Phrygian mother goddess Cybele is worshipped. She is the goddess of fertility who was important as the mother of gods even before Rome. The Saviour relates that the serpent was once friendly with Eve, and through it she led her husband astray. Through the serpent's poison in Eve that Cain had a share of at birth, Cain killed Abel. Mary must show clearly in her outward appearance that she is no longer a friend of the serpent. In contrast to the story in Genesis, from the beginning there was enmity between the man and the woman and through this the serpent gained the opportunity to make friends with Eve. Eve here is not the sinful seducer, as in many other writings, but the woman who has been made poor. The Saviour calls on Mary to escape this poverty and to enrich herself in herself. Her changed external appearance is an aid towards this.

The task of Philip, Mary and Bartholomew is immense: 'the pains of martyrdom and the redemption of the whole world' (ActPhil 8.3). John will support them in this. The roles are clearly distributed, but the book of the Acts of Philip at the same time gives Mary more space than any other writing. She baptizes the women, whereas Philip baptizes the men.

The longer version of The Martyrdom (Vaticanus Graecus 808) then reports that Mary also teaches the women. It is thought that this manuscript has kept the more original version of the role of Mary. Moreover this version shows that Mary's teaching is actually heard, both by women in general and by the wife of the proconsul Nicanora. In all the versions, Nicanora's conversion is the direct occasion of the martyrdom of Philip, Bartholomew and Mary. In the longer version the author allows Mary and Nicanora to speak at length and determines that the two women speak in public, out of doors, to an audience which is both male and female.

Nicanora speaks 'full of confidence' and bears witness that she has been healed 'by your preaching' (ActPhilMart 10). That includes Mary's preaching. Thereupon she makes known her resolve to live in purity, in abstinence and in true fear of the one God. She asks the same of her husband, the proconsul; otherwise she will leave him for good. However, the proconsul wants her to stay with him, but only confined to bed as before. The author relates that many other women have already separated from their husbands because of Mary's teaching and the girls have cut their hair, abandoned their jewellery and lavish clothing and resolve to remain with Philip, Bartholomew and Mary. With good reason the executioners say of Mary: 'She above all is the one who misleads the women' (ActPhilMar 19).

What is the content of that teaching? At all events it is that Christ is the Saviour who liberates. He liberates Nicanora from the influence of the serpent's poison, both literally, for she heals, but also figuratively, for she is redeemed from the bonds of sin and appointed heir of eternal life. So far it sounds quite orthodox, but the next sentence is special: 'You have forgotten your Father's house. You have forgotten the way that leads to your Mother's abode, you who were deceived and brought into confusion' (ActPhilMart 9). This recalls Gnostic thought, which points to ignorance as the cause of all misery: ignorance about the real Father who is exalted above all and about the mother, Sophia, Wisdom, who through her fall has set creation in motion. Lower deities try to keep people ignorant of this exalted divine origin by threatening them and confusing them. The highest lower god is the creator of heaven and earth.

It is clear that this interpretation is not possible in the context of the Acts of Philip. In the mission charge the Saviour is clearly talking about the God of creation when he speaks of 'my Father' and 'your Father' (ActPhil.8.5). The Father of Mary and Nicanora is thus the Creator God, as is also customary in Jewish faith. The Mother can point to Nicanora's and Mary's Jewish origin, which is through her mother. It is more probable that the Mother represents the Jewish Lady Wisdom in contrast to the Mother goddess, Cybele, the goddess of fertility and mother of the gods, who is worshipped in Hierapolis and also in Rome.[33] The portrait of Mary Magdalene in the Acts of Philip is thus far removed from the presentation of her as priestess of the goddess of fertility which we saw earlier in Chapters 1 and 2 of this book.

Nor is Mary a prostitute in the Acts of Philip. Instead, as a consequence of her teaching, wives leave their husbands and resolve to live in continence. But in the Acts of Philip, for the first time we come across the accusation that Mary Magdalene is adulterous. The proconsul sees the fact that she travels and works with men as proof of this (ActPhilMart 19). She does not fit into the usual male–female relationships. She travels and works with men who are not related to her by blood or married to her. Thus she is suspected of adultery. In this refusal to accept an independent relationship of women to men, in my view we see a deeper cause of the later image of Mary Magdalene as a prostitute.

Nevertheless it does not seem to be the intention of the Acts of Philip that women after Mary Magdalene should also travel and work with men. Both the short and the longer version of the Martyrdom relate how Philip gives Bartholomew his last advice about the Christian community in Hierapolis. Almost half of his words are devoted to the relationship between men and women. The intention is that the virgins who have come to believe shall remain in Stachys' house. They may leave it to visit the sick, but only in pairs. They may not speak with young men. In this connection Philip reminds Bartholomew of Jesus' words: 'Any man who looks at a woman and covets her has already committed adultery in his heart' (Matthew 5.28). In the longer version of the Martyrdom, Bartholomew puts the following question about the strict separation of men and women:

'Why did not the Saviour, at the time when he was with us, separate us from the holy virgins?' Philip answered him: 'Do you not know that while the sun is shining the world is filled with light? But when the sun disappears and leaves the world the whole world is filled with darkness. The wild beasts come out in the darkness and the snakes and scorpions and all reptiles bite. So too, while Christ was with us, we were in his glory. His grace and his gift surrounded us in every place that we were. And no shadow of sin could dwell in us because of the steadfastness and the loftiness of the Holy Spirit which he had breathed into us'. (ActPhilMart 36)

Thus according to Philip there is a distinction between the time when Christ lived on earth and the time afterwards. This above all influences the relationship between men and women. In the time of Christ they could travel together and work together. In the time after Christ they must remain separate.

In this context Philip also gives a striking view of Peter's relationship with women. Both in the short and the longer version of the Martyrdom, after quoting Jesus' words ('Any man who looks at a woman and covets her has already committed adultery in his heart'), Philip says: 'This is the reason why our brother Peter has fled from any place where a woman lived' (ActPhilMart 36). Moreover Philip relates that Peter has prayed to God to paralyse his daughter so that she does not form a temptation for men.[34] Are we here on the track of the ultimate reason for Peter's hostility to women, which also occurs in other writings like the Gospel of Thomas, the Gospel of Mary and Pistis Sophia? In the early Christian tradition was Peter known not only as a hothead who easily reacted unthinkingly? Was he perhaps also known for his sexual drives which he found it difficult to control? At all events, both in the short and the longer version of the Martyrdom Peter is presented as someone who has great difficulty in seeing a woman without desiring her and therefore he avoids every place where there is a woman.

Ann Brock has pointed out that the book of the Acts of Philip appears not only in several manuscripts in Greek but also in various dialects of Coptic, in Ethiopic and in Arabic. She shows that there is an important difference between the manuscripts over the role of Mary.[35] The Greek manuscripts also show great differences among themselves. In almost every Greek manuscript it is stated that Mary Magdalene baptizes the women and Philip the men. Only in the longer Greek version of the introduction to the Martyrdom does it emerge that Mary Magdalene teaches (Vaticanus Graecus 808). In another version she calls on people to listen to the teaching of 'the apostles', in this case Philip and Bartholomew (Vaticanus Graecus 824). In the short version of the Martyrdom Mary's teaching role at the entrance of the house of Stachys is not mentioned at all (Xenophontes 32).

The non-Greek manuscripts are not a literal translation of the Greek. The content of the Acts of Philip is retold. Mary does not appear in them as an apostle. It is Peter who stands beside Christ in the distribution of the lands and the cities. It is Peter who comforts Philip and Peter who accompanies Philip on his mission. We already saw earlier that Peter takes Mary Magdalene's place as the first witness to the resurrection in the Gospel of Luke. We also saw several times that Peter is described as someone who attacks Mary Magdalene and will not accept her role. I then suggested that various authors limit Mary Magdalene's role in favour of a greater role for men. This is the clearest example: in the non-Greek versions of the Acts of Philip, Mary Magdalene disappears and Peter takes over her role of apostle.

As early as the second century Celsus makes a disrespectful allusion to the apostolic career of Mary Magdalene. When he ridicules the great differences in belief among Christians and their appeal to various leaders, he mentions groups claiming to follow certain women, among them Salome, Mariamme and Martha. Origen indignantly objects that he does not know of such groups (*Against Celsus* 5.62). This does not mean that they did not exist. In the next chapters we shall see that in the tradition accepted by the church it became increasingly difficult to include the notion of women having authority, especially women having authority over men.

Chapter 6

Eve and Apostle of the Apostles

The church fathers do not add any new stories about Mary Magdalene. They mostly comment on what can be found about the resurrection in the first-century Gospels. The focus is on two subjects, the fact that according to John Mary Magdalene may not keep holding the risen Lord and the fact that she, a woman, brought the message of the resurrection to the male disciples. Both facts are connected with Eve, the woman from the creation story.

'Do not touch me'

'Do not cling to me,' says Jesus to Mary Magdalene in the Gospel of John. These words have entered history through the translation of them into Latin as *noli me tangere* as a prohibition to Mary Magdalene against touching the Lord. This 'Do not touch me' from the Gospel of John is a theme which occurs often in the church fathers. By way of an anthology there follow here three different views of the meaning of the words. Hippolytus of Rome, who lived *c.* AD 170–235, writes about them in his *Commentary on the Song of Songs*. In flowery language Hippolytus explains that Song of Songs 3.1-4, in which the bride tells of her search for the bridegroom, is an anticipatory reference to the women who seek Christ in the resurrection narrative. Jerome of Rome (*c.* AD 347–419) replies to a letter from the Roman scholar Marcella. She asks him why according to John Mary Magdalene may not touch the risen Lord, whereas according to Matthew she may. Ambrose of Milan (*c.* AD 333–397) also sees the problem and has a simple answer: there were two women called Mary, both of whom came from Magdala.

Hippolytus, Commentary on the Song of Songs *24.1–25.5*[1]

Therefore she calls: 'In the night I sought him whom my soul loves; I sought him and did not find him. The watchmen who guarded the city found me. "Have you seen him whom my soul loves?" And behold, when I had gone a little away from them I found him whom my soul loves. I found him and did not let him go until I brought him into my mother's house and into the chamber where she became pregnant with me.'[2]

2 O blessed voice! O blessed women who show that what has been seen before is a prefiguring. Therefore she calls out and says 'In the night I sought him whom my soul loves.'[3] See how that is fulfilled in Martha and Mary. With them the synagogue sought zealously for the dead Christ, whom she thought no longer to be alive. For this is what she teaches us and says: 'In the night I sought him and did not find him whom my soul loves.'[4]

3 It is written in the Gospels: 'The women came in the night to seek in the tomb.'[5] 'I sought him and did not find him.'[6] 'Why do you seek the living among the dead?'[7] And they found nothing that was his there, for the burial mound was not his abode, but heaven. Why do you seek him on this earth? The one who, after he has risen, is sitting on the throne? Why do you seek the most glorious of all in a contemptible tomb? Why do you seek the perfect one in a burial mound? Behold, now the stone has been rolled away; why do you seek him in this tomb? The one who, fulfilled by grace, is in heaven? Why do you seek the one who has been loosed as if he were bound there, as someone who is shut up in a prison?

4 See that there a new mystery has been fulfilled. For thus she calls out and says: 'I sought him and did not find him. The watchmen who guarded the city found me.'[8] Who other than the angels who sat there were those who found him? And what city did they guard other than the new Jerusalem, the body of Christ? 'The watchmen who guarded the city found me.'[9] The women asked this: 'Have you seen him whom my soul loves?'[10] But they said: 'Whom do you seek? Jesus of Nazareth? Behold, he is risen.'[11]

25. 1 'And when I had gone a little away from them.'[12] And while they were turning round and wanted to go away, the Saviour appeared to them.[13] Then was fulfilled what had been said: 'Behold, when I had gone a little way from them I found him whom my soul loves.'

2 But the Saviour answered and said: 'Martha, Mary.' And they said 'Rabbouni', which translated means 'my Lord'.[14] 'I have found him whom I love and I will not let him go.'[15] For at that moment she clings to him, embracing his feet. And he calls to her: 'Do not touch me, for I am not yet ascended to the Father.'[16] She continued to cling to him and said: 'I will not let you go until I have brought you in and have let you into my heart.' 'I will not let you go until I have brought you into my mother's house and into the chamber where she became pregnant with me.'[17] Because love of Christ had

gathered in her belly she did not want to go away. Therefore she cries: 'I have found him and will not let him go.'[18] O blessed woman who continued to cling to his feet, so that she could fly with him up in the air![19]

3 Martha and Mary said this to him. She showed Martha's secret beforehand through Solomon.[20] 'We do not permit you to fly upwards. Go to the Father and offer him a new sacrifice. Offer Eve, who is no longer straying, but full of longing clings to the tree of life with her hands. Behold, I clung to your knees. Not like a cord until it is broken, but I clung to the feet of Christ. Let me not return to the earth, so that I do not wander. Carry me off to heaven.'

O blessed woman, who did not want to depart from Christ.

4 Therefore she says: 'When I had gone a little way, I found him whom my soul loves.'[21] Take my heart to mix it with the Spirit! Secure it, fulfil it, until it can be united with the heavenly body! Mix this body of mine with the heavenly body! Drink it as wine! Take it and then reach it to heaven as a newly mixed drink. So that the woman follows the one whom she desires and does not go astray! She is no longer pierced in the heel[22] and no longer touches the wood of knowledge.[23] Instead, from now on she has been made a conqueror through the death on the wood.[24]

5 Take up Eve, so that she shall no longer give birth with pain, for the pangs, the pain and the sorrow have been driven away.[25] From now on, accept the Eve who walks according to the law. Receive her and recognize this gift which has been offered to the Father. Offer Eve as new, as no longer found naked. No longer is the leaf of the fig tree her clothing,[26] but she is clothed with the holy Spirit, for she has dressed herself with good clothing that is incorruptible.[27] She has Christ for he was not naked. Although the cloths lay in the tomb, he was not naked. Nor was Adam naked at first. He was clad in the renewed equipment of sinlessness, meekness and incorruptibility. But he was led astray and found naked. However, now that that has become clear to him, he is clothed anew.

Jerome, To Marcella, Letter 59.4[28]

The fourth question[29] that you put is how it is possible that in the Gospel of John after the resurrection Mary Magdalene is told, 'Do not touch me, for I am not yet ascended to my Father.'[30] Whereas in Matthew it is written that the women ran to the Lord and grasped his feet.[31] For it is clearly not the same after the resurrection to touch his feet and not to touch him. Mary Magdalene is the one out of whom he had driven seven demons,[32] so that where sin had abounded, grace should be even more abounding.[33] She is also the one who thought that the Lord was the gardener and spoke with him as with an ordinary person[34] and who sought the living among the dead. Therefore rightly she is told, Do not touch me.[35] That means: 'You do not deserve to remain in my footsteps. You do not deserve to worship me as Lord and to grasp the feet of the one whom you cannot believe to have risen, because for you I have not yet risen to my Father.'

But the other women who touch his feet confess him as Lord. And they deserve to remain in his footsteps, the footsteps of him whom they trust to have risen to the Father.

There should also be an easy solution when in the one Gospel it is said that she grasped his feet and in the other that she did not. For first she can be indicated as an unbeliever. And later possibly she would not have been rejected because she had undone her fault by a confession of guilt. That is what you can say also of the thieves.[36] The one Gospel relates that they both blasphemed him,[37] whereas the other relates that one of them confessed him as Lord.[38]

Ambrose, Commentary on the Gospel of Luke *10.153-155 and 164-165*[39]

153 It is early in the morning: Peter did not yet know, nor did John. But surely the Lord would not allow his disciples to be tormented longer by the uncertainty surrounding his death, when the women were directly chosen by the angel, directly chosen by the Lord to go and report to them what had happened?[40] To make you certain that it happened in the night, some women do not know about it and others do. Those who continued to look day and night know; those who have returned do not. According to John the one Mary Magdalene knows nothing of it, according to Matthew the other Mary Magdalene does. It is impossible that one of the two can first not have known and afterwards have known.[41] If there are more Maries, then there are also more Magdalenes, for Mary is the name of the person and Magdalene of the place where they come from.

154 Note therefore that a second Mary from Magdala is mentioned, the one who clung to the Lord's feet.[42] In Matthew the one may grasp the feet of the Lord; in John the other may not touch him.[43] The one deserved to see the angel, the other came early in the morning and therefore saw no one.[44] The one gave the disciples the message that the Lord had risen, the other gave it to be understood that he had been taken from the tomb.[45] The one is all joy, the other is ready to weep.[46] The one sees Christ coming to her in all his glory, the other still seeks him among the dead.[47] The one saw the Lord and believed, the other could not recognize him when she saw him.[48] The one fell on her knees before him in a spirit of faith, the other became all the more sorrowful through the doubt in her heart.[49]

155 Of course it was right that she was not allowed to touch Christ, for we do not touch the Lord through bodily contact but in faith. The Lord says: 'For I am not yet

ascended to my Father';[50] that means: in your eyes I am not yet ascended because you are still seeking the living among the dead. Therefore she is sent to those who are stronger.[51] Through their example she must learn to believe and have the resurrection proclaimed by them.[52]

164 Thus the Lord has no objection to allowing himself to be touched by a woman: it was also a Mary who anointed his feet with ointment.[53] He does not reject the touching but he shows the way to make spiritual progress. After all, not everyone can touch Christ as risen, although he has touched him during his abode in this life and in this body. Whoever wants to touch Christ must die to himself in his own members. Already bearing the traces of his future resurrection, he must clothe himself with tender mercy, and without hesitation renounce the earthly.[54]

165 So what does that mean: 'Do not touch me?'[55] Do not put your hand on what is too great for you, but go to my brothers, that is, to the more perfect persons – whoever does the will of my Father in heaven, he is my brother and sister and mother[56] – for the resurrection cannot come easily into one's reach, but only of those who have made further progress. The privilege of this belief is reserved for those who have firmer ground under them. However, 'I do not allow women to teach in the gathering.'[57] 'Let them question their man at home.'[58] So Mary was sent to her household and accepted the commandments prescribed.

Explanation

From the fourth century onwards, the church fathers refer to Mary Magdalene relatively often. Above all Jesus' words to her in the Latin translation of the basic Greek text, *noli me tangere*, 'do not touch me', from John 20.17 keep recurring. 'Do not touch me' has also become a specific theme in artistic depictions of Mary Magdalene. The great question of the church fathers is: why may not Mary Magdalene touch the risen Lord, whereas he invites Thomas to touch him? In the third century Origen of Alexandria expressed the view that perhaps the Lord was only partially risen when he appeared to Mary and was wholly risen when he let Thomas see him.[59] However, most church fathers think that Mary Magdalene did not yet believe in the divinity of Jesus whereas Thomas did. She says 'rabbouni' to Jesus, which means 'my Master', whereas Thomas says 'my Lord and my God'.[60]

Tertullian of Carthage, who lived *c.* AD 160–220 and mentions the theme in passing in his argument against Praxeas, is an exception. He praises the great piety of Mary Magdalene, who wanted out of love to touch Jesus, whereas Thomas wanted to do so out of curiosity and unbelief.[61] The customary answer is to be found in the fourth-century letter from Jerome to Marcella. Marcella was a widow of good reputation who after her conversion used her fortune for the poor and together with some other women led a life of prayer and study in simplicity. When Jerome arrived in Rome, Marcella had asked for him as their teacher. With him they read scripture in Hebrew and Greek and studied the first church fathers. In addition they wrote one another letters. The letters of Marcella and the others to Jerome have not been preserved, but those of Jerome to her and the other women of their company have. The letters show the exegetical questions with which they were occupied.

One of them is: why may Mary Magdalene not touch the risen Lord in the Gospel of John but may in the Gospel of Matthew?[62] Marcella presents this to Jerome. One wonders whether she found Jerome's answers satisfactory. He draws an unexpected distinction between Mary Magdalene and the other women. Only Mary Magdalene is said not to be able to touch the risen Lord; the other women may. However, that is not the case in the Gospel of Matthew: Mary Magdalene and the other Mary together cling to Jesus' feet and worship him. And John does not speak of other women, but only of Mary Magdalene. Thus Jerome does not take Marcella's question very seriously. As if Jerome also senses this, he gives a second answer in which he begins from Marcella's observation that there is a great difference between Matthew and John. Jerome suggests that before touching Jesus in Matthew, perhaps she had made a confession of guilt.

Elsewhere Jerome indeed clearly presents Mary Magdalene as a very pious woman. That emerges from the following quotation from a letter to Principia about a year later:[63]

> Priests and Pharisees crucify the Son of God, but Mary Magdalene weeps by the cross, prepares oils for anointing, seeks in the tomb, asks the gardener, recognizes the Lord, hastens to the apostles and proclaims him whom she has found. These (men) doubt, she trusts. (*To Principia*, Letter 65 1.3)

This fragment of text comes from a letter to Principia, one of Marcella's spiritual daughters, in which Jerome sends a commentary on Psalm 44 which he has made at her request. By way of introduction he defends himself against the accusation that 'he often writes to women and prefers the weaker sex to men'. He begins his defence with the ironic words: 'If men asked about the scriptures I would not speak with women.' He then presents a list of excellent women from the scriptures including Mary Magdalene. The last woman whom he mentions is Prisca, and he relates that the apostle Apollos was instructed by Prisca and her husband Aquila.[64] He concludes: 'If it was not reprehensible for an apostle to allow himself to be taught by a woman, why should it be reprehensible for me to teach women as well as men?' Again addressing Principia, he adds that he has given the women from scripture as models, 'so that you have no regrets about your gender'.[65]

Here Jerome's picture of Mary Magdalene is clearly different from that in the letter to Marcella quoted above (Letter 59). In this letter Mary Magdalene is presented as a woman with little faith at the moment of her encounter with the risen Lord. Her sins are many: she was possessed with seven demons, addressed the Lord as the gardener and sought the living among the dead. From the later letter to Principia (Letter 65) it is evident that Jerome has modified his picture of Mary Magdalene in the course of his life. In Chapter 7 we shall see that at the end of his life he sees her as an important example.[66]

Jerome's contemporary Ambrose dwells at more length on the differences between Matthew's Mary Magdalene and John's Mary Magdalene than Jerome does in Letter 59. Earlier Ambrose had pointed out the great differences in the four Gospel narratives of the resurrection. He then concludes:

> The only solution to the question seems to be to assume that the four evangelists were talking about four different circumstances. You must then begin from yet other women and yet other appearances. (*Commentary on the Gospel of Luke* 10.148)

So in our text he begins from two Maries, both of whom came from Magdala. One of them believed the Lord was risen, and the other did not. According to Ambrose, Jesus' words 'do not touch me' do not refer to the repudiation of physical contact nor to the repudiation of physical contact with a woman. For truly touching the risen Lord happens only in faith. They only touch the risen Lord who already bear the traces of their own future resurrection and thus without hesitation renounce the earthly and clothe themselves with tender mercy. According to Ambrose, the risen Lord in John 20.17 clearly does not repudiate Mary's physical contact. In this sense Ambrose is far less disparaging of Mary Magdalene than is Jerome in Letter 59.

According to Ambrose 'she had not yet come to believe, but she did have a good attitude towards believing' (10.162). With the words 'do not touch me' the risen Lord did not want sternly to reject Mary Magdalene because she believed too little. In Ambrose's view, the Lord is concerned to show Mary the way in which she can make spiritual progress by sending her to her brothers. They are advanced in the faith and they will preach the resurrection to her.

Thus, Ambrose says, Mary Magdalene accepts the prescribed commandments; he then quotes two 'silence texts' from the letters of Paul: 'I do not allow women to teach in the assembly'[67] and 'They must ask their man at home.'[68] The exposition of these words in the context of Ambrose's account is not immediately clear. What does he mean here by men and women? He interprets the word 'brothers' symbolically as 'the more perfect persons'. He then quotes a saying of Jesus which is not limited to the male sex: 'Whoever does the will of my Father in heaven, he is my brother and sister and mother' (Matthew 12.50; Mark 3.35). Moreover Ambrose earlier gave the word 'woman' a symbolic meaning when interpreting Jesus' question to Mary Magdalene, 'Woman, why are you weeping?' (John 20.15). Ambrose writes about this when explaining the difference from the other Mary Magdalene in Matthew 28.8-9:

> The differences between the two Maries are therefore underlined by the text. The one comes running to see Jesus, the other turns in the opposite direction. The one hears a greeting, the other a reproachful question. There you also read: Jesus said to her, 'Woman'. A woman who does not believe is just called woman and is always referred to physically, as she was born. But a woman who believes comes running to the perfect man, to the measure of the perfect Christ. From now on, it does not matter to this woman what name she has in the world, whether she is man or woman, whether she has the playfulness of youth or the verbosity of old age. (*Commentary on the Gospel of Luke* 10.161)

Thus, according to Ambrose the symbolic meaning of the word 'woman' is 'an unbelieving woman'. Once she believes, it no longer matters whether she is a man or a woman. But this does not mean that Ambrose uses the words 'man' and 'woman' only symbolically. He puts it like this: 'Not yet master of the faith in the full sense of the word, she is nevertheless sent as a herald to the disciples' (10.163). And 'But because women do not have the stamina for preaching and as women they lack the physical strength for it, the ministry of preaching of the Gospel has been given to men' (10.157). Thus Ambrose's picture of Mary Magdalene is also determined by what he thinks appropriate for women in general on the basis of their supposed lack of physical strength and persuasiveness. In addition he refers to precepts from the Pauline letters.

In the third century Hippolytus speaks quite differently about Mary Magdalene, as does his contemporary Tertullian, who praises Mary's piety. Hippolytus takes a positive view of Mary's gesture. He begins from the fact that Mary clasped Christ's feet and continued to grasp them even after he had said: 'Do not touch me, for I am not yet ascended to the Father.' She did that, too, out of love and therefore Hippolytus praises her. What is different about Hippolytus' interpretation is that he is not speaking about Mary Magdalene but about Martha and Mary. Then he has them working closely together and even appearing as one person. Together they are John's Mary Magdalene. Hippolytus seems to go as far as saying that Mary Magdalene and Mary the sister of Martha are the same person. However, he does this without presenting her as the sinner *par excellence*, as happens in the later church tradition.

In Hippolytus' view Mary continues to clasp the Lord's feet in order to go to the Father with him. Not only may Christ offer himself as a sacrifice to the Father but he must also take Mary with him as a sacrifice. Christ as the new Adam and Mary as the new Eve must both be offered as gifts to the Father. Just as the new Adam/Christ is no longer naked but clothed with incorruptibility, so too is the new Eve/Mary. The curse of the fall no longer holds. The new Eve/Mary desires the new Adam/Christ and is determined not to let go of him but to take him into her heart.

The tenor of Hippolytus' *Commentary on the Song of Songs* is that the Song of Songs expresses the love between Christ and the synagogue. This interpretation has hardly been adopted by church tradition. But Hippolytus' interpretation of the Song of Songs as the song of Mary Magdalene and her Lord and as the song of the church and Christ met with general approval. Through the centuries, following Hippolytus, Mary Magdalene's persistent search in the Gospel of John is seen as the desire of the bride who seeks her bridegroom in the Song of Songs. Thus Hippolytus' *Commentary on the Song of Songs* quite unintentionally laid the foundation for an eroticizing tradition about the love of Mary Magdalene for Jesus. The following texts show how things were with her apostleship.

Why a woman?

Hippolytus' *Commentary on the Song of Songs*, from the beginning of the third century, is the earliest writing in which Mary is presented as an apostle. Hippolytus is enthusiastic about this. He writes: 'O new comfort! Eve becomes an apostle.' However, for later church fathers this is not a fact which offers comfort, but one which calls for an explanation. Ambrose of Milan gives a succinct explanation of the importance of Mary in a text against the Arians, who are convinced that the Spirit must not be worshipped separately. Jerome of Rome mentions the topic in a short letter in which he points out to Antony, to whom he is writing, the importance of humility. In a sermon given during Easter Week Augustine of Hippo (AD 345–430) discusses the credibility of the women who came to bring the message of the resurrection alongside the unbelief of the disciples.

Hippolytus, Commentary on the Song of Songs *25.6-10*[69]

And after this the synagogue recognizes, crying about these women: 'Those bear us a good witness who, sent by Christ, became apostles for the apostles, to whom the angels said: "Go and tell the disciples: He is going before you into Galilee." There you shall see him.'[70]

However, so that the apostles should not doubt the angels, Christ himself also appeared to these apostles.[71] Thus it became clear that the women were apostles of Christ and were to make up through obedience the shortcomings of the old Eve. From now on she will show herself to be perfect by listening in obedience.

7 O new comfort! Eve becomes an apostle![72] Behold, from now on the deception of the snake is seen through and she (Eve) will no longer go astray. For from now on she has hated the one to whom she looked up at and has seen him as an enemy who led her astray through desire. From now on the tree of seduction will no longer seduce her. Behold, from now on she is gladdened by life, thanks to the confession of the tree. Now she has tasted of the tree through Christ. She has been made worthy of the good and has desired that as food.

8 From now on she will no longer be hungry, nor will people set corruptible food before her. She has received the incorruptible. From now on she is united[73] and a helpmeet,[74] for Adam guides Eve. O good helper, by bringing her spouse the good tidings! Therefore the women brought the good news to the disciples.

9 Therefore, too, they regarded her as misled and they doubted.[75] However, the cause was this, that Eve usually proclaimed lies and not the truth. 'What kind of a message about the resurrection is this, woman?' And therefore they regarded her as

misled. So that they should not seem misleaders but it should prove that they spoke the truth, at that moment Christ appeared and he said to them, 'Peace be with you'[76] and then he taught: 'I am the one who appeared to the women and I am the one who wanted to send them to you, apostles.'

10 Now that that has happened, beloved, see how from that moment the synagogue is silent and the church rejoices.

Ambrose, On the Holy Spirit 3, *11.73-75*[77]

73 Let us then here draw our conclusions and put an end to the impious questions of the Arians. For if they say that the Spirit must not be worshipped because God is worshipped in Spirit, let them also say that the Truth must not be worshipped because God is worshipped in Truth.[78] Assume that there are many truths. After all it is written: 'truths are diminished in number among the sons of men'.[79] Yet they are given by the Divine Truth, which is Christ, who says: 'I am the Way, the Truth, and the Life.'[80] If therefore they understand 'truth' in this passage in the ordinary sense, let them also understand the grace of the Spirit, and then there is no difficulty. Or if they accept Christ as the Truth, let them then also deny that he must be worshipped.

74. But they have been refuted by the acts of the pious and by the range of Scriptures. For Mary worshipped Christ, and therefore was appointed to be the messenger of the resurrection to the apostles.[81] In this way she loosened the hereditary guilt and the immeasurable transgression of the female sex.[82] For this the Lord has brought about secretly 'that where sin had exceedingly abounded, grace might more exceedingly abound'.[83] And a woman is rightly appointed before men, so that she who first proclaimed guilt to man should be the first to proclaim the message of the grace of the Lord.

75. And the apostles worshipped him, and therefore they who had rejected the testimony of the faith now received instruction in the faith.[84] And the angels also worshipped him, the angels of whom it is written: 'And let all his angels worship him.'[85]

Jerome, To Antony, Letter 12[86]

While the disciples were discussing who had precedence, our Lord, the teacher of humility, took a little child and said: 'Unless you are converted and become as little children you cannot enter the kingdom of heaven.'[87] And lest he should seem to preach more than he practised, he also followed it with his own example. For he washed his disciples' feet, he received the traitor with a kiss, he conversed with the woman of Samaria, he spoke of the kingdom of heaven with Mary at his feet, and when he rose again from the dead he showed himself first to some poor women.[88] Pride is opposed to humility, and through it Satan lost his greatness as an archangel.[89] The Jewish people perished in their pride, for while they claimed the chief seats and salutations in the market place, they were superseded by the Gentiles, who had previously been counted as 'a drop in a bucket'.[90] The fishermen, Peter and James, were sent out to refute the sophists and the wise men of the world. After all Scripture says: 'God resists the proud but gives grace to the humble.'[91] Think, brother, what an evil it must be which has God as its opponent. In the Gospel the Pharisee is rejected because of his pride, and the publican is accepted because of his humility.[92]

Now, unless I am mistaken, I have already written you many letters, affectionate and earnest, while you have not deigned to send me a single word. Although the Lord speaks to his servants, you, my brother, refuse to speak to your brother. 'It is too much for me, disturbing, unworthy.' Believe me, if restraint did not check my pen, I could show my annoyance in such a way that you would have to reply, even though it might be out of malice. But because malice is human and a Christian must not act abusively, I shall once again entreat you earnestly and beg you to love one who loves you, and to write to him as a servant should to his fellow-servant.

Augustine, Sermon 232.1-2[93]

The account of the resurrection of our Lord Jesus Christ has been read to you once again today, but now according to another Gospel, namely that of Luke.[94] The first time it was read according to Matthew, yesterday according to Mark and today it is read according to Luke. That is the order of the evangelists, just as his passion is also described by all the evangelists. But these seven or eight days give us space to read about the resurrection of the Lord according to all the evangelists. However, because his passion is read on one day, people are accustomed to reading it only according to Matthew. I wanted the passion narrative according to all the evangelists also to be read once a year at a given moment. And that has happened. But people did not hear what they were accustomed to and became confused. However, anyone who loves the literature of the Lord and does not want always to remain ignorant comes to know everything and zealously seeks out all things. But just as the Lord has distributed to each person a certain degree of faith, so everyone also progresses in it.[95]

2 Let us now look at what we heard today when it was read out. Today we have heard at even greater length, beloved, what I already entrusted to you yesterday: the unbelief of the disciples. This makes us understand how much, thanks to his benevolence, we enjoy the privilege of believing what we have not seen. He called them, he instructed them, he lived on earth with them, he did such marvellous things before their eyes that he even raised the dead. But people did not believe that he would make his own body rise. Women came to the tomb. They did not find the body in the tomb. They heard

from angels that Christ was risen. Women brought this report to men. And what is written? What have you heard? In their eyes these things seemed foolish talk.[96] What a great misfortune for human nature! When Eve related what the serpent had said to her she was immediately believed.[97] Belief was attached to a lying woman so that we should die. No belief was attached to women who spoke the truth so that we should live. If men must not believe women, why then did Adam believe Eve? If men must believe women, why did not the disciples believe the holy women?

Therefore in this circumstance we must see a benevolent disposition of our Lord. For the Lord Jesus Christ so directed it that the female sex should be the first to proclaim that he was risen. Because man has fallen through the female sex, man has been restored by the female sex. For a virgin brought forth Christ and a woman proclaimed that he was risen. By a woman came death, and by a woman came life. But the disciples did not believe what the women had said. They thought that they were talking foolishly, whereas they were proclaiming true things.

Explanation

Hippolytus' *Commentary on the Song of Songs* is the earliest extant writing, from the beginning of the third century, in which women (Martha–Mary/ Mary Magdalene) are explicitly called apostles. Hippolytus emphasizes here that the women who brought the message of the resurrection are apostles of Christ, appointed by Christ himself. Here too Hippolytus relates in flowery words that from now on a new time has dawned for Eve. From now on she will realize that the serpent is her enemy and that he led her astray through desire. As in the Gospel of Mary, according to Levi, Mary 'has been made worthy' by the Saviour, so has Eve in Hippolytus' view. She has been made worthy for the good and united with the new Adam/Christ, through whom she allows herself to be led in obedience. Moreover Hippolytus reports that the good witness of the women apostles silences the questions and doubt of the synagogue and causes the church to rejoice.

Whereas for Hippolytus it is a comfort that Eve has been made an apostle by Christ because that shows the liberation of the old Eve, for the later church fathers the main question is why the risen Lord appointed a woman as a messenger to men. Jerome keeps it simple in his pithy letter to Antony: the risen Lord appeared to 'some poor women' in order to show his humility. Jerome is not clear about whether the Lord also sent the women to the apostles with the message of the resurrection out of humility. However, Jerome does emphasize that Jesus' conversation with the

Samaritan woman, and his instruction of Mary, Martha's sister, show the humility of the Lord.

This does not mean that Jerome does not value these women. When he relates in the preface to the commentary on Zephaniah that he has written for Paula and Eustochium, two women from Marcella's community, he refers to a list of biblical women. He praises their excellence. Like Hippolytus, Jerome also praises the women to whom the risen Lord first appeared and calls them apostles, but he writes in a more daring way. He calls the women *apostolorum apostolae*: apostles of the apostles.[98]

Ambrose and Augustine increase the importance of the role of Mary Magdalene but do not call her an apostle. According to Ambrose, Mary looses the 'hereditary guilt' which has come about through 'the immeasurable transgression of the female sex'. She does this by worshipping Christ. Her worship then leads to her appointment as messenger of the resurrection to the apostles. And rightly so, Ambrose then adds, for in this way a woman was the first to proclaim the grace of the Lord, whereas earlier a woman was the first to proclaim guilt to the man. In this last formulation it is not Mary's active deed of worship which makes her messenger of the resurrection, but the Lord has ordained this beforehand. The risen Lord appoints her alone the messenger of the resurrection because she is a woman, since a woman was also the first to bring sin into the world. This last explanation, in which the Lord has the initiative and no active role is given to Mary Magdalene, could be about any woman, and met with a great response.

However, the first explanation, in which specifically the worship of Mary Magdalene does away with hereditary guilt, was not adopted, though the thought is echoed in Augustine. Augustine does not mention Mary Magdalene by name, but talks of the 'holy women' who proclaimed that the Lord was risen. Like Ambrose, in his second explanation he sees this as a disposition of the Lord. Augustine formulates this in a special way:

> Because humanity has fallen through the female sex,
> humanity has been restored by the female sex.
> For a virgin brought forth Christ
> and a woman proclaimed that he was risen.
> By a woman came death,
> and by a woman came life. (Sermon 232.2)

These words echo Paul's formulation of sin and redemption

> For since death came through a human being,
> the resurrection of the dead has also come through a human being.
> For as all die in Adam,
> so all will be made alive in Christ. (1 Corinthians 15.21–22)

Whereas Paul sums up the story of the fall and redemption in a line of men from Adam to Christ, Augustine does so in a line of women, from the first sinner, through the virgin who gave birth to Christ, to the woman who proclaimed that he was risen.

According to Hippolytus, Ambrose and Augustine, Mary Magdalene plays an important role in the settling of Eve's guilt. Mentioning Eve as a counterpart to Mary Magdalene met with a great response in later church tradition, but in an unexpected way. Through the centuries Mary Magdalene was increasingly identified with Eve. According to the later tradition, like Eve, Mary Magdalene led men astray. In this way, like Eve, she incurred great guilt. There is less and less emphasis on Mary Magdalene as the messenger of the resurrection; she is certainly not the one who redeems Eve by bringing the message of the resurrection. On the contrary, Mary Magdalene silences and kills the Eve in herself by converting from her life as a seductress and from then on living an asexual life. Thus Hippolytus, Ambrose and Augustine with their portrayal of Mary Magdalene as a counterpart to Eve quite unintentionally laid the first foundation for the later identification of Mary Magdalene with the seductive and sinful Eve.

However, the image of Mary Magdalene as apostle remained. The line taken by Hippolytus and Jerome did find followers. From the twelfth century, the usual title of Mary Magdalene as the one who proclaims the resurrection is *apostola apostolorum*, apostle of the apostles. However, that does not mean that from this time women may, like Mary Magdalene, perform apostolic tasks. The Lord's words to Mary Magdalene, 'do not touch me', are increasingly interpreted symbolically, but in a quite different way from that taken by Ambrose. In his symbolic interpretation the words are meant as a stimulus to make spiritual advances and to begin to experience the resurrection oneself by renouncing the earthly and clothing oneself with tender mercy. By contrast, in the symbolic exposition of the church tradition the words are specifically addressed to women. The church's interpretation does not contain any stimulus towards making spiritual advances, but limits spiritual development. Women may not touch the Lord. This means that women are not allowed to preach and to administer the sacraments. In the next chapter it will emerge that these limiting rules came into being at a very early stage with a reference to Mary Magdalene.

Chapter 7

Mary Magdalene as an Argument

In some early Christian texts Mary Magdalene is used as an argument for what women can and cannot do. Surprisingly, there are also texts which with a reference to Mary Magdalene show what is appropriate behaviour for men.

What women can and cannot do

The First Apocalypse of James is said to have been written at the end of the second century. It is a very damaged text which contains a secret Gnostic conversation between the risen Lord and James. According to James, all women must bless the Lord for what he has done for his seven women disciples. From the third century a number of church orders mention Mary Magdalene. The Instructions of the Apostles from the beginning of the third century forbids women to teach, certainly about the name of Christ and the meaning of redemption through his suffering. They are allowed to be women deacons, and especially to assist the women among their fellow Christians. The Apostolic Church Order from the beginning of the fourth century forbids women to assist at the eucharist or the Lord's supper. In the Apostolic Constitutions from the end of the fourth century the prohibition from the Instructions of the Apostles is reformulated and made more rigid. Thus the church orders from the beginning of the third to the end of the fourth century each limit the role of women with a reference to Mary Magdalene.

First Apocalypse of James 38.15-23 and 40.22-26[1]

38 Yet [another thing] I ask of you: who are the [seven] women who have [been] your disciples? And behold, all women bless you. I also am amazed how [powerless] vessels

have become strong by a perception which is in them. [The] Lord [said]: 'You [ ] well . . .'

[The rest of the Lord's answer is so damaged that little can be made of it.]

40 When you speak these words of this perception, be persuaded by these . . . Salome and Mary [and Martha and Ars]inoe . . .

Instructions of the Apostles 3.5-6 and 3.12-13[2]

5 When the Gentiles who are being instructed hear the word of God not fittingly spoken, as it ought to be, unto edification of eternal life – and all the more so in that it is spoken by a woman – how that our Lord clothed himself in a body, and concerning the passion of Christ, they will mock and scoff, instead of applauding the word of doctrine, and she shall incur a heavy judgement for sin. 6 It is neither right nor necessary therefore that women should be teachers, and especially concerning the name of Christ and the redemption of his passion. For you have not been appointed to this, O women, and especially widows, that you should teach, but that you should pray and entreat the Lord God. For he the Lord God, Jesus Christ our Teacher, sent us the twelve to instruct the people and the Gentiles; and there were with us women disciples, Mary Magdalene and Mary the daughter of James and the other Mary; but he did not send them to instruct the people with us.

12 As of old the priests and kings were anointed in Israel, do you in like manner, with the laying on of hands, anoint the head of those who receive baptism, whether men or women; and afterwards – whether you yourself baptize, or command the deacons or presbyters to baptize – let a woman deacon, as we have already said, anoint the women. But let a man pronounce over them the invocation of the divine names in the water. And when she who is being baptized has come up from the water, let the deaconess receive her, and teach and instruct her how the seal of baptism ought to be [kept] unbroken in purity and holiness. For this cause we say that the ministry of a woman deacon is especially needful and important. For our Lord and Saviour also was ministered to by women ministers, Mary Magdalene, and Mary the daughter of James and mother of Joses and the mother of the sons of Zebedee, with other women beside. And you also have need of the ministry of a deaconess for many things; for a deaconess is required to go into the houses of the heathen where there are believing women, and to visit those who are sick, and to minister to them in that of which they have need, and to bathe those who have begun to recover from sickness (. . .).

13 Let a woman rather be devoted to the ministry of women, and a male deacon to the ministry of men (. . .). It is required of you deacons therefore that you visit all who are in need, and inform the bishop of those who are in distress; and you shall be his soul and his mind; and in all things you shall take trouble and be obedient to him.

Apostolic Church Order 24–28[3]

24 Andrew said: It is a good thing to set apart women to be made deacons.[4]

25 Peter said: We have already defined this; but concerning the oblations of the body and the blood of the Lord we shall declare the thing with certainty.

26 John said: You have forgotten, brothers, on the day when our Master took the bread and the cup he blessed them, saying : 'This is my Body and my Blood.' You have seen that he did not give a place to the women to assist with them. Martha answered: That was because he saw Mary laughing. Mary said: Not because (of that) I laughed; for he said to us in his teaching : 'The weak will be healed by the strong.'

27 Peter said: Some say that it is right for women to pray standing up, and not to throw themselves upon the earth.

28 James said: Where shall we be able to set apart women for a ministry, except this ministry of this kind only, that they should help the needy?

Apostolic Constitutions 3 6.1-2[5]

We do not permit women to teach in the Church, but only to pray and listen to the teachers. 2 After all our Teacher and Lord, Jesus Christ himself, when he sent us the twelve to make disciples of the people and of the nations, nowhere sent out women to preach, although he did not lack women. For there were with us the mother of our Lord and her sisters; also Mary Magdalene, and Mary of James, and Martha and Mary the sisters of Lazarus; Salome, and certain others.

After all, had it been necessary for women to teach, he himself would first have commanded these also to instruct the people with us. For if the head of the wife is the man, it is not reasonable that the rest of the body should govern the head.

Explanation

The church orders limit the role of women with a reference to Mary Magdalene and the other women disciples. The First Apocalypse of James allows quite a different voice to be heard. All women must praise Jesus for making his seven weak women disciples strong through insight.

Probably the four women mentioned by name belong to the seven women disciples about whom the First Apocalypse of James speaks. Mary Magdalene would then be one of them. James must take counsel with her and the other women when it is a matter of preaching 'about this insight'. The seven women disciples have become strong through an insight that is in them and are no longer powerless vessels. Every woman must praise the Lord for this.

The powerless vessels which have become strong recall the Act of Peter from the first half of the second century in which a man by the name of Ptolemaeus kidnaps Peter's daughter. When Ptolemaeus is on the point of raping her, she is paralysed. When he bursts into tears about this, Christ addresses him in a vision and says:

> Ptolemy, God did not give his vessels for corruption and pollution. But it was necessary for you, since you believed in me, that you not defile my virgin, whom you should have recognized as your sister, since I have become one Spirit for you both. (Act of Peter 137.1–11)[6]

The Greek word *skeuos*, 'vessel', can mean 'body' generally or 'female body' in particular. It is an empty container into which one can put something. It is powerless, because it cannot do anything of itself. That is also an ancient image of the female body. It is not an active body but is like passive ground in which the male seed is sown. Men are the active principle. But in the vision in the Act of Peter Christ says that both Ptolemy's vessel and the vessel of Peter's daughter have been given the same content, namely the one Spirit. In the Apocalypse of James this content is 'insight'. In a culture in which the difference between men and women is that between the powerful and the powerless, for women this is indeed something to praise the Lord for.

Mary Magdalene says something comparable in the Apostolic Church Order. Here presented in the company of Martha, as in the Acts of Philip, Mary relates that during the sharing of bread and wine she was thinking of the teaching of Jesus that 'the weak shall be healed through the strong'. The thought of this instruction made her laugh. We are given no further explanation of what these words could mean. Probably 'the weak' is the human being, male and female, who is healed by 'the strong', the Lord. Exactly this teaching could be a reason why Martha and Mary and other women should have a role at the eucharist. After all, both sexes have been healed to the same degree. From the Acts of Philip it emerges that at that time in fact also a different opinion was held, since there it belongs to the specific responsibility of Mary Magdalene to prepare the bread and the salt and make ready the breaking of the bread.

The text from the Apostolic Church Order at least presupposes that women were present at the Last Supper. However, the Lord gave them no role then, so according to John now too they may not assist in preparing the body and blood of the Lord. Peter also still presupposes that women may pray standing, but James is inexorable: if women in the church have to do anything, it is to help the needy. It is striking that according to this text Martha and Mary are present and in this case can also take part in the discussions between the apostles about the course of the church to follow. However, their plea does not get a hearing.

The text from the Instructions of the Apostles begins from the assumption that women were also present at the missionary charge. Mary Magdalene, Mary of James and the other Mary are called 'women disciples' by the apostles. Here the twelve apostles use the same argument as in the Apostolic Church Order: the women were there but were not given any special commission by the Lord. Thus what he said was explicitly addressed to the twelve apostles. It is striking that the Instructions of the Apostles state so emphatically that women above all must not think that they have something to report about the name of Christ (Anointed) and redemption through his suffering. After all, in the New Testament Gospels women always play an important role specifically at these moments. A woman anoints Jesus' head and thus makes him the Anointed. And it is not the twelve apostles but Mary Magdalene and other women who are the witnesses to the crucifixion and resurrection. Do we perhaps have here the echo of a discussion from the time in which these two arguments were used to allow women to appear in the role of teachers and interpreters of scripture (prophetesses)?

Nevertheless, whereas with reference to Mary Magdalene women are not allowed to teach and preach, they are allowed to be women deacons, to be the soul and mind of the bishop. Here too we can detect a discussion in the background. Mary Magdalene's service to Jesus is used as an argument to defend the possibility that women can be ordained as deacons, and thus be of service to the bishop. Compared to the later church tradition, in which only male deacons were allowed, an ordained woman deacon is revolutionary. However, in both the prohibition against teaching and the permission to be ordained, to anoint and be the soul and the mind of the bishop, the background is conservative: Mary Magdalene is used to preserve the cultural boundaries between males and females. Women deacons are needed to minister to female fellow-Christians, especially when these Christians are married to Gentile husbands. But women cannot teach the faith, because since they are women their words will not be taken seriously by the Gentiles and they will make the faith ridiculous.

The Apostolic Constitutions from the fourth century consist of a collection of writings about church order. They have been rearranged and edited and made consistent. The author attributes the collection to Clement of Rome at the end of the first century and it is said to contain rules and agreements which the apostles and Paul made at the council in Jerusalem mentioned in the Acts of the Apostles (Acts 15.6-21). It is the best-preserved and most extensive church order to survive and consists of eight books. The first six books consist of a reformulation and expansion of, among other things, the Instructions of the Apostles. Where the ordination of women deacons is concerned Mary Magdalene's ministry to Jesus is no longer mentioned. The differences in the fragment about women teaching are also significant. No discussion can any longer be heard in the background. The fragment no longer addresses women but talks about them. Nor does it begin with the words 'it is not right and not necessary'. The later fragment has a more rigid approach to the authority of the apostles: 'we do not permit'. The argument is also put in a more prescriptive way. Nor only is the omission of the Lord to send out women central, but alongside it two sayings of Paul also play a role: 'I permit no woman to teach' (1 Timothy 2.12) and 'the man is the head of the woman' (1 Corinthians 11.3).

As in the Instructions of the Apostles, in the Apostolic Constitutions women seem to be present at the mission charge, even several women, but they are no longer called women disciples. However, it is striking that the twelve apostles assume that there are women. According to the Apostolic Church Order they are also present at the institution of the eucharist. This is not customary in later church tradition. It is then assumed that no women were present at the institution of the eucharist and the mission charge. In this later tradition and also in art the women have disappeared at these two moments. Moreover the argument changes: the women were not present, so the commission to preach and celebrate the eucharist was not addressed to them but to the male apostles. The later symbolic interpretation of Jesus' words to Mary Magdalene, 'do not touch me', strengthens this argument. It is said that these words show that the risen Lord himself forbade women to 'touch' him in a spiritual sense, meaning that women are not to be ordained and/or to preach and administer the sacraments.

What men can and cannot do

The following texts show that according to the early Christian tradition, men too must allow themselves to be instructed by Mary Magdalene. In the third century, Pseudo-Clement of Rome writes a letter against the cohabitation of male and female ascetics and gives the Lord's dealings with Mary Magdalene as an example. At Principia's request Jerome (*c.* AD 347–419) writes an obituary of Marcella, who had died in 411. Half-way through he realizes that not only the women of Marcella's community, but also men, will read his praise of Marcella.

Pseudo-Clement, Two Letters on Virginity *2.15*[7]

So as not to make our sermon too long: what is said about the Lord Jesus Christ? The Lord himself was always with his twelve disciples after he had come into the world. And not only this. When he sent them out, he sent them out two by two, in pairs, he sent out men with men.[8] However, he did not send out women with them. And while they were on the way, they did not stay in the same house with women or with virgins. And so they pleased God in all things.

Then, when the Lord Jesus Christ himself was speaking with the Samaritan woman apart there by the well, the disciples were amazed – after they had come and found him in conversation with her – that he stood by a woman and spoke with her.[9] Is not this the limit which may not be passed? Is not this the purpose and the model for all generations of human beings?

But this is not the only thing. The Lord himself also said to Mary, after he was risen from the dead and she had come running to the tomb and had prostrated herself at the Lord's feet and asked him whether she might hold him: 'Do not touch me, for I am not yet ascended to my Father.'[10] Is it not then surprising that the Lord did not allow Mary, that blessed woman, to touch his feet? You, however, live with them, and women and virgins serve you, and you sleep where they sleep and women wash and anoint your feet. Woe to this reprehensible disposition which is without fear! Woe to this brutality and folly which is without fear of God! Do you not then judge yourself? Do you not test yourself and your powers? This is part of the faith, this is just and righteous. Here are the limits which may not be passed by those who walk uprightly with God. However, many holy women served the saints with their possessions, as the Shulamite woman served Elisha, but she did not live with him. The prophet himself lived apart in a house. And when her son had died and she wanted to fall at the feet of the prophet, his servant did not allow it and repelled her. But Elisha said to the young man: 'Let her, for her soul is sorrowful.'[11] We must learn their way of life from this. Women served the Lord Jesus Christ with their possessions;[12] however, they did not live with him but walked before the face of the Lord, chaste, holy and without stain, and they ran their course and received their crown from the Lord, God, the Almighty.

Jerome, To Principia, *Letter 127 5.3*[13]

The unbelieving reader may perhaps laugh at me for being occupied with the excellences of mere women. Yet, let him but remember how the holy women, the companions of our Lord and Saviour, ministered to him of their substance, and how the three Maries stood before the cross and especially how Mary 'Magdalene' – who received the name 'fortified with towers'[14] because of the great effort and zeal of her faith – was privileged to see the risen Christ first of all before the apostles. Then he will convict himself of pride sooner than me of folly. For we judge of people's capabilities not by their gender but by their mind.

Explanation

As well as the obituary of Marcella Jerome wrote four other biographies of women whom he knew well.[15] In his description of Marcella's life, with a reference to Mary Magdalene and other women, Jerome shows that believing men must not judge women by their gender, as was customary at the time. According to Jerome, believing men must judge women by their minds. It is striking that Jerome interprets the name Magdalene with the Latin word *turritae*, which means 'towers'. The Hebrew word *migdal* in fact means 'fortress', 'stronghold' and 'tower'. But the word *turritae* is an epithet specifically applied to Cybele, the Phrygian goddess of fertility and mother goddess, who was also worshipped in Rome. Cybele was revered as the mother of the gods and was often depicted with towers on her head. This goddess is challenged in the Acts of Philip by Philip, Mary Magdalene and Bartholomew. Is it a coincidence that Jerome uses this particular word? It is clear that he sees Mary Magdalene as human and not as a mother goddess. Perhaps with the image he is alluding to Mary Magdalene as the fertile mother who has produced many believers.

At all events, Pseudo-Clement has quite a different image in mind. With a reference to Mary Magdalene and other women he shows that men may allow themselves to be served by women, but in all chastity. They certainly may not live in the same house as women. Nor may they allow themselves to be touched by women. The holy women who followed the Lord did not serve him physically nor did they live in the same house, but served him with their possessions.

There is a great difference between the two views. Pseudo-Clement uses the way in which the Lord acted towards Mary Magdalene as an argument for avoiding any physical contact between men and women. Jerome uses

Mary Magdalene's faith and commitment as an argument for not judging men and women by their gender but by their minds. Both writers admire Mary Magdalene and the other women greatly. However, the one begins from Mary Magdalene herself and the other begins from the way in which the Lord as a man dealt with Mary Magdalene as a woman. As a man, Pseudo-Clement warns other men against contact with women. The men might not be able to control themselves and might assault the women. By contrast, as a man, Jerome feels vulnerable towards other men because he is on familiar terms with women and even praises them.

The difference is probably to be explained by the fact that Pseudo-Clement is speaking to men who allow themselves to be served by women. Instead, Jerome has satisfactory spiritual contact with the women from Marcella's community. Pseudo-Clement is concerned with the body. Jerome sees the mind and defends the standpoint that this belongs to the faith. According to him, believing men need to judge women not by their bodies but by their minds. In the next chapter we shall see that Jerome finds Paul on his side, but that they are both voices in the wilderness.

Chapter 8

A Woman to Learn From?

We have now surveyed very different early Christian images of Mary Magdalene. How does it come about that this woman has provoked such divergent representations? According to the earliest text in which Mary Magdalene appears, the Gospel of Mark, she is the only person who is the witness both to Jesus' crucifixion and burial and to the empty tomb with the revelation that he is alive. Although she is associated in turn with different women, according to Mark, Mary Magdalene is the only constant factor. According to Matthew, together with another Mary she is the first to encounter the risen Lord. According to John, she is the only witness to the new revelation that the risen Lord gives at the empty tomb. Thus according to the first-century sources Mary Magdalene is an important witness, not to say the key witness, for the content of the Christian faith.

A woman who teaches women is all right. But a woman whose knowledge and insight could also be important for men is a problem in many cultures. That also applies to the Jewish and Hellenistic culture within which the Christian faith took shape. Each time in the history of Christianity it is firmly emphasized that women may not give instruction to men and time and again that is attacked. Here texts from Paul often are and have been quoted.

This chapter contains texts from the middle of the first century which show something of Paul's view of women and texts from the second half of the first century which elaborate Paul's view of women. Before them come some quotations from the work of Philo of Alexandria, which are typical of the view of women in Hellenistic and Jewish culture. Together, the texts in this chapter give an indication of the background against which the various early portraits of Mary Magdalene came into being.

Male and female

Philo, an older contemporary of Paul who lived in Alexandria in Egypt, was a Jewish exegete. As an interpreter above all of the first five books of scripture (the Torah), he looks both for the literal meaning of the text and also for a deeper meaning. In the deeper meaning we come upon his personal faith, but also upon convictions which played a great role at his time.

The first quotation is from Philo's exposition of the story of the flood in Genesis 6–9. Noah has understood from God that a great inundation (the flood) will come and has built a boat (the ark) to save as many species of animals as possible, along with his family. Through this, after the flood, when the earth dries out again, life will be able to progress on earth. In the second quotation Philo gives his exposition of the end of the menstruation of Sarah, Abraham's wife. Both quotations are about the soul, and show what was seen as typically male and female in Philo's time and culture.

Philo, Questions and Answers on Genesis *2.49*

Why, when they entered the ark, was the order (of words) 'he and his sons' and then 'and his sons' wives', but when they went out, was it changed ? For Scripture says, 'Noah went out and his wife' and then 'his sons and his sons' wives' (Gen. 8.18).

[Here follows the literal meaning.]

But as for the deeper meaning, this must be said. When the soul is about to wash off and cleanse its sins, man should join with man, that is, the sovereign mind like a father should join with its particular thoughts as with its sons, but not join any of the female sex, that is what belongs to sense. For it is a time of war, in which one must separate one's ranks and watch out lest they be mixed up and bring about defeat instead of victory. But when just the right time has come for the cleansing, and there is a drying up of all ignorance and of all that which is able to do harm, then it is fitting and proper for it to bring together those elements which have been divided and separated, not that the masculine thoughts may be made womanish and relaxed by softness, but that the female element, the senses, may be made manly by following masculine thoughts and by receiving from them seed for procreation, that it may perceive things with wisdom, prudence, justice and courage, in sum, with virtue.

But in the second place, in addition to this, it is proper to note also that when confusion comes upon the mind, and, like a flood, in the life of the world mounds of affairs are erected at one time, it is impossible to sow or conceive or give birth to anything good. But when discords and attacks and the gradual invasions of monstrous thoughts are kept off, then being dried, like the fertile and productive places of the earth, it produces virtues and excellent things.

Philo, Questions and Answers on Genesis *4.15*

What is the meaning of the words, 'There ceased to be to Sarah the ways of women' (Gen.18.11)? The literal meaning is clear. For Scripture by a euphemism calls the monthly purification of women 'the ways of women'.

But as for the deeper meaning, it is to be allegorized as follows. The soul has, as it were, a dwelling, partly men's quarters, partly women's quarters. Now for the men there is a place where properly dwell the masculine thoughts, that are wise, sound, just, prudent, pious, filled with freedom and boldness, and kin to wisdom. And the women's quarters are a place where womanly opinions go about and dwell, being followers of the female sex. And the female sex is irrational and akin to bestial passions, fear, sorrow, pleasure and desire, from which ensue incurable weaknesses and indescribable diseases. He who is conquered by these is unhappy, while he who controls them is happy.

And longing for and desiring this happiness, and seizing a certain time to be able to escape from terrible and unbearable sorrow, which is (what is meant by) 'there ceased to be the ways of women', this clearly belongs to minds full of the Law, which resemble the male sex and overcome passions and rise above all sense–pleasure and desire and are without sorrow and fear and, if one must speak the truth, without passion, not zealously practising apathy, for this would be ungrateful and shameless and akin to arrogance and reckless boldness, but that which is consistent with the argument given (namely) cutting the mind off from disturbing and confusing passions.

Explanation

Philo compares Noah's ark with the soul, which can purify itself from sins in the flood. That is a life-and-death struggle, in which the victory can be gained only by souls which temporarily allow themselves to be guided only by the mind and shut themselves off from the senses. In the Hellenistic thought-world to which Philo belonged, the soul consisted of a part that perceives the spiritual and a part that perceives the bodily. According to this view, a confusing multitude of impressions enters the soul through the senses: through sight, hearing, feeling, taste, touch, language and desire. A healthy person restrains and orders this confusion actively by the thinking part of the soul: the mind.

Philo and those of his time and culture call perception through the senses feminine. This perception after all is bodily and at that time the woman was also seen above all as body. The woman is like the (passive) earth which receives the seed and brings forth fruit. The seed comes from the man. He is the sower and the active principle. Therefore the mind that actively orders the perception of the senses is said to be masculine. On the basis of this division Philo makes a distinction between male thoughts and female opinions. It is evident from the second quotation that male thoughts are wise, healthy, righteous, judicious, pious, free and bold. By contrast, feminine opinions are impulsive and irrational and are given through animal thoughts such as fear, sorrow, pleasure and desire. They are unhealthy, because they cause unhealthy weaknesses and indescribable sicknesses.

The male mind must actively shut itself off from these female opinions and get sensual perception under control. The first quotation speaks of making the female element male, so that the soul produces a virtuous life. The male thoughts form the seed by which the female senses are made fruitful. Then the senses can perceive with wisdom, prudence, justice and courage.

In the first quotation the male and female elements seem to need each other to bring forth virtue, but it can temporarily be important to keep them separate from each other. In the second quotation the emphasis lies on the clear division. In the second quotation it also becomes more evident that Philo is not just speaking symbolically about male and female, apart from real men and women. Male is what belongs to the male sex and female what belongs to the female sex. It may be clear that this kind of thinking is no support in answering positively the question whether men might learn from women.

However, this does not mean that according to Philo women should only live confined to their houses and restrict themselves to caring for their families. On the contrary, Philo speaks very positively about a group of Jewish women and men near Alexandria (strictly separated and celibate) who live together to study scripture and to spend their life in prayer and singing. But these are women who have cut themselves off from all that is bodily. They have made themselves male.

Paul

In Chapter 5 it emerged that Paul worked with women and expresses his admiration for female co-apostles. Nevertheless, it is words of Paul that believers after his time quote and use as an argument for imposing silence on women. What does Paul say about female and male and about men and women? Is it like what Philo says?

Not all the letters in the New Testament attributed to Paul are by Paul. The first letter to the Thessalonians, the letters to the Corinthians, to the Philippians, to Philemon, to the Galatians and to the Romans are said really to come from Paul. The other letters are said to be by his disciples, who assumed that they were writing in Paul's spirit.[1] That happened often at this time and was also an accepted phenomenon. It is known as 'pseud-epigraphy'.

In the following quotations Paul talks about men and women. In the first letter to the Corinthians he answers questions from the community about being married and unmarried and discusses order in the assembly. In connection with both subjects Paul speaks of how men and women are to behave. It is thought that the letter was written in about AD 53. The letter to the Galatians contains a baptismal formula in which the words male and female occur. The letter is said to have been written about AD 55.[2]

1 Corinthians 7.1-40

1 Now concerning the matters about which you wrote: 'It is well for a man not to touch a woman.' 2 Because of cases of sexual immorality, each man should have his own wife and each woman her own husband. 3 The husband should give to his wife her conjugal rights, and likewise the wife to her husband. 4 For the wife does not have authority over her own body, but the husband does; likewise the husband does not have authority over his own body, but the wife does. 5 Do not deprive one another except perhaps by agreement for a set time, to devote yourselves to prayer, and then come together again, so that Satan may not tempt you because of your lack of self-control. 6 This I say by way of concession, not of command. 7 I wish that all were as I myself am. But each has a particular gift from God, one having one kind and another a different kind.

8 To the unmarried and the widows I say that it is well for them to remain unmarried as I am. 9 But if they are not practising self-control, they should marry. For it is better to marry than to be aflame with passion.

10 To the married I give this command — not I but the Lord — that the wife[3] should not separate from her husband 11 (but if she does separate, let her remain unmarried or else be reconciled to her husband), and that the husband should not divorce his wife.

12 To the rest I say — I and not the Lord — that if any believer has a wife who is an unbeliever, and she consents to live with him, he should not divorce her. 13 And if any woman has a husband who is an unbeliever, and he consents to live with her, she

should not divorce him. 14 For the unbelieving husband is made holy through his wife, and the unbelieving wife is made holy through her husband. Otherwise, your children would be unclean, but as it is, they are holy. 15 But if the unbelieving partner separates, let it be so; in such a case the brother or sister is not bound. It is to peace that God has called you. 16 Wife, for all you know, you might save your husband. Husband, for all you know, you might save your wife.

17 However that may be, let each of you lead the life that the Lord has assigned, to which God called you. This is my rule in all the churches. 18 Was anyone at the time of his call already circumcised? Let him not seek to remove the marks of circumcision. Was anyone at the time of his call uncircumcised? Let him not seek circumcision. 19 Circumcision is nothing, and uncircumcision is nothing; but obeying the commandments of God is everything. 20 Let each of you remain in the condition in which you were called.

21 Were you a slave when called? Do not be concerned about it. Even if you can gain your freedom, make use of your present condition now more than ever. 22 For whoever was called in the Lord as a slave is a freed person belonging to the Lord, just as whoever was free when called is a slave of Christ. 23 You were bought with a price; do not become slaves of human masters. 24 In whatever condition you were called, brothers and sisters, there remain with God.

25 Now concerning virgins, I have no command of the Lord, but I give my opinion as one who by the Lord's mercy is trustworthy. 26 I think that, in view of the impending crisis, it is well for you to remain as you are. 27 Are you bound to a wife? Do not seek to be free. Are you free from a wife? Do not seek a wife. 28 But if you marry, you do not sin, and if a virgin marries, she does not sin. Yet those who marry will experience distress in this life, and I would spare you that. 29 I mean, brothers and sisters, the appointed time has grown short; from now on, let even those who have wives be as though they had none, 30 and those who mourn as though they were not mourning, and those who rejoice as though they were not rejoicing, and those who buy as though they had no possessions, 31 and those who deal with the world as though they had no dealings with it. For the present form of this world is passing away.

32 I want you to be free from anxieties. The unmarried man is anxious about the affairs of the Lord, how to please the Lord; 33 but the married man is anxious about the affairs of the world, how to please his wife, 34 and his interests are divided. And the unmarried woman and the virgin are anxious about the affairs of the Lord, so that they may be holy in body and spirit; but the married woman is anxious about the affairs of the world, how to please her husband. 35 I say this for your own benefit, not to put any restraint upon you, but to promote good order and unhindered devotion to the Lord.

36 If anyone thinks that he is not behaving properly towards his fiancée, if his passions are strong, and so it has to be, let him marry as he wishes; it is no sin. Let them

marry. 37 But if someone stands firm in his resolve, being under no necessity but having his own desire under control, and has determined in his own mind to keep her as his fiancée, he will do well. 38 So then, he who marries his fiancée does well; and he who refrains from marriage will do better.

39 A wife is bound as long as her husband lives. But if the husband dies, she is free to marry anyone she wishes, only in the Lord. 40 But in my judgement she is more blessed if she remains as she is. And I think that I too have the Spirit of God.

1 Corinthians 11.2-16

2 I commend you because you remember me in everything and maintain the traditions just as I handed them on to you. 3 But I want you to understand that Christ is the head of every man, and the man[4] is the head of the woman,[5] and God is the head of Christ. 4 Any man who prays or prophesies with something on his head disgraces his head, 5 but any woman who prays or prophesies with her head unveiled disgraces her head — it is one and the same thing as having her head shaved. 6 For if a woman will not veil herself, then she should cut off her hair; but if it is disgraceful for a woman to have her hair cut off or to be shaved, she should wear a veil. 7 For a man ought not to have his head veiled, since he is the image and reflection of God; but woman is the reflection of man. 8 Indeed, man was not made from woman, but woman from man. 9 Neither was man created for the sake of woman, but woman for the sake of man. 10 For this reason a woman ought to have a symbol of authority on her head, because of the angels. 11 Nevertheless, in the Lord woman is not independent of man or man independent of woman. 12 For just as woman came from man, so man comes through woman; but all things come from God. 13 Judge for yourselves: is it proper for a woman to pray to God with her head unveiled? 14 Does not nature itself teach you that if a man wears long hair, it is degrading to him, 15 but if a woman has long hair, it is her glory? For her hair is given to her for a covering. But if anyone is disposed to be contentious — we have no such custom, nor do the churches of God.

1 Corinthians 12.12-13

12 For just as the body is one and has many members, and all the members of the body, though many, are one body, so it is with Christ. 13 For in the one Spirit we were all baptized into one body — Jews or Greeks, slaves or free — and we were all made to drink of one Spirit.

1 Corinthians 14.20-40

20 Brothers and sisters, do not be children in your thinking; rather, be infants in evil, but in thinking be adults. 21 In the law it is written,

'By people of strange tongues and by the lips of foreigners
I will speak to this people;
yet even then they will not listen to me,'

says the Lord. 22 Tongues, then, are a sign not for believers but for unbelievers, while prophecy is not for unbelievers but for believers. 23 If, therefore, the whole church comes together and all speak in tongues, and outsiders or unbelievers enter, will they not say that you are out of your mind? 24 But if all prophesy, an unbeliever or outsider who enters is reproved by all and called to account by all. 25 After the secrets of the unbeliever's heart are disclosed, that person will bow down before God and worship him, declaring, 'God is really among you.'

26 What should be done then, my friends? When you come together, each one has a hymn, a lesson, a revelation, a tongue, or an interpretation. Let all things be done for building up. 27 If anyone speaks in a tongue, let there be only two or at most three, and each in turn; and let one interpret. 28 But if there is no one to interpret, let them be silent in church and speak to themselves and to God. 29 Let two or three prophets speak, and let the others weigh what is said. 30 If a revelation is made to someone else sitting nearby, let the first person be silent. 31 For you can all prophesy one by one, so that all may learn and all be encouraged. 32 And the spirits of prophets are subject to the prophets, 33 for God is a God not of disorder but of peace.

As in all the churches of the saints, 34 women should be silent in the churches. For they are not permitted to speak, but should be subordinate, as the law also says. 35 If there is anything they desire to know, let them ask their own men[6] at home. For it is shameful for a woman to speak in church. 36 Or did the word of God originate with you? Or are you the only ones it has reached?

37 Anyone who claims to be a prophet, or to have spiritual powers, must acknowledge that what I am writing to you is a command of the Lord. 38 Anyone who does not recognize this is not to be recognized. 39 So, my friends, be eager to prophesy, and do not forbid speaking in tongues; 40 but all things should be done decently and in order.

Galatians 3.23-29

23 Now before faith came, we were imprisoned and guarded under the law until faith would be revealed. 24 Therefore the law was our disciplinarian until Christ came, so

that we might be justified by faith. 25 But now that faith has come, we are no longer subject to a disciplinarian, 26 for in Christ Jesus you are all children of God through faith. 27 As many of you as were baptized into Christ have clothed yourselves with Christ. 28 There is no longer Jew or Greek, there is no longer slave or free, there is no longer male and female; for all of you are one in Christ Jesus. 29 And if you belong to Christ, then you are Abraham's offspring, heirs according to the promise.

Explanation

Galatians 3.28 is a very special verse in the work of Paul that has been preserved. Are there no male and female in Christ, whereas Paul himself writes regulations about the behaviour of men and women? What can that mean?

It is striking that in his letter to the Corinthians, in a similar text Paul does not refer to male and female (1 Corinthians 12.13). Is the addition unimportant, is it taken for granted in the Corinthian community, or does it perhaps cause too many misunderstandings?

It is evident from the letter to the Corinthians that in the community of Corinth there is little difference between men and women when they assemble. Both men and women pray and prophesy (1 Corinthians 1.3-4). The only comment that Paul makes is that as distinct from men, women must cover their heads (1 Corinthians 11.5). It appears from a later part of the letter that everyone in the assembly is taught and encouraged by means of prophecy (1 Corinthians 14.31). Thus we get the impression that both men and women teach and encourage one another during the assembly.

However, 1 Corinthians 14.34-35 says that women must keep silent during the assemblies and that it is shameful for a woman to speak during the assembly. How is this possible? Some exegetes assume that the praying and prophesying by women in 1 Corinthians 11.2-6 is not necessarily related to the assembly, whereas that is the case in 1 Corinthians 14.34-35. In that case there would be no conflict between 1 Corinthians 11.2 and 1 Corinthians 14.34-35. It is also thought that Paul specially added verses 34 and 35 in 1 Corinthians 14 because he was concerned about the impact that the assembly made on outsiders (1 Corinthians 14.23). Others think that the women in verses 34 and 35 are only the married women, since they are expected to ask their 'own men' about things at home.

The fact is that this 'silence text' seems strange in a letter which gives no further reason for thinking that Paul gives men more rights than women. On the contrary, in 1 Corinthians 7 it is striking that Paul begins from a freedom for women which is great for his time. Women can evidently themselves decide whether to marry or remain unmarried, to separate from their husbands or remain with them. That is the situation to which Paul is alluding. In Paul's own view they have as much right to the bodies of their husbands as the husbands have a right to the bodies of their wives. There seems to be no question in Paul of a special subjection of wives to their husbands; rather, there is mutuality. Throughout this passage about being married or unmarried Paul elucidates his statements about women in the same way as he does those about men.

It is also striking that in 1 Corinthians 11.1-16 Paul explicitly does not use the words 'Christ is the head of every man, and the man is the head of the woman, and God is the head of Christ' (1 Corinthians 11.3) as an argument for the subjection of women to men but exclusively as an argument about whether or not the head should be covered in praying and prophesying. He does the same thing with the words 'man was not made from woman, but woman from man. Neither was man created for the sake of woman, but woman for the sake of man' (1 Corinthians 11.8-9). Paul does not associate these words with the superiority of the man, which would already have been determined at the beginning of creation. Instead, he states that the glory of man is the woman and that of God the man. Moreover, immediately afterwards he puts the order of creation in perspective with the words 'nevertheless, in the Lord woman is not independent of man or man independent of woman. For just as woman came from man, so man comes through woman; but all things come from God' (1 Corinthians 11.11-12). Thus according to Paul the order of creation, too, is a matter of mutuality.

The alienating verses 34 and 35 in 1 Corinthians 14.20-40 are absent from a number of manuscripts. They then stand after the closing words in v. 50. This could indicate that they are a later addition, a so-called gloss. The person who copied a manuscript in order to distribute it sometimes commented on it in the margin. In a number of cases it has been shown that such a commentary was added to the main text by subsequent copyists, and then turns up in different places. It is indeed quite possible to read 1 Corinthians 14.20-40 without verses 34 and 35. The unexpected opposition between 1 Corinthians 7 and 1 Corinthians 11.1-16 would then disappear.

Thus it seems that in the letters attributed to Paul himself there is no mention of an imposed subjection of the woman to the man. This would fit in with what we know of Paul's convictions. After all, he is the apostle to the Gentiles and breaks down the dividing walls between Jews and Greeks:

the Jewish law is not fulfilled in all kinds of differing rules, but in love. Jews are no longer superior to Greeks and free men and women are no longer superior to slaves. This should also apply to men and women. Under the law one is superior to the other, but not in faith.

In Galatians 3.28 Paul in fact says that there is no male and female in Christ. According to some interpreters this is an old baptism formula:

> As many of you as were baptized into Christ
> have clothed yourselves with Christ.
> There is no longer Jew or Greek,
> there is no longer slave or free,
> there is no longer male and female;
> for all of you are one in Christ Jesus.

In this view the words male and female refer back to the first creation story, in which God does not make the woman from the man's rib but makes the human being male and female immediately. 'So God created humankind in his image, in the image of God he created them; male and female he created them' (Genesis 1.27). Reference is then made to Philo with the argument that with baptism the conflict between the female (unbridled sensual perception) and the male (the sound mind) is past. They have become one. The objection to this is that nowhere in his letters does Paul speak about male and female in such a figurative way. The only place where Paul uses the words male and female once more is about actual men and women who 'commit shameless acts' with their own sex (Romans 1.26-27).

Thus it seems reasonable to assume that in Galatians 3.28 Paul literally means men and women. That would mean that in his view, with baptism not only the superiority of Jews to Greeks and the free to the slave, but also that of men to women, has an end in Christ. The question, however, is what that means in practice. Some exegetes say that that end comes only in the future. 'In Christ' means: when everything is completed. This standpoint seems untenable because Paul is certainly thinking of radical new relations between Jews and Greeks and slaves and free in the present. At the same time it is clear in Paul that Greeks do not become Jews and slaves do not become free. So following on from this one could say that women do not become men. Where then is the difference? On the basis of what we know from Paul's letters, we can only say that at all events the difference between man and woman does not lie in the superiority of man to woman.

Deutero-Pauline letters

The letters which do not come directly from Paul but from authors after him are called Deutero-Pauline. They come as it were from a second Paul. They form the earliest interpretation and adaptation of Paul's preaching in a new time. They are more general in tone and no longer go into the concrete situations of those to whom they are addressed. These letters sometimes contain the opposite to the thought that is attributed to Paul himself. The second Paul is also somewhat more peremptory in 'his' thinking about the relationship between man and woman than the first. Woman must be subject to man and keep silent. For this reason it is assumed that the 'silence text' added later in the first letter to the Corinthians was originally a Deutero-Pauline commentary in the margin.

In the Graeco-Roman world and in early Judaism many writers ventured a code of behaviour for domestic life. The following quotations show such codes of behaviour for Christian life. The first quotation is from the letter to the Colossians. The letter to the Ephesians is said to be an extended commentary on this. These letters come from the second half of the first century, somewhere between AD 70 and AD 100. The first letter to Timothy is said to have been written between AD 100 and AD 125.

Colossians 3.5-21

5 Put to death therefore, whatever in you is earthly: fornication, impurity, passion, evil desire, and greed (which is idolatry). 6 On account of these the wrath of God is coming on those who are disobedient. 7 These are the ways you also once followed, when you were living that life. 8 But now you must get rid of all such things — anger, wrath, malice, slander, and abusive language from your mouth. 9 Do not lie to one another, seeing that you have stripped off the old self with its practices 10 and have clothed yourselves with the new self, which is being renewed in knowledge according to the image of its creator. 11 In that renewal there is no longer Greek and Jew, circumcised and uncircumcised, barbarian, Scythian, slave and free; but Christ is all and in all!

12 As God's chosen ones, holy and beloved, clothe yourselves with compassion, kindness, humility, meekness, and patience. 13 Bear with one another and, if anyone has a complaint against another, forgive each other; just as the Lord has forgiven you, so you also must forgive. 14 Above all, clothe yourselves with love, which binds everything together in perfect harmony. 15 And let the peace of Christ rule in your hearts, to which indeed you were called in the one body. And be thankful. 16 Let the word of Christ dwell in you richly; teach and admonish one another in all wisdom; and with

gratitude in your hearts sing psalms, hymns, and spiritual songs to God. 17 And whatever you do, in word or deed, do everything in the name of the Lord Jesus, giving thanks to God the Father through him.

18 Women,[7] be subject to the men, as is fitting in the Lord. 19 Men, love the women and never treat them harshly. 20 Children, obey your parents in everything, for this is your acceptable duty in the Lord. 21 Fathers, do not provoke your children, or they may lose heart.

Ephesians 5.21-33

21 Be subject to one another out of reverence for Christ.

22 Women,[8] be subject to your own men as you are to the Lord. 23 For the man is the head of the woman just as Christ is the head of the church, the body of which he is the Saviour. 24 Just as the church is subject to Christ, so also the women ought to be, in everything, to the men.

25 Men, love the women, just as Christ loved the church and gave himself up for her, 26 in order to make her holy by cleansing her with the washing of water by the word, 27 so as to present the church to himself in splendour, without a spot or wrinkle or anything of the kind — yes, so that she may be holy and without blemish. 28 In the same way, the men should love the women as they do their own bodies. He who loves his woman loves himself. 29 For no one ever hates his own body, but he nourishes and tenderly cares for it, just as Christ does for the church, 30 because we are members of his body. 31 'For this reason a man will leave his father and mother and be joined to his own woman, and the two will become one flesh.' 32 This is a great mystery, and I am applying it to Christ and the church. 33 Each of you, however, should love his woman as himself, and the woman should respect the man.

1 Timothy 2.8-15

8 I desire, then, that in every place the men should pray, lifting up holy hands without anger or argument; also that the women should dress themselves modestly and decently in suitable clothing, not with their hair braided, or with gold, pearls, or expensive clothes, 10 but with good works, as is proper for women who profess reverence for God. 11 Let a woman learn in silence with full submission. 12 I permit no woman to teach or to have authority over a man; she is to keep silent. 13 For Adam was formed first, then Eve; 14 and Adam was not deceived, but the woman was deceived and became a transgressor. Yet she will be saved through childbearing, provided they continue in faith and love and holiness, with modesty.

Explanation

In contrast to Paul, the authors of the letters to the Colossians and to the Ephesians are agreed that there certainly is such a distinction in the relationship between men and women that it amounts to superiority. Whereas the relationship in 1 Corinthians 7 is mutual, here it is out of balance. The writers explicitly call on the man to love his woman. However, the woman must recognize the authority of the man. In the letter to the Colossians the author refers to the baptism formula from the letter to the Galatians, but the superiority done away with in baptism does not apply to men and women (Colossians 3.9-11). Nevertheless the author of Colossians puts the submission to the man required of the woman in perspective with the words 'as is fitting in the Lord' (Colossians 3.18).

In the letter to the Ephesians the author elucidates the relationship of authority further. Now the woman must recognize the authority of the man 'in everything' (Ephesians 5.24). Whereas according to Paul in 1 Corinthians 7.4 married couples have the right to each other's bodies, here the woman is the body of the man (Ephesians 5.28). According to the letter this is the mystery of their unity in the marriage. The man is the head and the wife is his body. That is how the Deutero-Pauline author interprets the meaning of Paul's words about the unity of male and female (Galatians 3.28). In this interpretation of Paul we see once again the view of Philo and his contemporaries, in which the male represents perception through the mind and the female perception through the body. As Philo presupposes, for this Deutero-Pauline author too the becoming one of the two means that the male leads and guides the female.

The author argues that the man is the head of the woman, as Christ is the head of the church. Just as the church worships Christ, so the woman must worship her man (Ephesians 5.23). Thus the position of the man is compared with, and in a certain sense identified with, that of Christ. The thought that Christ is the head of the man, the man is the head of the woman and God is the head of Christ in connection with whether or not the head should be covered is abandoned (1 Corinthians 11.3). So is Paul's thought that the church is the (whole) body of Christ (1 Corinthians 12.12-31). Now Christ is the head and the church (the rest of) the body. This new, hierarchical relationship between Christ and the church is the argument for the hierarchical relationship between man and woman. Here much attention is paid to the love that is required of the man, a love which is in fact self-love. He is required to love his own body.

At first sight the author of the first letter to Timothy seems to limit himself to the behaviour of men and women in the assembly. However, the author devotes only one verse to the assembly, and this is addressed to men (1 Timothy 2.8). The letter to Timothy then moves quickly from the man and worship to the behaviour of women in general (1 Timothy 2.9-15). They must dress soberly and stand out only for their good deeds. The author then explicitly devotes several verses to his view that women may not have any authority over men. He argues for his prohibition with a reference to the order of creation and adds that the woman was led astray and not Adam. The woman will be saved only by bearing children. Women must combine this with a believing, loving, holy and modest life.

This interpretation of Paul contrasts greatly with Paul himself, who praises a life without family not only for men but also for women. Another difference is that Paul does not see Eve or the woman but Adam as the first sinner. Moreover Paul does not use the order of creation as an argument for the relationship of authority between husband and wife. He relativizes the order of creation and uses it only as an argument for a difference in clothing.

Let us assume that the Deutero-Pauline authors in all honesty think that they are continuing Paul's line of thought. How then does it come about that the Deutero-Pauline interpretation deviates so much from what is known of Paul himself? This specific line of interpretation bears witness to the tendency of Christians to adapt themselves to what the Jewish and Graeco-Roman rules of behaviour require of men and women. Households were seen as the smallest unit and as the basis of the hierarchical structure of society, even of the whole cosmos. Master and slave, husband and wife, father and children formed the elements of this microcosm. If the master/husband/father governed his household well and in accordance with that the senate governed the land well, then human life could be a reflection of the harmony produced by the divine governance of the universe. People thought it very important that, in order to be able to reflect this harmony, women, slaves and children should know their places in relation to men, masters and fathers. If they did not keep to their subordinate positions, they were a danger to society.

Although Paul himself does not talk like this about women and men, he does not argue for a revolution in social relationships. He regularly calls on Christians not to give offence. 'However that may be, let each of you lead the life that the Lord has assigned, to which God called you,' he says (1

Corinthians 7.17). And he also says, with the eating of meat offered to idols as an example:

> 'All things are lawful', but not all things are beneficial. 'All things are lawful', but not all things build up. Do not seek your own advantage, but that of others. Eat whatever is sold in the meat market without raising any question on the ground of conscience, for 'the earth and its fullness are the Lord's'. If an unbeliever invites you to a meal and you are disposed to go, eat whatever is set before you without raising any question on the ground of conscience. But if someone says to you, 'This has been offered in sacrifice', then do not eat it, out of consideration for the one who informed you, and for the sake of conscience — I mean the other's conscience, not your own'. (1 Corinthians 10.23-29a)[9]

Perhaps the Deutero-Pauline authors would have independently applied such an argument to the relationship between men and women. A woman who teaches men, bears no children or is not subject to her husband could cause offence to the hierarchical order which is called for in Graeco-Roman and Jewish rules for domestic behaviour. And finally, completely different behaviour could be seen as a danger to the welfare of the state.

However, the Deutero-Pauline authors did not explain their choice by a wish to cause no offence, as Paul would probably have done. On the contrary, they emphasize the importance and general validity of their rules of behaviour with a reference to the relationship between Christ and the church and a reference to the order of creation from scripture. Thus they elevate the rules of behaviour for women, which had been determined by the time and culture, into timeless and eternally valid religious commands. This was reinforced in the course of the history of early Christianity by the fact that the Deutero-Pauline letters themselves also became part of holy scripture. The rules of behaviour for women determined by time and culture were thus increasingly seen as the Word of God. In the next chapter we shall see that with respect to the required behaviour of women the Deutero-Pauline rules in particular had a great impact on the church fathers.

Chapter 9

Two Forces

In the previous chapter, important differences came to light between Paul's view of how women should behave from the middle of the first century and the view of interpreters of Paul from the second half of the first century. This chapter contains texts from subsequent centuries which show the influence of Paul's words and the Deutero-Pauline interpretation of Paul on the role of women in the building-up of the church. Although at this time the modern distinction between Pauline and Deutero-Pauline letters is not made, a clear line can be discovered. The Deutero-Pauline view of how women should behave increasingly becomes an integral part of 'right doctrine'. At the same time women seem to be active in many areas. The texts in this chapter show how much these two forces clash. It also becomes clear how the portrayal of Mary Magdalene changes under the influence of the Deutero-Pauline texts.

The Deutero-Pauline tradition as authoritative

How are Paul's words quoted later, when it is a question of the right of women to speak and their active part in the building-up of the church? Origen of Alexandria, an important interpreter of scripture, who lived between about AD 185 and AD 253, comments on Romans 16.6, in which Paul greets Mary, who has done much hard work for the believers in Rome. Then follows a text from Didymus the Blind, from Alexandria (c. AD 310–389) and part of a dialogue between a Montanist and an orthodox believer. The prophetesses Priscilla and Maximilla had an important role among the Montanists, a movement which gave prophecy a central place. Both texts come from the fourth century and investigate the meaning of 1 Corinthians 11.5, where Paul requires women to keep their heads covered when praying and prophesying. In the Dialogue, the Montanist argues for a literal interpretation of the words: if women may pray, then they may also prophesy. The orthodox gives examples to show that a literal interpretation is untenable. Both the orthodox believer in the Dialogue and Didymus the Blind want to interpret this text figuratively, allegorically: women may not write books under their own names. Finally, Epiphanius of Salamis, also from the fourth century (*c.* AD 310–403), tells of a Christian movement in which Galatians 3.28 plays a major role in the abolition of the inequality between the sexes. Epiphanius counters this by citing 1 Corinthians 11.8, where Paul quotes the order of creation from Genesis. It emerges from these texts that in the 'right faith' Paul's words are interpreted quite differently from the way in which they are interpreted in the faith which is less 'right'.

Origen, Commentary on the Letter to the Romans *10.20*[1]

'Greet Mary, who has laboured much among you.'[2]

   Paul is teaching even in this that women likewise ought to labour for the churches of God. For they labour when they teach young women to be modest, to love their husbands, to raise children, to be pure and chaste, to govern their homes well, to be kind, to be submissive to their husbands,[3] to receive in hospitality, to wash the feet of the saints, and all the other things written that are recorded concerning the services of women to do with all purity.[4]

Didymus the Blind, On the Trinity *3 41.3*[5]

Scripture recognizes as prophetesses the four daughters of Philip, Deborah, Miriam the sister of Aaron and Mary the mother of God, who says, as is written in the Gospel: 'From now on all women and all generations shall call me blessed.'[6] But Scripture contains no books written in their name. On the contrary, the apostle says in 1 Timothy, 'I do not allow women to teach', and also in 1 Corinthians: 'Every woman who prays or prophesies with her head uncovered dishonours her head.'[7] He means that he does not allow a woman shamelessly to write books on her own authority, or to teach in the assemblies. Because when she does that she insults her head, the man: for 'the head of the woman is the man and the head of the man is Christ'.[8] The reason why women are commanded to keep silent is clear: the teaching of a woman caused notable harm to the human race, for the Apostle writes: 'It is not the man who is misled, but the woman.'[9]

Dialogue between a Montanist and an Orthodox[10]

Montanist: Why do you reject the holy Maximilla and Priscilla and say that women are not allowed to prophesy? Did not Philip have four daughters who prophesied and was not Deborah a prophetess?[11] And does not the apostle say: 'Every woman who prays or prophesies with head uncovered'? Why then are women not allowed to prophesy and to pray?[12] If they pray, then they may also prophesy.

Orthodox: We do not reject the prophesies of women. For holy Mary also prophesied when she said: 'From henceforth all generations shall call me blessed.'[13] And as you yourself also say, the holy Philip had four daughters who prophesied and Miriam, the sister of Aaron, prophesied.[14] But we do not allow women to speak in the assemblies or to have authority over men,[15] even so that books would be written under their own name. For that means that they are praying and prophesying with head uncovered. And they may not shame their head, that is, the man.[16] For could not the holy Mother of God, Mary, have written books under her own name? But she did not, in order not to shame her head by exercising authority over men.

Montanist: So praying and prophesying with head uncovered means that they may not write books?

Orthodox: Indeed.

Montanist: When the holy Mary says, 'From henceforth all generations shall call me blessed', is she speaking in public, and is her head uncovered or not?[17]

Orthodox: She has the evangelist as a covering, for the Gospel is not written under her name.

Montanist: Do not count allegories as dogmas![18]

Orthodox: Above all the holy Paul also used allegories as pillars of dogmas when he said: 'Abraham took two wives. That is meant as an allegory, for these are the two covenants.'[19] Suppose that the covering of the head is not meant as an allegory, allow me to interpret the following allegorically. If there is a needy woman and she has nothing to put round her, may she then not pray or prophesy?

Montanist: And is she so needy that she has nothing to put round her?

Orthodox: We have often seen women who were so needy that they had nothing to put round them – what do you do with people who are being baptized? Must women not pray when they are being baptized? And what do you say about men who cover their heads because of an ailment? Do you prohibit them too from praying and prophesying?

Montanist: At the moment when he prays or prophesies, he takes off this covering.

Orthodox: So he does not need to pray without ceasing? But he must listen to the apostle who instructs him and says: 'Pray unceasingly.'[20] But you advise the woman not to pray when she is being baptized?

Montanist: So is it because Prisca and Maximilla have composed books that you do not recognize them?

Orthodox: It is not for this reason only but also because they were false prophetesses with their leader Montanus.

Montanist: Where do you discover that they were false prophetesses?

Orthodox: Did they say the same as Montanus?

Montanist: Yes.

Orthodox: It has been proved that Montanus said things which contradict the divine scriptures and thus they will be rejected along with him.

Epiphanius of Salamis, Medicine Chest *49.1-3*[21]

Now the Quintillians again, who are also called Pepuzians, and those called Artotyrians and Priscillians are the same as the Cataphrygians, and have their origin from them, but differ in a certain way.[22] For these Quintillians, or Priscillians, say that in Pepuza either Quintilla or Priscilla, I cannot say precisely, but one of them, as I said before, had been asleep in Pepuza and the Christ came to her and slept with her in the following manner, as that deluded woman described it. 'Having assumed the form of a woman,' she says, 'Christ came to me in a bright robe and put wisdom in me, and revealed to me that this place is holy, and that it is here that Jerusalem will descend from heaven.' For this reason, they say, even to the present some women and men are thus initiated there, at that place, that, if they wait, they may behold the Christ. Women are called prophetesses among them, but I do not know very clearly whether it is among them or the Cataphrygians. For, they are together and hold the same doctrine.

2 They use the Old and New Testament, and likewise say that there is a resurrection of the dead. And they have Quintilla as their leader, together with Priscilla who was also with the Cataphrygians. And they bear many vain testimonies, granting grace to Eve because she first ate of the tree of knowledge.[23] And they consider Moses' sister as a prophetess, in support of the women appointed to the clergy among them.[24] 'Moreover,' they say, 'Philip had four daughters who prophesied.'[25] And frequently in their assembly seven virgins dressed in white and carrying torches enter, coming, of course, to prophesy to the people. And these, by manifesting a certain kind of frenzy, produce deception in the people present, and make them weep; they pour forth tears as if they were sustaining the sorrow of repentance, and with a certain bearing they lament the life of men. And women are bishops among them, and presbyters, and the other offices as there is no difference, they say, for 'in Christ Jesus there is neither male nor female'.[26]

These are the things which we have grasped. But they call them Artotyrians from the fact that they set forth bread and cheese in their mysteries, and in this way celebrate their mysteries.

3 Men are totally absurd when they separate from the orthodox faith and turn to illogicality and the disagreements which stem from enthusiastic inspiration and secret rites. For the thought of those who do not retain the anchor of the truth, but deliver themselves to one who carries them about for any cause whatever, is subject to Bacchic frenzy. For even if women among them are appointed to the office of bishop and presbyter because of Eve, they hear the Lord saying: 'Your resort shall be to your husband, and he shall rule over you.'[27] And the apostolic word has also escaped their notice: 'I do not permit a woman to speak, nor to have authority over a man'.[28] And again: 'For man is not from woman, but woman from man,'[29] and: 'Adam was not deceived, but Eve was first deceived and transgressed.'[30]

Explanation

Epiphanius' *Medicine Chest* was written in AD 374–377 and is meant as a medicine chest against all heresies. It is the most extensive reference work for the various views and customs of early Christianity and contains descriptions of all kinds of groups which do not observe the 'right doctrine'. It is clear from the quotation printed here that there is also a 'right doctrine' about the behaviour of women.

The movement which Epiphanius describes appeals to words of Paul, namely Galatians 3.28, in which Paul quotes the baptismal formula which says that there is neither male nor female in Christ. This group has concluded from it that women can be bishops and elders. The Deutero-Pauline interpretation from other letters is not mentioned. It would have been interesting to hear the view of this movement on them. It would also have been interesting to get to know Epiphanius' view on Galatians 3.28. However, he does not refer to this text. By contrast, later on in the text Epiphanius declares that this group consecrates bishops and elders on the basis of Eve's role.

Moreover, it is striking that Epiphanius also refers to Paul, but then goes on to interpret him in a Deutero-Pauline way. He quotes Paul's words, 'For man is not from woman, but woman from man'(1 Corinthians 11.8). However, Epiphanius omits the following sentences, in which Paul himself relativizes the order of creation. 'Nevertheless, in the Lord woman is not independent of man or man independent of woman. For just as woman came from man, so man comes through woman; but all things come from God' (I Corinthians 11.11-12). Instead of this Epiphanius affirms the given order of creation with his own quotation from Genesis and with the Deutero-Pauline interpretation of Paul from the first letter to Timothy.[31]

Epiphanius does not see, or does not want to see, that the words from 1 Corinthians 11.8-12 are in opposition to what he quotes from Genesis and Timothy. The movement which ordains women elders and bishops cites words of Paul and does not mention the Deutero-Pauline interpretation. Epiphanius twists Paul's words and gives priority to the Deutero-Pauline interpretation. Where the role of women is concerned, for Epiphanius the Deutero-Pauline interpretation expounds the 'right faith'. As in that interpretation, the view that the man needs to rule over the woman is thus elevated to become a religious rule.

Moreover Epiphanius describes the movement in a confusing and obscurantist way. Are they Quintillians, Pepuzans, Artoturians, Priscillians or Cataphrygians? And precisely what do they do wrong? Like the 'right doctrine', they base themselves on the Old and New Testaments and confess the resurrection from the dead. Exactly these are the three topics which are attacked by the 'heresies'. The word Cataphrygians gives us some information. It literally means 'those who are (called) after Phrygia'. This name has been corrupted into Cataphrygians and is used by the opponents of this movement to make people believe that they were limited to Phrygia. From the fourth and fifth centuries people began to call this movement Montanism after one of the male prophets, Montanus, about whom little is known. The movement called itself 'New Prophecy', with the town of Pepuza in Phrygia as a holy place. The vision mentioned by Epiphanius was had by Priscilla and stands at the beginning of the movement, in around AD 170. Quintilla is a woman, a leader, from a later period of the movement. Given the Hellenistic and Jewish views of man and woman in the quotations from Philo in Chapter 8, the special and offensive feature of the vision is that Christ appears to Priscilla in the garb of a woman. He places Wisdom in her as a woman.

Prophecies were greatly valued in the 'New Prophecy'. Like Paul, people within this movement saw prophecy as a gracious gift from the Spirit and an important possibility for understanding the word of God. In the growing church a discussion was already under way about when God's revelation was complete: with the coming of Jesus on earth, with Pentecost and the twelve apostles, with Paul, or with scripture as the word of God. But according to the believers who felt attracted to the 'New Prophecy', Christ was still speaking. The words of Priscilla and also of Maximilla were carefully recorded in books. These books have not been preserved. From the moment that Christianity became the official religion in the Roman Empire, 'Montanism' was combated with every possible means. The

Montanists were so disadvantaged that in a number of instances they burned themselves and their churches. However, for a long time this movement was part of the growing church, and someone like Tertullian felt very much part of it in the course of his life; he strove for the recognition of this form of faith.

It is evident from the Dialogue between a Montanist and an Orthodox that the Montanists did not appeal only to Galatians 3.28 but also to another text from Paul, namely 1 Corinthians 11.5. In it Paul requires women who pray and prophesy to cover their heads with a veil. The Montanist cites this text as proof that women may prophesy. However, the orthodox believer cites 1 Corinthians and the Deutero-Pauline text from 1 Timothy 2.12 which forbid women to speak during the assembly; women may not have any authority over men. So the orthodox believer concludes that they may not write books under their own name. This, then, seems to be the allegorical interpretation of prophesying with head uncovered. The orthodox shows that a literal interpretation of 1 Corinthians 11.5 is untenable given Paul's words 'pray without ceasing', so the text must be interpreted allegorically. Priscilla and Maximilla have written books under their own names. This is the reason why they are to be rejected. A further reason for rejecting them, according to the orthodox, is that they are false prophets because they say the same as Montanus.

The quotation from Didymus the Blind, one of Jerome's teachers, shows that this allegorical interpretation of 1 Corinthians 11.5, which fits seamlessly within the Deutero-Pauline interpretation, is also shared by others. Whereas the Dialogue between a Montanist and an Orthodox probably comes from Antioch in Syria, Didymus the Blind comes from Alexandria in Egypt. His way of looking at things also gives a new perspective on the question why the Gospel of Mary is not counted as part of scripture. According to Didymus, scripture does not contain any books which are written under the names of women who give instruction. Didymus the Blind also interprets Paul's remarks (1 Corinthians 11.3, 5) from the Deutero-Pauline interpretation (1 Timothy 2.12-14).

The same thing emerges from Origen's Commentary on Romans 16.6, where Paul praises a Mary for all the work that she has done for the believers in Rome. Here Paul uses the same word as he does for his own apostolic work (*kopiao*). However, Origen thinks that this passage is about a woman who has taught girls to be sober, chaste and submissive to their husbands. All the duties of woman which Origen sums up come from 1 Timothy 5.10 and Titus 2.3-4. Both are Deutero-Pauline letters. Origen thinks that this must also be the content of women's contribution to the church.

All women must be silent

The texts quoted above could give the impression that women were active above all in Montanist circles and that in more orthodox circles they remained obediently in the background. Only heretical women were silenced. The following texts, however, show that this was not the case. Origen (*c.* AD 185–253) reports that women, even if they say holy and wonderful things, may not be listened to in the assembly. In his treatise on baptism, Tertullian of Carthage (*c.*160–220) states that women must not only refrain from teaching heretical things, but should not teach at all, even if they are teaching sensibly. Both church fathers appeal to the Deutero-Pauline tradition.

Origen, Commentary on 1 Corinthians *14.34-35*[32]

[Women must be silent during your assemblies. They may not speak, but must remain subordinate, as is also written in the law. If they want to teach, they must ask their own men at home, for it is a disgrace for a woman if she speaks during an assembly.]

Whereas all in the community speak and can speak when they receive a revelation, Paul says: 'Women must be silent during your assemblies.'[33] But that command did not apply to the disciples of the women, those who had received instruction from Priscilla and Maximilla! And it did not apply to the disciples of the bride of the man Christ! But let us be benevolent enough to meet their arguments. They say that the evangelist Philip had four daughters and that these prophesied.[34] And if these prophesied, would it then be more preposterous that our 'prophetesses', as they call themselves, prophesied? We shall answer that argument as follows: first, by saying: 'You say, our prophetesses prophesied' – show us that what they said was really prophecy. And secondly: 'If the daughters of Philip prophesied, then they did not speak during the assemblies.' At least we read nothing about that in the Acts of the Apostles. Nor do we read it in the Old Testament: there it is certainly testified that Deborah was a prophetess. And also that Miriam, the sister of Aaron, took the cymbals and went out before the women. But nowhere will you find that Deborah gave a speech to the people, like Jeremiah and Isaiah.[35] And nowhere in the Old Testament will you also find that Huldah, though she was certainly a prophetess, addressed the people, except an individual who came to her.[36] And also in the Gospel it is written about Anna, a prophetess, the daughter of Phanuel from the tribe of Asher – but she did not speak during the assembly.[37] So that, even though it becomes clear from a prophetic sign that a woman is a prophetess, it is equally clear that she is not allowed to speak during the assembly. When the prophetess Miriam spoke, she was the leader of some women. 'For it is a disgrace for a woman if she speaks during an assembly, and I do not allow the woman to teach or to have authority over the man.'[38]

And I shall also show this from another place in Scripture. There it is said even more clearly that the woman may not play a leading role in respect of the word of the man. 'Older women too must behave modestly. They must give good advice and know how to give the young women guidelines,'[39] but that does not mean that they give instruction. For women, too, can be good teachers, but not in such a way that men sit at women's feet and listen, as if men, who can serve the Word of God, do not count.

'And if they want to learn something, they must ask their own man at home, for it is a disgrace for women if they speak during an assembly.'[40] It seems to me that 'their own man' does not refer only to the married. For in that case the virgins might certainly speak during an assembly, otherwise they would have no one to teach them. And that would also be the case with the widows. But could not 'their own men' also mean the brother, or the housemate or the son? Let a woman understand the expression 'her own man' as the general term 'man' as opposed to 'woman'. 'For it is a disgrace for a woman if she speaks during an assembly.'[41] Whatever she says – even if she says wonderful things and even if she says holy things – the fact is that it comes from the mouth of a woman.

A woman during the assembly – it is clear that with reference to 'disgrace' this is said categorically about the whole church.

Tertullian, On Baptism *1.1-3 and 17.1-5*[42]

1.1 This discussion of the sacred significance of that water of ours in which the sins of our original blindness are washed away and we are set at liberty unto life eternal will not be without purpose. It provides equipment for those who are at present under instruction, as well as those others who, content to have believed in simplicity, have not examined the reasons for what has been conferred upon them, and because of inexperience are burdened with a faith which is open to temptation.

2 And in fact a certain female viper from the Cainite sect, who recently spent some time here, carried off a good number with her exceptionally pestilential doctrine, making a particular point of demolishing baptism. Evidently in this according to nature: for vipers and asps as a rule, and even basilisks, frequent dry and waterless places.

3 But we, being little fishes, as Jesus Christ is our great Ichtus,[43] are born in the water, and only while we abide in the water are we safe and sound. Thus it was that this very monstrous woman, who had no right to teach even sensibly, knew very well how to kill the little fishes by taking them out of the water.

17.1 To round off our slight treatment of this subject it remains for me to advise you of the rules to be observed in giving and receiving baptism. The supreme right of giving it belongs to the high priest, which is the bishop: after him, to the presbyters and deacons, yet not without commission from the bishop, on account of the church's dignity: for when this is safe, peace is safe.

2 At the same time, even laymen have the right: for that which is received on equal terms can be given on equal terms. Unless perhaps you are prepared to allege that our Lord's disciples were already bishops or presbyters or deacons. As the Word ought not to be hidden by any man, so likewise baptism, which is no less declared to be 'of God', can be administered by all. Yet the rules of humility and restraint apply to laymen, as they apply to more important persons. Therefore, they must not arrogate to themselves the function of the bishop. Opposition to the episcopate is the mother of schisms. The holy apostle has said that all things are lawful but all things are not expedient.[44]

3 This means it is enough that you should use this right in emergencies, if ever conditions of place or time or person demand it. The boldness of a rescuer is acceptable when he is constrained to it by the necessities of the man in peril. After all, he will be guilty of a man's destruction if he forbears to give the help he is free and able to give. But the impudence of that woman who assumed the right to teach is evidently not going to arrogate to her the right to baptize as well. Unless perhaps some new beast appears, like that original one. So that as that woman abolished baptism, some other should of her own authority confer it.

5 And if women, with a reference to the Acts of Paul, which are mistakenly so named, claim the example of Thecla for the licence of women to teach and to baptize, let them know that an elder in Asia compiled that document, adding the so-called title 'of Paul' to it. Convinced of his error he confessed that he had done it for love of Paul. Subsequently he renounced his position. Moreover, how could we believe that he (Paul) should grant a woman authority to teach and to baptize? He (Paul), who did not even allow a woman to learn by her own right? 'Let them be silent,' he says, 'and ask their men at home.'[45]

Explanation

Tertullian maintains that all may baptize, but then goes on to emphasize that women may not. Origen does the same thing. He says that all may speak in the assembly. Then he devotes lengthy attention to the position that women may not.

Tertullian expresses his abhorrence at a woman who with her teaching robs baptism of its force. She says that the Lord did not baptize, nor did Paul. Moreover, she thought that water, one of the basic elements of matter,[46] could not bring about spiritual renewal. In a parenthesis, Tertullian mentions at the beginning of his work that a woman may not teach, even about intelligent things. At the end of his work he again returns to her (the 'beast') when he assures his readers that anyone may baptize. Only women may not baptize, just as they may not teach.

Before adhering to Montanism, Tertullian thus seems already to have given a clear opinion about the role of women in the church with a reference to the Deutero-Pauline 1 Corinthians 14.34-35. They must keep silent. But at the same time Tertullian's writing *On Baptism* shows that Tertullian knew women who did not keep silent but taught and baptized, and like Tertullian, did so with a reference to Paul. However, this was not to the Paul who is known from Paul's letters, the Deutero-Pauline interpretation and the Acts of the Apostles, which became part of the New Testament, but to the Paul from the Acts of Paul, which was still valued in Tertullian's time.

The women about whom Tertullian speaks appeal to the model of Thecla. In the Acts of Paul from the beginning of the second century, Thecla leaves her fiancé to become a disciple of Paul. Not that Paul wants this. He leaves her to her fate in Antioch, whereupon she is assaulted and defends herself so fiercely that she is brought to trial and the judges decide to throw her to the lions. She baptizes herself with water from a basin in the arena. The lions cannot do anything to her. This happens first through divine intervention, then by the women of Antioch throwing soporific herbs from the platform into the arena. Later Queen Tryphoena, a member of the imperial family with whom Thecla had found temporary lodging, faints when looking at Thecla and the lions and the women assert that Tryphoena has died during the games. Thereupon the contest is stopped. Thecla proclaims the gospel and the governor no longer sees her as godless but as a handmaid of God. Thecla, who then becomes an itinerant apostle, again seeks Paul. Now he has to recognize her as a servant of God. He grants his permission to her: 'Go and teach the word of God' (Acts of Paul and Thecla 41).[47]

The Acts of Paul and Thecla were not rejected until the sixth century. Nevertheless, for a long time Thecla was revered in the Western church, and in the Eastern Orthodox Church to the present day she is celebrated as the first woman martyr and as apostolic. But already in the second century, at the time when there was still no clear distinction between canonical and non-canonical writings and the Acts of Paul was disseminated in many manuscripts, Tertullian declares the writing to be non-canonical. He vaguely speaks of 'an elder in Asia', who is said to have compiled it for love of Paul. Didn't all the pseudepigraphical writings arise in this way, including the Deutero-Pauline letters? And weren't they nevertheless regarded as valuable? His second argument is more important: Tertullian thinks it incredible that the writing is really about Paul, given that the remark in the first letter to the Corinthians shows quite a different Paul. So for Tertullian it is the Deutero-Pauline tradition which determines who Paul was and whether a writing about him is trustworthy or not. Perhaps that is one of the reasons why no women who baptize and preach appear in the writings which begin to form part of the New Testament. And when they are said to teach, as for instance Prisca taught Apollo (Acts 18.26), then their teaching is omitted.

After his conversion to Montanism, Tertullian assumes that women may prophesy. But then he also says: 'A woman is not allowed to speak in the assembly, far less to teach, to baptize, to celebrate the eucharist or perform any other male task, let alone the office of priest.'[48]

Origen, too, bases himself on the Deutero-Pauline tradition. Evidently there are people in Origen's time and environment who think that 1 Corinthians 14.34-35 is only about married women. Other women, for example widows and virgins, may speak in the assembly. Against this Origen states explicitly that although all may speak during the assembly, all women must keep silent during it, unmarried women and also women who say holy and wonderful things. He then adds the striking words: 'For women, too, can be good teachers, but not in such a way that men sit at women's feet and listen, as if men, who can serve the Word of God, do not count.'

As if the men who can serve the word of God do not count! It is as if Peter from the Gospel of Mary is speaking. Is it then a matter of the men's fear and jealousy? Does Origen with these words betray the deeper reason behind the vigour with which the 'silence texts' from the Deutero-Pauline letters are repeated time and again?

Opposition

Women played an active part in the building-up of the church. At the same time, according to the Deutero-Pauline letters they had to keep silent. How did women and men deal with the fact that the Deutero-Pauline tradition began to belong to the 'right doctrine'? An excursion into a twelfth-century sermon by Theophanes Kerameus about the resurrection narrative in the

Gospel of Luke shows how the Deutero-Pauline texts influenced the image of Mary Magdalene. Theophanes opposes this interpretation and in contrast to Tertullian, as late as the twelfth century, points to the example of Thecla. Jerome of Rome (*c.* AD 347–419) describes how the learned woman Marcella of Rome (*c.* AD 335–411), who was regarded as an important interpreter of scripture, dealt with the rule that women were not allowed to teach. He relates how she nevertheless taught and how he valued her teaching.

Theophanes Kerameus, Sermon 31 (part)[49]

At the same time as they (the angels) spoke, the women remembered his words.[50] So they returned, full of faith and joy, and became apostles for the apostles and messengers for the messengers. They overcame their nature and showed themselves more than the men. For these had hidden themselves for fear of the Jews, but they proclaimed the resurrection with more than apostolic courage with the zealous and courageous Magdalene to lead the way.

It is known to me that some do not hesitate to criticize what is written. They assert that the women who came with sweet-smelling herbs were not evangelists and preachers of the resurrection because Paul, they say, did not allow women to teach. And they did not teach the apostles, but were submissive to them. Some of the flatterers say that. However, these thoughts must not be regarded as honest opinions but as fabrications of childish souls. For at that time it was not a matter of Paul's legislation, nor was it the intention that the first fall of the woman should again be brought forward. But because the primal mother in paradise taught her husband in a perverse way, her descendants now taught the apostles in a good way. Paul himself also brought forward Thecla, the first athlete,[51] as a teacher and proclaimer of the faith. But the author of the Compilations writes better than I do about this in a particularly attractive way.[52]

'But that tale seemed to them to be idle talk and they did not believe them.'[53] It seems that the disciples were overcome with such great despondency that they regarded the announcements of the women loved by God as rubbish. For a jealous feeling goaded them because they felt they had been slighted compared to the women.

Jerome, To Principia, *Letter 127.7*[54]

When the needs of the church at length brought me to Rome, in company with the bishops Paulinus and Epiphanius (one was leader of the church of Antioch in Syria and the other of the church of Salamis on Cyprus), and in my modesty I avoided the eyes of noble ladies, Marcella acted, as the apostle says, 'in season and out of season,'[55] so that her zeal overcame my shame. Because I then had something of a reputation and was esteemed for my zeal for the scriptures, we never met without her asking something about scripture. Nor was she ever satisfied immediately. On the contrary, she continued to ask questions, not for the sake of a discussion but so that by questioning the answers she learned to know any further objections that might be made.

I hesitate to say how much virtue, how much spirit, how much holiness, how much purity I found in her, so that I do not exceed the bounds of credibility and so that I do not cause you more pain when you remember what a great good you have lost. This much only will I say, that whatever in me was the fruit of long study that had become part of my nature by repeated imprints, she tested, learned and made her own. Thus after my departure from Rome, when there was a discussion of any kind about the testimony of scripture, people turned to her as an arbiter. She was very wise and familiar with what the philosophers call *to prepon*, that is, that what one does must be fitting. So when she was asked, she answered in such a way that she did not present her opinions as her own but as from me or some one else. In this way she made it clear that she herself was a pupil in the teaching she gave. After all, she knew the saying of the apostle, 'I do not allow a woman to teach'.[56] Thus she wanted to avoid the impression that she was doing an injustice to the male sex, many of whom (often also including priests) questioned her about obscure and doubtful passages of scripture.

Explanation

In the year AD 382 Jerome came to Rome and went away again three years later. There he got to know Marcella and her community. This issued in a lifelong exchange of thoughts about her and his passion: the interpretation of the scriptures. Finally he settled in Bethlehem. Two women from Marcella's company, Paula and her daughter Eustochium, founded a community of women there. The three of them tried in vain also to persuade Marcella to settle in Bethlehem. Marcella saw it as her task to remain with her community and her poor in Rome.

Jerome is certainly not what today we would call an emancipated man. In 394, when he had already known Marcella for many years, he writes to Paulinus with the intention of stimulating him to a close study of Scripture:

> The art of interpreting the Scriptures is the only one of which all men claim to be masters. To quote Horace again: 'Taught or untaught we all write poetry.' The chatty old woman, the doting old man and the wordy sophist, all take in hand the Scriptures, rend them in pieces and

teach them before they themselves have learned them. Some with brows knit and bombastic words, others philosophizing about the sacred writings surrounded by weak women. Others – I blush to say it – learn from women what they must teach men; and as if even this were not bad enough, they are still so impudent as to explain to others what they themselves by no means understand. (Letter 53.7)

The meaning of this quotation is evident: women are not to teach men. Yet Marcella has made such an impression on Paul that he esteems her teaching greatly. In the letter *To Principia* he mentions her great wisdom, her excellent scholarship and her ascetic way of life. She was a widow, refused a second marriage and was not concerned to please men. She dressed very simply. Her wealth she devoted to the care for the poor. She did not eat meat, nor did she drink wine except when she was sick. She guided her community and under her leadership the study of the scriptures flourished in it. She collected an extensive library to which Jerome sent many scholars from his abode in Bethlehem. And many people came to her for the exposition of scripture. People turned to her as an arbiter over the correct interpretation. Priests also allowed themselves to be instructed by her.

How could that be? Jerome praises her for her teaching. He praises her learning, but how does that fit with the view that it is shameful for a man to be taught by a woman? How does it fit with the Deutero-Pauline words 'I do not permit a woman to teach'? Here, according to Jerome, Marcella's great wisdom was evident. She did not set herself up as a teacher but as a pupil. Even when she was giving her own view she made it seem as if she was repeating the view of Jerome or another male teacher. The double meaning of this remark is evident. Not only does Jerome emphasize Marcella's befitting behaviour, but he also frankly states that Marcella had her own opinions and that they were so elaborate that they could pass for his opinions or for the opinions of other very learned men. Moreover, with this remark Jerome reveals that the official clergy allowed themselves to be taught by a woman. Doubtless Jerome, who was himself attacked so often because he took women seriously as conversation-partners in the study of the scriptures, is being ironic here.

We cannot discover whether Marcella, while giving her own opinions, not wanting to do any injustice to the male sex, in fact deliberately pretended that she only passed on the teaching that she received from learned men. She was indeed known not only for her learning but also for her modesty. However, it is most probable that Jerome is describing Marcella's 'very wise' attitude in order to anticipate and ward off the expected criticism of his male readers, as we saw in Chapter 7 in a quotation from the same letter to Principia about Marcella. Against the scorn of men which he expects, earlier in the letter Jerome refers to the excellence of Mary Magdalene as evidence for his view that women must not be judged according to their bodies but according to their minds.

It is evident from the quotation from the twelfth-century Eastern Orthodox Theophanes Kerameus how much the formation of the image of Mary Magdalene is connected with the view of the role allowed to women in the building-up of the church. Theophanes tells of people who insist that Mary Magdalene and the other women cannot have been the evangelists of the resurrection, because Paul did not allow women to teach. About a century later, it is for example no less a figure than Thomas Aquinas who does the same when he says: 'It is the preaching that makes this witness public, and this preaching is not granted to women.'[57]

As we already saw in Chapter 6, Ambrose of Milan did the same thing earlier, in the fourth century. Ambrose and Thomas Aquinas show that the Deutero-Pauline view of women makes decisive changes to the portrayal of Mary Magdalene as a preacher and as the one who teaches the apostles. Theophanes rejects this idea and rates it among 'fabrications of childish souls'. Contrary to the Deutero-Pauline view, Theophanes states that Paul himself also presents a woman as a teacher and proclaimer of the faith. Evidently even in the twelfth century the story of Thecla could also be regarded as an important argument in a debate about Paul. Theophanes explains that the unbelief of the apostles derives from their despondency and their jealous feeling that they are being put in the background.

In the next chapter it emerges that this difference becomes a tendency. The church in the East emphasizes Mary Magdalene's apostleship. The church in the West recognizes this aspect but does not emphasize it. The Western church puts forward quite a different picture of Mary Magdalene.

Chapter 10

The East and the West

From the sixth century a new image of Mary Magdalene arises. Over the centuries it will prove to be the most popular of all the images that we have seen so far, at least for the Western tradition. The churches in the East maintain the early Christian images. Mary Magdalene takes her place in the calendar of saints in the Eastern Orthodox tradition as 'equal to the apostles'. Down to the 1960s the Roman Catholic calendar of saints had her as 'penitent'. The brain behind this title is Pope Gregory the Great, who in Easter week 591 gave a sermon on Mary Magdalene at the empty tomb. An Easter sermon by his namesake Gregory, Bishop of Antioch, shows that things could still be quite different in the same century. In the sermon from Rome Mary Magdalene bewails her sins. In the sermon from Antioch she is 'ordained apostle' by Christ. In Rome Mary Magdalene is the model for people who 'have lost the purity of the flesh' through sensual desire. In Antioch she is witness to the resurrection and the 'first teacher of the teachers' for people who long to know more about the mystery of death and life.

Ordained apostle

Gregory, Bishop of Antioch, lived from the first quarter of the sixth century to the end of it. The Easter sermon is one of the few of his sermons to have been preserved. We do not know where or when the sermon was given. It was perhaps given following Easter Eve, because Gregory speaks of 'you who watch'. The hearers were also near the tombs. This is a ritual which took place at the end of Easter night. There is also mention of the newly baptized, who could have been baptized in the night before Easter.

Gregory calls on his hearers, who are sitting packed together as if they were in tombs, to see the tombs which they have visited as temporary resting places, as 'tents'. One day the day of judgement will come on which the dead will be called from their tombs. Gregory calls the tombs 'bride chambers of life'. He encourages the churchgoers to reckon that like Christ they will rise from death. He then talks of the 'mystery of death desired by you that ultimately no one can comprehend'. He does this by means of the Gospel of Matthew. Gregory relates Matthew's account from the death and burial of Jesus up to and including his encounter with Mary Magdalene and the other Mary (see Chapter 3).

It is characteristic of Gregory's style that as well as quoting texts from Matthew he also identifies with the various figures from the text and introduces them as speakers. Joseph of Arimathea speaks to Pilate, Gregory himself to the Jews, Pilate to the Jews, death to itself, the two Maries to each other, the Lord to the angel, the angel to the guards at the tomb and to the women, and last of all the Lord to the women. These parts are rhythmic and almost poetic in style. The last monologue emphasizes the message of immortality and mercy. With the death and resurrection of the Lord the judgement on Adam and Eve and their expulsion from paradise are revoked.

The sermon ends with the summons of the two Maries to the disciples to go to Galilee. There they will see the risen Christ. Through the Sea of Galilee and Jesus' promise to make his disciples fishers of men, Gregory arrives at the newly baptized and the font. Just as the risen Christ will encounter the disciples by the Sea of Galilee, so he encounters the newly baptized at the font. He himself has invisibly washed the newly baptized with the water from the font. He himself has anointed them with the Holy Spirit and he himself is the bread and wine which the newly baptized may now taste for the first time.

Gregory concludes the sermon with a prayer, conscious of the sinful hands which will touch the holy body of the Lord in the eucharist. He prays for mercy and refers to the mercy which Christ showed to the sinful woman who anointed Jesus' feet and to Paul who persecuted the Christian community. God also saved them. 'Make us ready to celebrate this day with a pure conscience.'

Gregory of Antioch, Sermon on the Bearers of Ointment[1]

Dedicated to the women who brought fragrant ointment and to the tomb of the divine body of our Lord Jesus Christ. Dedicated to Joseph of Arimathea and to the resurrection on the third day of our Lord Jesus Christ.

1 We praise the law of the church. This prepares us to celebrate in the precious treasury of memories that we have of our dead the memory of the three-day death of our Saviour.

For does not whoever gives his account of the life-bringing death of the Saviour become convinced that the dead lie in their resting-places as in tents?

In this way they await the heavenly trumpet which will call us all from the tombs to the fearful day of judgment.[2]

And would not whoever sees the tomb that brings redemption approach the tombs as bride chambers of life?

And has not whoever believes that Christ is risen from the dead trusted that he himself will also gain the resurrection, through him who has raised himself?

You who watch, having hastened to those who sleep in the tombs, are obedient to the fair law of the church. And packed into this small space, you have made this place broad by your longing. And now you, the people that love Christ, still so packed together, listen to the mystery of the death which you desired, that ultimately no one can grasp, even after one has allowed it to penetrate oneself.

2 Christ the Lord, the only begotten Son of God, went to the cross of his own free will, without being compelled to do so. And through his outstretched hands he justified the whole creation. And through his own bodily suffering he nailed all the invisible and evil powers to the tree of shame.

He wanted to taste his own holy flesh by being three days dead for the whole of nature, so that through this he would give immortality to the generation that was dead. And after he had bent his sacred head, he commanded the end of life to come to his flesh as though it were a little slave girl. And immediately death appeared as a slave and served the Lord at his command. And after death had taken the body, he kept it, because the body had been entrusted to him.

The body, terrifying for the cherubim and making the seraphim shudder, was dominated by death. And as the Lord of the body wanted, the soul of the Saviour also hastened to proclaim to other souls the good news of their redemption. He was God, both according to the body and according to the soul, for after the union his divinity is never separated from his humanity. Together they were in heaven and, without suffering, also in the tomb, where they kept the bodily clothing incorruptible.

While these things were being done, a certain Joseph went to Pilate. Joseph was a distinguished and rich man, he came from Arimathea and was a disciple of the Crucified. By going to Pilate he gave the Master right at his end the last honours. He said to Pilate: 'I make this request for this dead man. This dead man was reviled by his enemies and abandoned at the moment of his suffering. About him I make this request. This dead man has earned neither gold nor silver. He had no soldiers, no allies and no body-guards. He had only a poor mother, who was rich through his birth. I come to negotiate for this dead man who died voluntarily. For, had he not willed it, he would not have died. Let what is left of him be taken down from the cross. He never did wrong to anyone but has honoured people with tens of thousands of gifts. You cannot do me a greater favour.

Give me that dead body which brings life.
When I have it, I shall hide it in the earth.
Give me that thrice-blessed body.
For when the creation saw that it had died, the creation mourned.[3]
Give me the body.
For when the temple saw that it had given up the spirit, it rent its own curtain down the middle.[4]
Give me the body,
for which the splits of the rent rocks showed their sorrow.[5]
I shall kiss the wounds of the sacred hands through which the wounds of my soul will be healed.
I shall caress that pure side from which the mystic blood flowed and the water of rebirth.[6]
These hands shall bury him who will loose the linen wrappings of death.[7]
These sinful fingers will care for him who does all righteousness and educates others to it.
I shall touch the sinless flesh which makes thrice blessed anyone who touches it with faith.
I shall bear to the tomb him who will open the tombs for the dead.
I shall bring the fount of the resurrection to those who have entered death.
I shall light the candle of the resurrection for those who have been held fast in the realm of the dead.'

3 Joseph said this full of piety. And Pilate listened benevolently. For the divine force of the body sought by Joseph works in a divine way on those who obey it. It made the soul of Pilate tender, so that he wanted to listen. And immediately Joseph showed himself to be the envoy and the one who would see to the burial. For, after he had received the body that he desired he put it down and kissed it. He touched the sacred members with his own lips, thinking to himself: if the woman with an issue of blood made the source of the blood dry up by piously touching his garment,[8] shall I not gain gifts by touching his divine body? After that he wrapped the pure pearl with a pure, precious cloth. And he laid it in his new tomb. And after he had laid a stone before the entrance to the tomb, he turned away in tears. But time and again he turned round to the tomb and grieved the loss of the Master.

But Joseph's piety was far surpassed by the godlessness of the Jews. For those who fight against God again thronged together on the sabbath day, went to Pilate and said: 'Lord, we recall that this deceiver, when he was still alive, said: "After three days I shall be raised." Now give the order for the security of the tomb to be ensured until the third day, so that his disciples do not come in the night, steal him, and tell the people that he is risen from the dead. Then the last error shall be worse than the first.'[9]

What do you say, wandering and lawless Jew?

Was he a deceiver who healed your leprous fellow-countrymen?

Was he a deceiver who brought the blind who are of the same tribe as you out of the
   night in which they had to wander around from their birth?

Was he a deceiver who freed those possessed by demons from their diabolical craziness?

Was he a deceiver who in the barren desert set a table before you?

Was he a deceiver who unbound Lazarus from his tomb and with his word called
   back again from sleep the dead man as one who slept?[10]

Was Christ a deceiver? And who then was truthful?

Was Christ a deceiver? Why then were you afraid of what the deceiver proclaimed?

Was he a deceiver? Why then are you afraid of the voice of the dead man?

Was it perchance because he said something about the resurrection while he still
   lived? Do you perhaps believe what he said earlier?

Why are you so opposed to the outcome?

If this dead man by whom you are so troubled does not rise, then he is a deceiver, as
   you assert in such a blasphemous way.

4 And what did Pilate say to them? 'You can have a guard. Impose your security measures as seems good to you.'[11]

If you so shudder before that godless and lawless man – which is what you call him,
if you, the living, are so afraid of that dead man,
then you can have a guard,
then you can have soldiers,
then all of you go against him alone.

Impose your security measures on the dead man who causes you fear, as seems good
   to you.

Do you want to seal the tomb? Seal it.

Do you want to put iron chains around it? Put them around,

so that, when everything is done, you do not say: "Had we been allowed to guard the
   tomb, we would not have lost the body."

Come, impose your security measures as seems good to you.

If Peter shows himself there, seize him with your weapons.
If one of the disciples of the Nazarene pops up, then kill him immediately.
Be watchful and careful, so that no one shall be suspected of stealing your enemy
  secretly.'

After the enemies of the Saviour had been equipped in this way with words and
weapons and soldiers, they guarded the tomb with much zeal and frenzy. And after they
had provided the cave tomb with iron seals, they began to sit by it watching it, as long
as the one whom they guarded wanted that.

5 At that moment, when the second day had dawned, death turned his plunder round,
just as on the first day. When he wanted to devour this plunder with the teeth of
corruption, he did not succeed. And when he wanted to try again and taste it the
following day again he did not succeed. He faced a riddle and probably thought this to
himself:

'What kind of strange dead body is that, which is not easy to get?
What kind of body is that, dead according to the law of nature,
which is preserved in incorruptibility against the law of nature?
It is not God. For it did not die while it was incorporeal.
It is not an angel. For it has a human form.
He was subject to me as Adam, but he is not subject to corruption like Adam.
As a human being he underwent death, but he did not bear it in order to undergo it
    as a mortal. His flesh is stronger than corruption. None of the dead from the
    world which is ruled by me came to me while he had received such a body.
Is this body then perchance some garment from God?
And is that why it offers such stubborn resistance to my mouth?
Is this perchance the tent of the Word of God?
Is this then perchance the temple of him who said to the Jews:
"Break down this temple and in three days I shall raise it up again?"[12]
Has he than perchance been preserved incorruptible for the resurrection?
Is he perchance spying out the dead, this alien dead one?
Will he perchance also take away with him the dead who have long been in my power
    here?
And is it perchance that like Jonah, who camped in the belly of the whale without
    undergoing danger,[13] he is thus spending some time with me, and on the third day will
    wake up so as then, as the first to rise, to show the gates to the other dead?'

  Death spoke in this way, with deeds, not with words.

6 After these events, and after the Jews and the guards had begun to sit together by the tomb, late after the Sabbath, at the dawning of the first day of the week – that is said to be the day of the Lord – Mary Magdalene and the other Mary came to look at the tomb.[14]

O strange and improbable wonders!
Peter, Christ's first commander, denied his living Lord, out of fear for the tongue of
    the maidservant![15]
And the women, weak and fearful, were present at the dawn of this day to honour
    their beloved Master!
They came to look at the tomb.
They did not yet precisely believe the word of the resurrection.
They came to look at the tomb.
They looked at the tomb to gain comfort in their despair.
Seeing the tomb and the tears which then appear can give comfort to souls full of
    sorrow.
They came to look at the tomb.

They wanted to come closer but they dared not, for fear of the Jews. After with misleading movements in secret they had reached the entrance, they sprinkled fragrant oil on the tomb. And after that they returned secretly. And while they were standing so far off, with their eyes full of tears directed at the tomb, they thought that they were serving the Lord with their sighs and laments. With a soft voice they also expressed to one another accusations of the blameworthy role of the Jews. They said:

'How dared they assert such things about our Lord?
And that when they had nothing substantial to bring against him?
How is it possible that they did not shrink to nail him to the cross,
him for whom the sun took flight when it saw him hanging there on the cross?[16]
How did they not shrink from delivering him over to death,
him who had done nothing by which to deserve death?
How was it possible that they did not tire of their own wrath,
even after the death of him who had been vainly attacked by them?
During his lifetime they may have turned against him with foolishness,
but why did they also besiege his tomb after the end of his life?
And why did they hinder those who wanted to do good to him from coming to the
    tomb,
so that they could not worship him in freedom at the tomb?
When only with tears they wanted to return a small gift of what they had received?'

7 Thus the women lamented and mourned over Christ. They thought that he was dead. But the Lord himself, he who was being bewailed by them, had left the tomb marked by the cross without the eyes of the guards seeing it. He had gone away from it as he alone knows how, and said to an angel:

'Go to those brave and believing women who are standing there mourning and who
    think that I am still dead.
Explain to them that I have overcome death and that I am alive, as you see.
Change them from being sorrowful to death into exalted people.
With your right hand remove the stone which the right hands of many have fixed
    there. Convince them by this of how much one soldier loyal to the law of a king
    can do, as compared to many soldiers of a lawless tyrant.
Bring the women into the tomb,
so that they can begin to sing of my power with songs of praise,
after they have been able to see the place where I have lain in a voluntary death.
But show yourself as a deterrent to the guardians of the tomb.
Strike all down through the fear that your countenance arouses.
So that they learn from your force that I have undergone their hardship not out of
    weakness but out of loving kindness.
Also go inside with them, with the banner of the kingdom on your face.
And I shall go with you and make the earth quake again,
so that the earthquake shall be the confirmation of your message.'

8 The angel went quickly to the tomb of the Lord, for he dared not be disobedient when the Lord gave a command. And as soon as he was inside, the earth shook from its foundations, so that he, after waking the guards from their sleep, could tell them before witnesses of the reason for his coming. Then he rolled away the stone from the entrance to the tomb before their eyes and began to sit on it.[17] He laughed at the iron seals and mocked the Jews, because they had entrusted the security to a stone.

And his countenance was like lightning.[18]
For where a cloud of sin casts no shadows, there is multiform splendour there.
And his garment was white as snow.[19]
For the form and the clothing must also be appropriate to the things that he is going
    to proclaim.
For it must be that the messenger of such a glorious thing was glorious in all things.
After he had cast down the guards through great terror and he had been close to
    making all the Jews present dead men, he said to them:
'Why are you afraid, Pharisees?

Why do you quake, and why have you all fallen on your faces like dead men?[20]
To me, the servant, you are dead, but in the face of the Lord you are daring?
Is the soldier regarded as terrifying but the King of heaven as contemptible?
You cannot bear the appearance of one angel – which is quite without danger.
And how do you think you can obscure the full force of the Creator of the angels?
You who could not prevent me, the labourer from heaven, from moving the stone.
How could you have prevented it when the maker of the whole of creation wanted to
    recreate the temple of his body,
you who cannot hold back the creature,
how could you try to strive against the Creator?
But stand up and look carefully around you.
Is Peter now with me?
Has any of the fishermen together with me stolen the dead body?
Does God perchance need help?
Does the divine Word need a fellow-worker for the resurrection of his own body?

9 After the angel had said this to the Pharisees and had left them solitary and quaking, he turned his face to the women. First he allowed them to enjoy the sweetness of the dawning day. After that he drove the fear from their souls by crying to them:

'You must not be afraid.[21]
They were anxious and afraid, for they are haters and enemies,
But you need not be afraid.
You must dance and rejoice,
for you have done things that deserve a garland.
You must not be afraid,
for we are subject to one rule, we praise the same Lord.
I know that you seek Jesus, the crucified.[22]
– He did not say, "Jesus, the dead man," for then he was no longer dead, but "Jesus
    the crucified."
– You seek him who through you has withstood the shame of the cross.
You seek him who seeks those who seek him.
You seek him who is close to those who call on him.
I know that you seek Jesus, the crucified.
He is not here. He is not where you think. He is not where he lay.'
'What do you say, angel?
Is our Master and Lord not here?
Is he who is the cause of our tears not here?
Have we wept for him for nothing?

Have we brought the gifts for the dead for nothing?

Is he not here?

Have those of evil will taken him somewhere else?

Did they not grant him even his tomb, those who did not grant him his life?

Is he not here?

But where is he then?

Tell us quickly, we are asking you.

Make our trembling souls more peaceful again.

Do not pile one pain upon another.

Show us the place where we must seek the dead body,

so that we can take away somewhat the sorrow that comes from our eyes by there
quickly.

10 And the angel said: 'Do you want to know where he is, he whom you seek? And how he is risen? I shall tell you. For that is why I have been sent to you by him, the dead man whom you sought, to explain his resurrection to you, to heal your souls, to stop your tears and to raise you up in joy by what I shall say.

He is risen, as he has said.[23] Even now the truth has become truth, according to God's custom. And what he said in words he has fulfilled in deeds. His immortal divinity has remained immortal. And at the moment of the end of his flesh, his mortal body, he received with his bodily eyes the sleep of the dead. He lay down and lay like a lion, royally.[24]

But he came back; he appeared from there, full of divine majesty. The guards of the garrison did not notice that he arrived. For, they were not worthy to see him, whom they had treated as an enemy, again as the Risen One. The tomb did not prevent the resurrection of the Almighty. Death was not able to bind him who had not been bound by sins. The unwilling tyrant had to yield before the King. Even hell itself was seized by fear and quaked. The guardians of the gates of hell threw away their keys, let the doors stand open, and did not dare to say anything to even one of those who stood by them.

So he is risen, as he has said.

How can I tell you unspeakable things?

How shall I proclaim things which transcend all reason and understanding?

How shall I expound the resurrection of the mystery of the Lord?

The cross too is a mystery.

And his three days long death is a mystery.

And all things relating to the Saviour are mysteries.

For, as he was born while the doors of virginity were closed, so he has risen while the
tomb was closed.

And as he was born the firstborn from his mother, he, the only-begotten son of God,
   so he becomes the firstborn who has risen from the dead.
As at his birth he did not nullify the virginity of his virgin mother,
   so at his resurrection he left the form of his tomb completely intact.
Therefore – I cannot explain either his birth or his resurrection in words.
I see the place of the resurrection and I worship the resurrection.
I cannot explain the details of the resurrection.
I worship the place of wonder, though I cannot understand anything vital about it.
But what I see I can also show you.
Come, see the place where the Lord has lain.[25]
For that is why I have put the stone in another place.
Not benevolently to open the door through which Jesus could come out.
For he, the Help of all, did not need my help.
For before I had rolled the stone away, the stone with sharp corners rolled back,
   as he wanted.
But so that you could learn to know the place and sing songs of praise to the risen
   Christ,
come, see the place where the Lord lay.
Hitherto you have seen the place and also the strange fruit of the place.
Come, see the place where the devil received the deadly blow.
Come, see the place on which the symbols of your resurrection were written.
Come, see the place where death lay as a corpse.
Come, see the place on which the seed of the body, not yet sown, fell and made
   countless seeds of immortality grow.
Come, see the place, more enjoyable than the whole of paradise.
Come, see the place, more glorious than any royal bridal chamber.
Come, see the dumb tomb that loudly sings the power of him who is buried there.
Bend towards the hole of the tomb which has become the gateway of incorruptible
   life.
Bend towards the cave from which you will move to heaven.
Stop your sighs and your tears.
Stop looking for the Living among the dead.
Dancing with joy, speak negatively about death.
Where, death, is your sting? Where, kingdom of the dead, is your victory?[26]
And now quickly go and tell his disciples that he is risen from the dead.
And look, he goes before you to Galilee.
There shall you see him. Behold, I have told you.[27]
See that you do not hide the wonder by keeping silent.

For it is not without danger for servants to be silent about the wonders of the Lord.' And after they had gone away from the tomb quickly, with fear and great joy, they hastened to his disciples to report to them that he was risen from the dead. 'And look, he goes before you to Galilee. There shall you see him. Behold, he has told you.'

11 Because the Holy Spirit urged the women to run faster, they fulfilled the words which he spoke by the prophet Isaiah:

You, women, who come from what you have seen, come here.
For the people has no understanding.[28]

The women ran there with their anointing oil in fear and great longing.[29] They vied with one another over the quickest way, because each wanted before the other to bring to the apostles the good news entrusted to them. Suddenly the Lord stood there before them and sealed the words of the angel with the seal of his own bodily presence. He gave their souls wings by saying to them:

'Rejoice.[30]
The condemned Eve is justified.
The banished Adam is recalled.
The judgment is revoked.
The bad serpent is trampled underfoot.
The devil has fallen.
The defenders of the devil are put to shame.
The enemies are routed.
The Jews have sorrow and cannot be comforted.
The Pharisees regret that they ventured it.
My cross proved a shield.
The tomb has become a witness to my power.
Death concedes defeat.
Immortality is set down in writing for human beings.
In me human nature is renewed.
In me all the dead came to new life.
In me prevails the steadfastness in which you have support.
In me is my image garlanded.
These are the fruits of my three-day stay in the tomb.
These are my garlands for the victory over death.
These are the royal pearls of my kingship
which I have taken with me from the depths of the kingdom of the dead

and I shall bring to my beloved.

Therefore be full of joy. Dance. Rejoice. Feast.

Go, tell my disciples.

See that I bear not hate, but loving-kindness.

I call them brothers, who left me alone at the moment of the crucifixion.[31]

I know how to be generous when I am violated.

I know how to bear it when I am treated ungratefully.

I know how to be lenient for the weaknesses of my friends.

I know how to show compassion to those who sin and weep about it.

Go, tell my brothers that they must go to Galilee and that they will see me there.[32]

Tell my disciples the mysteries that you have seen.

Be the first teachers of the teachers.

Let Peter, who has denied me, learn

that I can also ordain women to be apostles.

Let them go to Galilee and see the humble sea

from which I fished when I fished for thinking fishes.[33]

Let them see the sea from which I made them march to the sea of men.'

12 That is what the Lord said to the women.

Invisible he now also stands by the faithful at the baptismal font.

He himself embraces the newly baptized as friends and brothers and says to them,
    'Rejoice.'

He himself fills their hearts and souls with gladness and joy.

He himself washes them, who have become dirty, with the flowing water of grace.

He himself anoints them, who are reborn, with the unguent of the Spirit.

He himself is the one who feeds them and at the same time he is the food.

He himself provides the spiritual food for his own servants.

He himself says to all the pious:

'Take, eat the heavenly bread.

Take the fountain from my side, from which water can always be drawn, and which
    never runs dry.

You who are hungry, be satisfied,

and you who thirst, be drunk with a drunkenness which makes wise and offers
    redemption.'

But, O King of the heavens, you who sit at the right hand of the Glory in the highest,

you, the Lord of the incorporeal powers,

you, who guide creation as you will,

you, who have given us this day and this assembly,

have mercy on us, as you had mercy on the prostitute
and do not reckon it to us when we,
without awe for your loving kindness,
are bold to take your holy body with sinful hands.
And as you were not offended at the sinner, the prostitute,
for clasping your pure feet,[34]
withhold your wrath from us, unworthy.
You who rule, protect us all in your loving-kindness,
and in your love of human beings also encircle us with the net of reverence for you,
as you sent the thrice blessed Paul,
after you had saved his life from heaven,
out as an apostle.[35]
Also save us, so that with pure conscience
we may celebrate the day of your life-giving resurrection on the third day.
For you alone are the Lord, good and loving, Christ our God.
For to you is the praise, and the power,
together with your spotless Father,
and the life-making Spirit,
now and always, for ever and ever. Amen.

Explanation

Gregory of Antioch introduces Mary Magdalene and the other Mary half-way through his sermon. He does so with a quotation from Matthew (Matthew 28.1). Gregory himself does not mention the two Maries by name once in this sermon. He always calls them 'the women'. He is obviously quite aware that they are women. In accordance with current thinking he describes the women in their 'femininity' as 'weak and fearful' (6). The words *imbicillimae* and *timidae*, from which our words 'imbecile' and 'timid' are derived, appear here in the Latin translation of the Greek. The eyes of the women are 'full of tears' and they did not go to the tomb because of the message of the resurrection, as Matthew suggests, but to seek comfort in their despair (6).

Gregory sees a great contrast between these women and Peter, 'Christ's first commander' (6), who had said about Jesus on the eve of his crucifixion, 'I do not know this man.' The strong Peter proves to be afraid of 'the tongue of a serving maid' and denies the Lord, whereas despite their fear the weak women go to the guarded tomb and thus confess Jesus as their Master. Gregory makes Christ call the women 'these brave and believing women' in conversation with the angel (8). And the angel says to them: 'You have done things which deserve a garland' (9). But even their encounter with the angel does not make the women think of the resurrection in the first instance. On the contrary, they ask, 'Show us the place where we must seek the dead body' (9). The angel's task is to make the sorrowful women elated. After the appearance of the angel, the Lord himself appears.

It is striking that Gregory of Antioch does not make a single attempt to explain why the Lord first appears to women. Moreover both the angel and the Lord himself tell the women in detail about the meaning of Christ's death and resurrection. In contrast to their role in Mark, Matthew and Luke the women are thus not the vehicles of a short message that all the disciples already know. The angel then says explicitly that they are not to keep silent about it: 'For it is not without danger for servants to be silent about the wonders of the Lord' (10). As well as the meaning of his death and life, the women must also announce the generosity of the risen Lord to the male disciples, his forgiveness for the fact that they had all abandoned him at the crucifixion. Then follow the striking words:

> Tell my disciples the mysteries that you have seen.
> Be the first teachers of the teachers.
> Let Peter, who has denied me, learn
> that I can also ordain women to be apostles. (11)

No echo of the Deutero-Pauline prohibition 'I do not permit women to teach' can be found in these words. Moreover, Gregory of Antioch gives the women a greater role than they have in Matthew. They are not only thought worthy to relate what the disciples already know, namely that they must go to Galilee to see the risen Lord there. The women must also tell the men about the mysteries that they have seen. The risen Lord himself ordains the women apostles and makes them the first teachers of the teachers, without any explanation, without any excuses. Seen in the light of the texts which we read in Chapters 7, 8 and 9, this is a hammer blow to the male ego of this time. Christ's words are opposed to what is increasingly beginning to belong to 'right doctrine', namely the command that women must keep silent.

Why does Gregory of Antioch put these words in Christ's mouth, and what do they mean for his audience? We know nothing about this. Did Gregory as Bishop of Antioch want to ordain women and include them in the apostolic tradition? Did he defend women as teachers in his diocese?

Was he critical of an exclusively male hierarchy? 'Let Peter, who denied me, learn that I can also ordain women to be apostles.' Such a statement also reminds me of the words of John the Baptist in the Gospel of Matthew: 'God is able from these stones to raise up children of Abraham' (Matthew 3.9). John the Baptist says that to the leaders of the people who boast that they are children of Abraham. Perhaps Gregory of Antioch also means his words in this way, opposing those who claim to be successors to Peter.

Be this as it may, Peter and his men need the Lord's mercy. So do Paul and the sinful woman who anointed Jesus' feet, the newly baptized and all churchgoers. They all need Christ's mercy because of their sins. But Mary Magdalene and the other Mary are the brave and believing women who deserve a garland for what they have done. They are the teachers who must tell of the mysteries of faith and preach the message of mercy. Gregory the Great, the Pope of Rome and as such Peter's successor, in the city where Peter and Paul lie buried, sketches out a very different picture.

Penitent

The great difference between Gregory of Antioch and Gregory of Rome is that the latter identifies Mary Magdalene with Luke's anonymous woman who was a sinner and the former does not. In the preceding chapters we saw that Mary Magdalene is identified with Martha's sister, but not yet that she is the same person as the sinful woman from Luke. Gregory the Great makes this identification in his sermon on Luke 7.36-50. The first fragment of text from Sermon 33 shows this. The second fragment of text comes from the same sermon and shows Gregory's mystical interpretation of the anointing of Jesus' feet. In this sermon Mary Magdalene is the symbol of the pagan church, in which penance and conversion are central. She is also a symbol of individual believers who bewail their sins and do good works; who love their disadvantaged neighbours with all their hearts and assuage their need from their own superfluity.

Sermon 25, the whole of which is quoted here, shows what this image of Mary Magdalene means for Gregory's interpretation of the resurrection story in the Gospel of John. Gregory examines the text verse by verse and interprets it both literally and figuratively. The most important characteristic of Mary Magdalene in this sermon is her ardent and tenacious love. This is a passionate sermon in which Gregory the Great summons his hearers to penitence and conversion.

Gregory the Great, Sermon 33.1, 5 (Luke 7.36-50)[36]

When I think about the penitence of Mary, I would rather weep than say anything. For whose heart, however hardened, would not be so softened by the tears of this sinner that he follows her model of penitence? She had reflected on what she had done and did not want to be stopped from what she had planned. While they were reclining at the meal she entered. She came uninvited and she brought tears. Recognize how she burns with pain who does not hesitate to weep during the meal.

Luke describes her as a sinner, but John as Mary. We believe that she is that Mary of whom Mark attests that seven demons were driven out of her. What is meant here by the seven demons other than the totality of all vices? For because seven days embraces all time, the number seven is rightly interpreted as 'totality'.

So Mary had seven demons, filled as she was with all the vices. But look, because she recognized the shamefulness of her wickedness, she ran to the source of mercy to wash herself. She was not ashamed before those who were at the meal. For because she was inwardly deeply ashamed for herself, she believed that there was nothing for which she must be outwardly ashamed.

So what should we admire more, brothers, that Mary comes or that the Lord receives her? Must I say that he receives her or that he draws her to him? I shall rephrase it: it is better to say that he draws her to him and receives her, because he evidently drew her to himself inwardly full of mercy, whereas outwardly he received her full of meekness.

But now let us go through the text of the holy Gospel and reflect on the order of events in which the healing came.

5 Beloved brothers, this was the interpretation in the historical sense of the text that we have been through. But now, if it pleases you, we shall also look at what is said in its mystical meaning.

What is meant by the Pharisee, who makes himself stand out for his perverse righteousness, other than the Jewish people? And who is the converted sinner who goes to the Lord's feet and cries, other than converted paganism? She came with an alabaster jar, poured out the anointing oil, put herself behind the Lord's feet, made the feet wet with her tears, dried them with her hair, and did not stop kissing the feet that she had anointed and dried.

So we, we are meant by this woman when after sins we turn to the Lord with all our heart, when we take the sorrow of her penitence as an example.

What is meant by the anointing oil other than the fragrance of good works? Therefore Paul says: 'We are in every place before God the good aroma of Christ.'[37] So when we do good works in this way, what do we do other than pour anointing oil over the

Lord's body? But the woman stood at the Lord's feet. We stand opposite the Lord's feet when in a sinful state we turn from his ways. But whenever we convert to true penitence after sin, we stand behind his feet, because we then follow the footsteps that we first opposed.

With tears the woman makes his feet wet. We also do that in all truth when we bend with a feeling of compassion to the least members of the Lord, when we have compassion on his saints in oppression, when we believe their sorrow to be ours.

With her hair the woman dried the feet that she had made wet. Hairs are abundantly present on the body. Has the abundance of earthly possessions another symbol than the hairs? When possessions are greater than what is necessary for life, we do not notice when we lose some of them. With our hairs we dry the Lord's feet, when we also by means of our abundance have mercy on his saints whom we pity out of love, we do this so that out of compassion the spirit experiences suffering in such a way that a generous hand also shows the feeling of suffering. Whoever has compassion on the suffering of the neighbour, but does not have compassion on him out of his abundance, makes the feet of the Lord wet without drying them. Whoever only utters words of suffering but does not lighten suffering in any way by showing the care that is lacking weeps, but does not dry.

The woman kisses the feet which she dries. We also do that perfectly when we zealously love those whom we support, so that the need of our neighbour does not become heavy, so that the need of those whom we support does not become a burden on us. And so that, while the hand offers what is necessary, the heart does not grow rigid in love.

Gregory the Great, Sermon 25 (John 20.11-18)

[Given before the people in the basilica of St John, which is called the Constantinian, on the fifth day of Easter.]

1 Because she loved the truth, Mary Magdalene, who was a sinner in the city, washed away with tears the stains of her guilty state. And the word of the Truth was fulfilled, in which it is said: 'Her sins are forgiven her, though they were many, for she has shown much love.'[38] For she, who beforehand had remained cold through sinning, afterwards burned ardently because she loved. For, after she had come to the tomb and did not find the body of the Lord there, she thought that he had gone away and reported that to the disciples. When they came, she told it to them and they believed that it was as the woman had said. And about them directly after that is written: 'Then the disciples returned.'[39] And thereafter has been added: 'But Mary stood outside the tomb weeping.'[40] Here we must remember how great was the power of love which had set the spirit of this woman aglow. For even when the disciples went away, she did not depart

from the tomb. She continued to seek him whom she had not found. She wept while seeking and, kindled by the fire of her love for him, she burned with longing for him who she thought had been taken away.

And so it happened that only she, who had remained to seek, saw him: because the force of doing good lies in persistence. And through the voice of the truth it was said: 'But he who persists to the end shall be saved.'[41]

It is also commanded by a precept of the law that in a sacrifice the tail of a sacrificial animal must also be offered.[42] Now the tail is the end of the body. And only he sacrifices in a good way who performs the sacrifice of a good work to the end. Therefore it is written of Joseph that in the midst of the other brothers he wore a garment that fell to the ankles.[43] For a garment falling to the ankles is a good work that is performed completely.

2 But while Mary was weeping, she bent down and looked in the tomb. She had already seen that the tomb was empty, she had already reported that the Lord had been taken away – what made her bend down again, again desire to look? For someone who loves, looking once is not enough. For the force of love multiplies the desire to investigate. So first she sought and did not find him. But she persisted in her search and so succeeded in finding. The unsatisfied desires grew, and the constantly growing longings could seize what they had found. For this is also what the church in the Song of Songs says about the same bridegroom: 'By night in my bed I sought him whom my soul loves: I sought him and did not find him. I shall rise and go round the city, through the alleys and through the streets I shall seek him whom my soul loves.'[44] And once again she repeats her fruitless search, when she says: 'I sought him, and did not find him.'[45] But because the finding is no longer so far away if the seeking does not stop, she adds: 'I was found by the watchmen who guard the city. Have you perchance seen him whom my soul loves? Scarcely had I passed them, when I found him whom my soul loves.'[46] We seek the beloved in bed when in the short rest of this life we languish with desire for our Saviour. We seek by night because, although when awake the soul is busy with him, our eye is hitherto darkened. But for the one who does not find his beloved, there is nothing but to rise and go around in the city. That means he traverses the holy church of the elect already seeking in his thought, that he seeks him through alleys and streets. That means that he looks at those who go along the narrow and broad way to see whether he can somehow find traces of him. Because in the worldly life too there are sometimes people who act so virtuously that they have to be followed. If we seek in this way, the watchmen who guard the city find us: because the holy fathers, who guard the welfare of the church, come to help our good efforts. For they teach us with their words and with their writings. And when we have gone only a little way further, we find him whom we love. Since our Saviour, although in lowliness a man among men, was above

men in his divinity. When the watchmen have been passed, the beloved is found. For when we see that the prophets and the apostles stand beneath him, we see him who by nature is God, standing above human beings. For first he is sought, whereas he does not allow himself to be found, so that after having been found he is held on to more steadfastly. For holy desires grow, as we have said earlier, because the fulfilment is postponed. However, if they perish through delay, they were not longings. Everyone who could come to the truth burned with this love. For that is why David said: 'My soul thirsts for the living God: when will I come and appear before God's face?'[47] So he also urges us: 'Seek his face always.'[48] That is also why the prophet said: 'My soul longed for you in the night. And with my spirit, in my innermost parts I shall wait for you from the early morning.'[49] That is why the church also says again in the Song of Songs: 'I am wounded by love.'[50] It is after all right that she is healed by seeing the physician, she who through the glow of longing for him bears a wound of love in her heart. Therefore she says again: 'My soul was melted when my beloved spoke.'[51] For the spirit of a person who does not long to see his Creator is much hardened, because it remains ice-cold in itself. But when it already begins to burn with longing to follow him whom she loves, then she hastens, melted by the fire of love. She becomes restless through the longing and everything that previously was pleasing in the world becomes worthless. There is nothing outside the Creator in which she takes pleasure. And things with which previously the spirit diverted itself later become a heavy burden. Nothing comforts her sorrow as long as he who is longed for is not seen. The spirit mourns, the light itself is a torment, and by such fire in the spirit the rust of guilt is consumed. And the inflamed spirit which, like gold, has lost its splendour through use, begins to shine through the glow.

3 However, she loves so much that again she bends down towards the tomb into which she had already looked once. Let us see how the force of her love duplicates the result of her search. There follows: 'She saw two angels sitting in white clothes, one at the head and one at the feet, where the body of Jesus had lain.'[52] What does it mean that two angels are seen at the place of the body of the Lord, one sitting at the head and one at the feet? In Latin, angel means proclaimer. He who is God before all ages and man to the end of the ages must be proclaimed because of his suffering. It is as if an angel were sitting at the head when the apostle of John proclaims: 'In the beginning was the Word, and the Word was with God and the Word was God.'[53] And as if an angel were sitting at the feet when the apostle says: 'The Word has been made flesh and has dwelt among us.'[54] By the two angels we can also recognize two testaments, the first by the one and the following one by the other. The angels are bound together by the place of the Lord's body. Both testaments proclaim that the Lord has been made flesh, has died and risen. And the first testament has its place at the head and the later testament at the feet.

Hence, too, the two cherubs which cover the mercy seat look at each other with their faces turned towards the mercy seat.[55] Cherub means fullness of knowledge. And what is indicated by the two cherubs other than the two testaments? What else is depicted by the mercy seat than the incarnate Lord, of whom John has said: 'He is a propitiation for our sins?'[56] And whereas the Old Testament declares that this will happen and the New Testament proclaims that it has been done by the Lord, the two cherubs look as it were at each other simultaneously, while they turn their face to the mercy seat. For whereas they see the incarnate Lord lying between them, they do not turn away from their own gaze, because they relate in agreement with each other in what way the mystery has been accomplished.

4. The angels ask Mary: 'Woman, why are you weeping?' And she says to them: 'Because they have taken away my Lord and I do not know where they have laid him.'[57] Truly, these holy words which arouse in us tears of love, comfort the same tears because they promise that we shall see our Saviour. But in this report it must be noted that the woman does not say: 'They have taken away the body of my Lord,' but 'They have taken away my Lord.' It is customary in holy Scripture that this sometimes makes the whole clear from a part, but sometimes also a part from the whole.

The whole is evident from a part as when it is written of the sons of Jacob: 'Because Jacob went down to Egypt with seventy souls.'[58] And of course no souls went down to Egypt without bodies, but the word soul alone denotes the whole person. For the total is expressed from a part. And only the body of the Lord had lain in the tomb. And Mary did not seek the body of the Lord, but the Lord who had been taken away. In this way of course she interpreted a part from the whole.

'When she had said that, she turned round and saw Jesus standing, and she did not know that it was Jesus.'[59] It must be noted that Mary, who up to that moment doubted the resurrection of the Lord, turned round so that she might see Jesus. Because of her doubt she had turned her back on the face of the Lord, whom she could not believe to have risen. But because she both loved and doubted, she saw him and did not recognize him. Love made her see him, whereas doubt kept him hidden from her. And her not knowing up to that moment is expressed by the incidental remark: 'And she did not know that it was Jesus.' And he said to her: 'Woman, why are you weeping? Whom do you seek?' He asks about the cause of her sorrow to make her longing grow. So that when she mentions the name of him whom she seeks, she should burn even more ardently for love of him: 'Thinking that he was the gardener, she said to him: Sir, if you have taken him away, tell me where you have laid him, so that I can take him with me.'[60] Perhaps this woman was wrong, without being wrong, in believing that Jesus was the gardener. Or was he perhaps for her the gardener in a spiritual sense, he who in her heart planted the seeds which blossomed with virtues through love of him?

5 But why, after she had seen him whom she took to be the gardener, did she say, when she had not told him whom she sought: 'Sir, if you have taken him away?'[61] For as if she had already said whom she so desired that she wept for him, she spoke of him of whom she had not yet said who he was. But the force of love ensures that you cannot believe of the one of whom you are always thinking that anyone else does not know him. So this woman, too, rightly does not say whom she seeks. Yet she says: 'If you have taken him away.' For, she thinks that the one over whom she herself so weeps with longing cannot be unknown to the other. 'Jesus said to her: "Mary."'[62] After first addressing her with the general term which denoted only her sex, he called her now by her name, as if he was openly saying to her: recognize the one by whom you are recognized. The perfect man is also told: 'I know you by your name,'[63] because 'man' is a word that refers to all of us in common. But Moses is a proper name and to him it is rightly said that he is known by name. As if the Lord were openly saying to him: I do not know you in general like the rest of human beings, but particularly. Because Mary is named by her name, she recognizes the master and also directly calls him 'Rabbouni', which means master. Because he both was the one who was sought outwardly and he who taught her that she must seek him inwardly.

The evangelist does not now tell us what the woman did, but that incidentally becomes known to us through what she heard. She is told: 'Do not touch me, for I am not yet ascended to my Father.'[64] In these words it is made clear that Mary wanted to embrace the feet of him whom she recognized. But the Master said to her: 'Do not touch me.' Not because the Lord refused to be touched by women after the resurrection. It is written about the two women who came to his tomb: 'They came to him and clasped his feet.'[65]

6 The reason why he may not be touched is also added. It is said: 'For I am not yet ascended to my Father.'[66] In our heart Jesus ascends to the Father when we believe that he is like the Father. But the Lord does not yet ascend to the Father in one who does not believe that he is like the Father. Thus he truly touches Jesus who believes that the Son is as eternal as the Father. Jesus was already ascended to the Father in Paul's heart when the selfsame Paul said: 'He who was then in the form of God did not think that he must hold grimly on to the fact that he was like God.'[67] Therefore John also touched our Saviour with the hand of faith when he said: 'In the beginning was the Word and the Word was with God and the Word was God. This was in the beginning with God. All things were made through him.'[68] Thus the one touches the Lord who believes that he is like the Father through the eternity of his being. But perhaps someone feels the silent question arising in him how the Son can be equal to the Father. In this matter it is the case that what cannot be understood by wondering at it can only become credible through wondering at something else. Human nature has something through

which it can give itself a brief answer. For, it is certain that he himself created the mother in whose virginal womb he was prepared for his humanity. What then is more wonderful than for him who was before his mother to be like God? We have also learned through the testimony of Paul: 'Christ the power of God and the wisdom of God.'[69] Thus whoever thinks that the Son is less, does an injustice to the Father in particular, of whom he confesses that this wisdom is not like himself. What powerful man would bear it without becoming agitated if someone said to him: 'You are great, but your wisdom is less than you'? The Lord also himself says: 'I and the Father am one.'[70] And on another occasion he says: 'The Father is greater than I.'[71] And it is also written of him that he 'was submissive to his parents'.[72] What then is there more wonderful than that from his humanity, in which he was also subject to his parents on earth, he concedes that he is less than his Father in heaven? And from that humanity Mary is now told: 'Go to my brothers and say to them: I am going to my Father and your Father, to my God and your God.'[73] When he says 'my' and 'your', why does he not say quite generally 'ours'? But by making that distinction in speaking he indicates that he himself has the same Father and God, but in a way which differs from ours. 'I am going to my Father' – of course by virtue of his nature; 'and to your Father' – by grace. 'To my God' – because I have descended: 'to your God' – because you will rise. 'Because I am human, for me he is God. Because you are freed from error, for you he is God. Thus he is Father and God for me in a different way. Because he created me, whom he brought forth before the ages as God, at the end of the ages with me as human being.'

Mary Magdalene came to proclaim to the disciples: 'I have seen the Lord and he has said these things to me.' [74] Behold, the guilt of the human race is here cut off where it sprouted. For because in paradise a woman gave a man death to drink, from the tomb a woman gave men life.[75] And she tells what he who gives life has said to her, who had once related the words of the death-bringing serpent. As if the Lord says to the human race, not with words but with concrete things: 'Receive now from the hand with which the drink of death was offered you the cup of life.'

7 We have briefly discussed these things from the Gospel reading. Now, with the help of the same Lord about whom we are speaking, we shall consider the glory of his resurrection and the deepest essence of his love. For he wanted to rise from the dead as quickly as possible, so that our soul should not remain too long in the death of mistrust. And that is also expressed by the psalmist: 'On the way he shall drink from the brook, therefore he shall raise up his head.'[76] In the human race, from the very first beginning of the world the brook of death had flowed. The Lord drank from this brook on the way – he tasted death in passing. But in that way he lifted up his head so that in his resurrection he raised above the angels what he put dying in the tomb. And through that he smote the age-old enemy on earth eternally, after he had first allowed the hands

of those who persecuted him to rage against him for a while. And the Lord openly points to that through the blessed Job: 'Can you catch Leviathan with a fishhook?'[77]

8 Leviathan, which means 'their added gift', denotes the sea monster that swallows up the human race. The one who promised to make man divine took his immortality away from him. He saddled the first man with the guilt of sin. And by making the transgressions ever greater, he loaded punishment upon punishment on him without ceasing.

However, in the fishhook the bait is visible but the hook is hidden. So the almighty Father caught him with a fishhook, since he sent his only-begotten incarnate Son to kill Leviathan. In him the flesh capable of suffering was visible, but the divinity incapable of suffering was invisible. And when the serpent bit him in the visible flesh through the hand of those who persecuted him, he was pierced by the hook of his divinity. For first he had recognized God in him in the miracles, but he began to doubt when he saw that he was capable of suffering. As with a fishhook he held the mouth of the swallower fast, while in him the bait of the flesh was visible. And the swallower very much wanted to eat that up. But the divinity which would kill him remained hidden during the time of suffering. He was caught in the fishhook of his incarnation. For while he bit into the flesh of his body, he was pierced by the hook of his divinity. Thus on the one hand it was the humanity that the swallower took to himself, on the other hand the divinity that pierced him. On the one hand it was the clear weakness which had to exercise the force of attraction; on the other hand the hidden force which had to pierce the mouth of the robber. Thus he is caught in the fishhook, so that he perished where he had bitten. And he lost the mortals whom he rightly held fast because he did not have the right to hold him, whom he expected to be able to attack his immortality with death.

9 Hence too she, Mary, lives. Because he who in no way owed anything to death died for the human race. Hence also every day when we have made ourselves guilty we return to life. Because the Creator, who was innocent, descended to our guilt. Behold, the old enemy already has lost the prey which he had snatched from the human race. And he has lost his victory. Every day sinners return to life, every day they are snatched from his mouth by the hand of the Saviour. Hence it is also right that through the voice of the Lord the blessed Job is again told: 'or can you pierce his jaw with a ring?'[78] For a ring is made to hold together what is within it. What is denoted for us by the ring except that the divine mercy embraces us? The divine mercy which pierces Leviathan's jaw shows us, after we have done what it had forbidden, the remedy of repentance. With a ring the Lord pierces Leviathan's jaw. And through the inexpressible power of his mercy he so resists the maliciousness of the old enemy that this one perhaps also loses those whom he already has in his grasp. And they fall as it were from his mouth, those who return to innocence after committing sin. For who, once having been seized

by his mouth, could escape his jaws were they not pierced? Or did not he hold Peter in his mouth when Peter denied the Lord?[79] Or did he not hold David in his mouth when David steeped himself in the whirlpool of vice?[80] But whereas both returned to life through penitence, this Leviathan lost them in one way or another through the gap in his jaw. Through the gap in his jaw they escaped from his mouth, those who after committing such a great injustice returned through penitence. But which human beings shall escape the mouth of that Leviathan?

From this we come to know how guilty we are before the Saviour of the human race, who did not prevent us from perishing in Leviathan's mouth but also allowed us to return from his mouth. He has not taken hope away from the sinner. To indicate Leviathan's jaw as an escape route, he pierced it, so that the one who, carelessly, did not want to guard against being bitten, could flee immediately after the bite. So everywhere he encounters us with the heavenly medicine. For he has given human beings precepts that they should not sin, but he gives to anyone who has sinned remedies, so that he does not despair. Therefore extreme caution is required that no one is seized by the mouth of that Leviathan through the seduction of sin. But – if he is caught, let him not despair. For if he regrets his sin in a perfect way, he will still find in his jaw a gap by which he can escape.

10 She, of whom we speak, Mary, is herself present as a witness to the divine mercy. Of her the Pharisee said when he wanted to block the source of mercy: 'If this man was a prophet, he would know who and what sort of a person the woman is who is touching him, because she is a sinner.'[81] But she washed away with her tears the stains in her heart and her body. And she touched the feet of her Saviour, she who had left her bad ways. She sat at Jesus' feet and she heard the Word from his mouth.[82] When he was alive, she had clung to him. When he was dead, she sought him. As the Living One she found him whom she had sought as dead. And she found in him such a great place of grace that she herself had to go and proclaim him to the apostles – note well, his proclaimers.

What, then, brothers, must we see here but the immeasurable mercy of our Creator? He who shows us as a sign of mercy those whom after penitence he made alive after the fall. For I look at Peter, I regard the murderer, I see Zacchaeus, I look at Mary, and I see in them none other than examples of hope and penitence which are set before our eyes. Perhaps someone in the faith has fallen into sin – let him then look at Peter, who wept bitterly, because he had denied him when he was afraid.[83] Someone else is consumed with malicious cruelty towards his neighbour – let him look at the murderer who even at the moment of death received the reward of life through penitence.[84] Someone else, panting in ardent avarice, has stolen the goods of others – let him look at Zacchaeus, who, if he had taken anything from anyone, gave it back fourfold.[85] Someone else, inflamed with the fire of passion, has lost the purity of his flesh – let him look at Mary, who in herself melted the fleshly love through the fire of the divine love. See, the almighty God has everywhere set people before our eyes whom we must follow. Everywhere he shows examples of his mercy. So let us turn away from evil, above all from that which we ourselves have experienced. The almighty God gladly forgets that we were guilty. He is ready to reckon our penitence as innocence. Stained as we are again after the waters of salvation, let us be born again from our tears. Therefore, according to the word of the Supreme Shepherd 'as newborn children desire milk.'[86] Return again, little children, to the bosom of your mother, the eternal Wisdom: suck on the great breasts of the love of God; regret what is past, avoid what is threatening. Our Saviour will comfort our present weeping with eternal joy, he who lives and reigns with God the Father in the unity of the Holy Spirit, God, for ever and ever.

Explanation

'When I think about the penitence of Mary, I would rather weep than say anything.' Gregory the Great begins his sermon about the sinful woman who anointed Jesus' feet with these words. Here a man is talking who is really gripped by his subject, a man who knows himself to be truly inspired by the decisiveness of the sinful woman. He is a man, I think, who knows what it is to make mistakes and feel guilty. Here too speaks a leader to whose preaching the mercy of God is central, a leader who is convinced that the personal recognition of guilt and the personal penitence and conversion of believers is of great importance for the church that is coming into being in Europe. For him, it is true that:

> See, the almighty God has everywhere set people before our eyes whom we must follow. Everywhere he shows examples of his mercy. (Sermon 25.10)

In the eyes of Gregory the Great, Mary Magdalene is also 'a witness to the divine mercy' (25.10). By appearing to her, although she is a sinner, and by entrusting to her in particular the message of the resurrection, Christ shows God's mercy.

Gregory the Great has often been referred to as the great culprit who changed the picture of Mary Magdalene as apostle into that of the penitent *par excellence*. And indeed from his time Mary Magdalene is no longer characterized by her witness to the resurrection, but by her 'life story' of sin, penitence and conversion. Gregory the Great composed her 'life story'.

He fused Mary Magdalene with other biblical figures to make one figure. In this fusion there is not a great deal of Mary Magdalene herself, but all the more of the anonymous sinful woman who anointed Jesus' feet, of Mary the sister of Martha and Lazarus who anointed Jesus' feet, and of Mary the sister of Martha who listened to Jesus' words at his feet (see Chapter 2). Thus Mary Magdalene not only gets a sinful past, but her sins are also clearly marked out. She is consumed by the fire of passion and because of that has lost the purity of her flesh (25.10). And in what does her redemption consist? The physical love she leaves behind and she turns to spiritual love (25.1-5). She burns so ardently with spiritual love of the Lord that the rust of her guilt burns bright (25.2).

Gregory the Great mentions four examples of guilt and penitence. Peter has denied the Lord but wept bitterly as a result. The murderer on the cross next to Jesus is 'consumed with malicious cruelty' but asked the Lord for forgiveness. Zacchaeus has stolen, but repaid everything fourfold. Gregory the Great mentions one woman, and her sin is sexual by nature. The suggestion is clear: women are above all sexual beings and their sexuality has to be controlled and tamed.

What is left of the woman who knows and proclaims the mystery of faith? What remains of Gregory of Antioch's teacher of the teachers? In Gregory the Great's sermon Mary Magdalene is at the empty tomb only 'as a witness to the divine mercy' (25.10). Gregory the Great says: 'And she found in him such a great place of grace that she herself had to go and proclaim him to the apostles – note well, his proclaimers' (25.10). Her conversion from physical love to ardent spiritual love for the Lord gives Mary a role of honour. Thus the message of the resurrection is no longer her central characteristic, but a by-product.

From Gregory the Great onwards, for fourteen centuries Mary Magdalene has been a model of penitence, at least in the Western church. She is a model of penitence for all believers, indeed for the whole church. Moreover she is the model of the rejection of physical love by means of spiritual love for the Lord. And in this way the image is strengthened that the woman's sin is her sexuality.

Susan Haskins investigated the formation of the image of Mary Magdalene down the ages. With reference to Gregory the Great's two sermons she says in her book *Mary Magdalene. Myth and Metaphor*:

And so the transformation of Mary Magdalene was complete. From the gospel figure, with her active role as herald of the New Life – the

Apostle to the Apostles – she became the redeemed whore and Christianity's model of repentance, a manageable, controllable figure, and effective weapon and instrument of propaganda against her own sex. (pp. 96–7)

At a stroke, Gregory the Great resolved all early Christian wrestling with Mary Magdalene as first witness to the resurrection through his picture of her as a penitent. Haskins assumes that he did this on purpose. With his picture of Mary Magdalene as penitent Gregory the Great is said deliberately to have shown all women their place. They are sexual beings whose unbridled passion must be tamed by love for the Lord.

I cannot discover such a purpose in reading the two sermons. Gregory the Great seems above all possessed with the theme of penitence and conversion. Moreover his picture of Mary Magdalene has also been a positive inspiration to people in the history of the church. However, the fact remains that at the same time it had a disastrous effect and has ruined lives. In particular those who focus on the latter can concur whole-heartedly with Gregory's words, 'When I think about the penitence of Mary, I would rather weep than say anything.' But what is more important is that Gregory the Great's image of Mary Magdalene has nothing to do with the Mary Magdalene who appears in the early sources. Gregory the Great's image of Mary Magdalene as a penitent and a reformed prostitute is a construct and must be rejected not only on moral, but also on historical grounds.

Chapter 11

'Has he Chosen her Above us?'

What is fact and what is fiction about Mary Magdalene? Was she a prostitute or a goddess priestess, was she Jesus' wife, did Jesus entrust the leadership of the church to her? Was she an initiate who had already gone
through many reincarnations and did she give her esoteric teaching in
France? Above all: was she the victim of a cover-up by the church?

Now that we have surveyed the early Christian texts about Mary Magdalene, it is at all events clear that the image of her as the penitent sinner is
fiction, however passionately Gregory the Great may write about her. Nor
are there any points of contact in the early sources for seeing her as a
goddess priestess, as the wife of Jesus or as the one to whom Jesus had
entrusted the leadership of the church. Nor do the sources tell of initia-
tions, reincarnations or France. But the texts do show that she is the victim
of a cover-up. However, it is not so much a cover-up by the church alone,
but a cover-up that is part of a whole culture: a culture dominated by men.

Various descriptions of Mary Magdalene

The texts from early Christianity show a perplexing diversity of images of
Mary Magdalene. She is a witness to the crucifixion, burial and resurrection of Jesus. But the texts differ in their story about precisely what she is
witness to and whether that is important. She is a follower of Jesus. But in
some texts she forms part of a large group of women and in others she
belongs to the core group of the disciples.

According to a number of texts she kept silent about her experiences, but
other texts have her telling about them. Here she turns only to the eleven
remaining apostles or also to everyone. She relates what the apostles could
already know or brings a new message which is revealed only to her. She
withdraws and no one hears any more of her, or, like Paul, she sets out to
preach the gospel.

Her gospel has a Gnostic character, as in Pistis Sophia. Or it is more orthodox, but then it is above all ascetic, as in the Acts of Philip, where, because of her teaching, girls remain virgins and married women leave their husbands. Or she teaches that the Lord lives despite death and what that means for believers and their lifestyle, as in the Gospel of John and the Gospel of Mary, where there is no special emphasis on ascetic or Gnostic teaching.

In Chapter 1, I asked what a historically reliable picture of Mary Magdalene might look like. But can one argue from this diversity of early Christian images to the contours of a historical figure? I think that this is possible, because in the early Christian texts one clear motif shines out which has played a central role in the formation of these images.

Various texts demonstrate without any restraint that the view of the role of women determines how Mary Magdalene has been seen. At the beginning of the second century it is Peter in the Gospel of Mary and in the Gospel of Thomas who couples his view of Mary Magdalene with his view of women generally. Ambrose and Augustine in the fourth century wrestle with Mary Magdalene's precise role, on the basis of their picture of what women are allowed. Jerome in the fourth century and Theophanes in the twelfth also show that the image of Mary Magdalene is connected with the image of what a Christian woman must be. From the texts it is evident that the most important stumbling block in the conceptualization of Mary Magdalene is the notion that women are not allowed to instruct men.

Because this motif did not begin to play a part from a particular time but belongs to the culture in which Mary Magdalene came into the world, it is not possible simply to assume that the earliest sources sketch the most trustworthy picture of her. In Chapters 3 and 4 we saw that this motif already plays a part in, for example, the Gospels of Matthew, Luke and John. Perhaps we can say that it is most probable that the images of Mary Magdalene which seem to be determined by this motif, even if they occur in the earliest texts, are furthest removed from historical reality.

If we begin from this criterion, it is more probable that Mary Magdalene was an important witness than that she was not. It is more probable that she belonged to the core group of disciples than to a large group of women. It is also more probable that she told of her experiences than that she kept silent, that she told something new rather than that she confirmed what the eleven already knew, and that she went out to proclaim the gospel rather than that she withdrew. But what was the content of her teaching? Here too interests play a role: Gnostic thought in Pistis Sophia and an ascetic lifestyle in the Acts of Philip. These interests seem to play no role in the Gospel of Mary, which is more concerned with a creative expression of the gospel than with doctrinal certainties that must be defended.

Thanks to the early Christian texts, however, we do not need to stop at these presuppositions. The texts make it possible to give the different images of Mary Magdalene a place in historical reality, and moreover to discover something about the motivation which played a role in their formation.

General explanations and the appeal to scripture

Why must women keep silent? An answer which is often heard points to the structure of society in Hellenistic culture. In the second century Celsus saw the Christian faith as a danger to the stability of the society of his time (Chapter 3). That emerged even more clearly from the Deutero-Pauline texts quoted in Chapter 8. The household was seen as the smallest element of society and as the basis of its hierarchical structure. If a husband, father or master governed his household well, and in a corresponding way the senate governed the land well, human life could be a mirror of the divine harmony in the universe. To be able to reflect this harmony, people thought it very important that women, slaves and children knew their place in relation to husbands, masters and fathers. If they did not keep to their subordinate position they posed a danger to society.

Another answer to the question why according to Christian doctrine women have to keep silent which is often heard refers to religion in Hellenistic culture. Not only gods, priests and prophets but also goddesses, priestesses and prophetesses played a role in this culture. This contrasts with the Jewish rite, in which only one God is worshipped and a prophetess can be seen only here and there alongside priests and prophets. With the exclusion of women the Christian church is said to have wanted to follow Jewish religious customs markedly more than Hellenistic ones. Our present-day culture is so steeped in this that the words goddess, priestess and prophetess are associated directly with heresy and then above all with the fertility religions.

What answer do the early Christian texts give to the question why there is a rule that women must keep silent? The authors appeal to scripture, to the creation narrative in Genesis in which Eve leads Adam astray, to the behaviour of Mary the mother of Jesus and other women, and to Paul (Chapters 8 and 9). But we have seen that another appeal to scripture is also possible. In the texts of Paul the reference to the creation story functions as a means of indicating the equality of men and women (Chapter 8). The Montanists appeal to Eve and other women from scripture, and to Paul when they admit women to functions in the church such as prophetess, elder and bishop (Chapter 9). The book The Instructions of the Apostles from the third century suggests a discussion in which reference is made to Mary Magdalene and the other women disciples, in order to defend the right of women to give teaching (Chapter 7). In the fourth century Jerome uses scripture to encourage women not to experience their femininity as a hindrance. He refers to outstanding women in scripture, including Mary Magdalene and the other female followers of Jesus (Chapter 6). He praises Marcella, precisely because she uses her learning for building up the church and because by her modest attitude she spares the feelings of men, giving the impression that she is respecting the prohibition against women instructing men (Chapter 9).

The question precisely which books belong to scripture also plays a role in the appeal to scripture. Didymus the Blind points out that no biblical writings are attributed to a woman. Rightly, he says, for according to 'right doctrine' women may not have authority over men and thus may not write books under their own name. Tertullian refers to the Acts of Paul and Thecla as untrustworthy, because in it Paul allows a woman to appear as an apostle, whereas in his letters he says that he does not allow women to do so. In the twelfth century Theophanes Kerameus uses that argument in quite the opposite way, since he refers to the example of Thecla to show that Paul did allow women to teach (Chapter 9).

Thus the appeal to scripture is not an objective matter. First comes the choice of which standpoint scripture must defend. It is not scripture that determines whether women must keep silent. The choice whether women should be silent or not has already been made before the appeal to scripture.

Superiority, rivalry, sexuality and shame

Women may not exercise authority over men. What considerations play a role in the choice of this prohibition? The early Christian texts show that it is not a matter of balanced arguments, but of sentiments.

There is a sense of superiority. Women are associated with the physical and earthly and men with the spiritual and supernatural, as Philo shows (Chapter 8). Peter expresses the extreme consequence of this thought in the

Gospel of Thomas: 'Let Mary leave us, for women are not worthy of life' (logion 114; Chapter 3). Along the same line the Deutero-Pauline letter to the Ephesians asks male readers to love their wives as their own bodies. If this were mutual, it might perhaps sound attractive. But women may not love men as their own bodies; on the contrary, in every respect they must recognize the authority of their husbands as the authority of Christ (Chapter 5).

Men have more knowledge than women. In the Gospel of Mary, Andrew points out to his brothers that Mary's words sound different from what the brothers already know. Something new cannot come just from a woman (Chapter 3).

Men are more important than women. Jerome gives his brother Antony dealings with women as an example of Jesus' humility (Chapter 6).

Men are stronger than women. Ambrose points to the lesser stamina and physical strength of women in order to demonstrate that the preaching of the gospel has not been entrusted to them but to men (Chapter 6).

As well as the sense of superiority there is also the sense of rivalry. The Gospel of Mary contains Peter's words:

> He did not speak with a woman
> apart from us and not openly.
> Are we to turn and all listen to her?
> Has he chosen her above us? (GosMar 17.18-22; Chapter 3)

Origen speaks his mind when he says:

> For women, too, can be good teachers,
> but not in such a way that men sit at women's feet and listen,
> as if men, who can serve the Word of God,
> do not count. (Commentary on 1 Corinthians 14.34-35; Chapter 9)

In the Instructions of the Apostles we can hear the rivalry between the apostles and the women who have told them about the resurrection. Later women must not think that they too can teach on the basis of this:

> For he the Lord God, Jesus Christ our Teacher, sent us the Twelve to instruct the people and the Gentiles; and there were with us women disciples, Mary Magdalene and Mary the daughter of James and the other Mary; but he did not send them to instruct the people with us. (Instructions of the Apostles 3.6; Chapter 7)

The rivalry is also expressed in the Gospel of Philip when the disciples ask Jesus about Mary: 'Why do you love her more than all of us?' (GosPhil 64.1-2; Chapter 2). And in Pistis Sophia Philip says:

My Master, we cannot endure this woman
who gets in our way,
and does not let any of us speak,
though she talks all the time. (Pistis Sophia 36; Chapter 3)

As well as the senses of superiority and rivalry, feelings of a sexual kind also play a role. In the Acts of Philip Mary Magdalene is seen as a prostitute because she travels and works with men who are not of her family, although on Christ's advice she goes clothed as a man and makes sexual continence part of her teaching. In the same writing Philip relates that Peter flees every house in which there is a woman because of the Lord's words: 'Everyone who looks at a woman with lust has already committed adultery with her in his heart' (Matthew 5.28). Moreover Peter has prayed to God to make his daughter paralysed so that through her paralysis she may no longer be an object of desire (Chapter 5). Pseudo-Clement warns men not to live unmarried with women and allow themselves to be served by them. Otherwise men put their self-control too much to the test (Chapter 7). According to Gregory of Antioch the nameless sinner from Luke is a prostitute and according to Gregory the Great Mary Magdalene burns with passion (Chapter 10).

These feelings of men about women of a sexual nature, of rivalry and superiority, produce a sense of shame in the men who see women as their equals or more than their equals, shame not towards women but towards other men. Jerome expresses this feeling when he speaks of the ignorance of men in interpreting scripture. He then says: 'Others – I blush to say it – learn from women what they must teach men' (Letter 53.7; Chapter 9). And when Jerome praises Marcella in his obituary of her he is aware of the scorn of other men that he is provoking with it (Chapter 7).

When they are talking about the choice of men not to regard women as equals in the building-up of the church, the early Christian texts do not mention balanced arguments, but these sentiments of superiority, rivalry and sexuality. This choice leads to the appropriate appeal to scripture and also determines which books begin to belong to Holy Scripture; it also determines the picture that is painted of Mary Magdalene. But at the same time it is evident that this choice belongs within a historical reality in which other choices were made. The great diversity in the early Christian pictures of Mary Magdalene can be explained from these different choices and the clash between them.

A historically reliable picture of Mary Magdalene

To be able to detect something of a historical reality, it is important in reading the texts to make a distinction between what the author in question *prescribes* as desirable behaviour and what the author *describes* as the existing situation. Even if the author does not describe the existing situation explicitly, we may assume that a particular regulation has been made with good reason. Evidently the situation requires it. For example, the regulation that women must keep silent is relevant only where women are speaking (or want to speak).

The prescriptive elements in the texts from Chapter 9 show that an active role of women is criticized from the perspective of 'right doctrine'. Above all the Deutero-Pauline interpretation of Paul's words seems to have been authoritative (Chapter 8). According to the 'right doctrine' women may not teach, baptize, write books under their own names or occupy the positions of prophet, elder or bishop, because they are women. Women may not undertake anything by which it seems as if they had authority over men. They must show themselves to be subservient and obedient. Those who behave otherwise by definition do not belong to the 'right faith'. Thus active women are silenced, not because of the unholy things they said but simply because they were active without being men (Chapter 9).

Against this background it is not surprising that the Gospel of Mark produces a silent Mary Magdalene and that the Gospel of Matthew draws a distinction between her proclamation to the apostles and the proclamation of the apostles to the nations (Chapter 3). The fact that in the Gospel of Luke it is not Mary Magdalene but Peter who is the first witness to the resurrection (Chapter 3) and that Peter replaces Mary Magdalene as an apostle in the Acts of Philip (Chapter 5) fits in here. The rise of the 'right doctrine' also makes more credible the thought that the Gospel of John has attributed the role of Mary Magdalene as chief witness to an anonymous male figure (Chapter 4).

At the same time it is also clear that the active participation of women is defended. Women and men appealed to the female figures of the scripture of the time. They appealed to Eve, Miriam, Deborah, Huldah, the four daughters of Philip and Thecla. They also appealed to Paul (Chapter

9). The texts in which Peter, as a jealous hothead, attacks an active role for Mary Magdalene, as in the Gospel of Mary, the Gospel of Thomas and Pistis Sophia, fit in against this background of attack and defence (Chapter 3). There and also in the First Apocalypse of James reference is made to the Lord himself, who has made Mary Magdalene worthy to play an active role (Chapter 7). Hippolytus too emphasizes that Christ himself sent out Mary Magdalene as an apostle and Ambrose and Augustine explain the role of Mary Magdalene by a special commission from the Lord (Chapter 6).

Not only the texts from Chapter 5 and 7, but above all the texts from Chapter 9 show that women also really had an active role in the building-up of the early church. They taught, they preached the gospel, they baptized and they wrote books. They were prophets, elders and bishops. They were learned women who expounded scripture and adapted it towards less learned brothers who nonetheless had important functions in the church. It is evident from the texts that this applied not only to Montanists and perhaps especially to the region of Phrygia, where the movement of the 'New Prophecy' began with the revelation of Priscilla. Origen from Alexandria also knows of women who say holy things and of believers who think that Paul does allow unmarried women to speak in the assembly. Tertullian from Carthage knows women from his own circle who baptize and teach, and for this they appeal to the Acts of Paul and above all to the example of Thecla. And Jerome of Rome praises Marcella's learning and her teaching to men within the orthodox church.

So not only in Asia Minor but also in Egypt, Africa and in the heart of the Roman Empire women have been active, both in Montanist and in more orthodox circles. Against the background of the fact that women played an active part in the building-up of the early church, the portrait of Mary Magdalene as disciple and apostle is not surprising. The image of Mary Magdalene in the Acts of Philip as someone who bears witness to the words of Jesus and expounds them, who also teaches and baptizes, fits against this background (Chapter 5). In addition, it is credible from this perspective that she had disciples who set down her witness in writing, as the Gospel of Mary and the Gospel of John suggest (Chapter 4).

One cannot make out precisely who Mary Magdalene was from the early sources. Was she a young woman with long golden or copper hair, as she is often depicted in art? Or could she have been of the same age as Jesus' mother with a grey bun? Was she married? Did she have children? How was it for her to learn from Jesus and follow him?

No diary or early biography of Mary Magdalene has been preserved. There are only the early Christian texts which diverge so much in their images of her. But anyone who reads them patiently is rewarded with an insight into an intriguing discussion about the role of women in rising Christendom. This is a discussion which is not dated but it is still being carried on. Women still play their part in the building-up of the church, and in most churches there is still a male hierarchy which puts limits on women, determines what the content of the faith is and what rules are part of it. The early Christian texts show that this is not a historical necessity or a divine ordinance. There are not even any balanced arguments. It is a matter of a choice which is determined by sentiments. Anyone who has noticed that can only be amazed at the fact that to the present day there are still churches which want to keep their male hierarchy.

The early Christian discussion about the role of women also makes it possible to see the contours of a historically reliable picture behind the various images of Mary Magdalene, moreover a picture which is inspiring. Mary came from Magdala, a town on an international trade route in which different cultures met. It was a fortified town where opposition to Roman domination was brewing and was put down with a heavy hand. Mary Magdalene knew what it was to see crucified people. It was also a city where Hellenistic culture flourished, and alongside it the more orthodox Jewish laws were applied.

In the beginning of the Gospel of John the first disciple of Jesus is an anonymous figure who together with Andrew belongs to the circle of John the Baptist's disciples (John 1.35-42). Perhaps this figure was Mary Magdalene and so she was a former disciple of John the Baptist. It is certain that she became a disciple of Jesus, at an early stage, when he had only just appeared with his teaching and his preaching. His gospel had a liberating effect on her. And then it happened: he was crucified. Almost every source about her from the first century relates how she was a witness to that, how she was also a witness to his burial, and after a few days, to her bewilderment, found his tomb empty. There she received a revelation. 'I have seen the Lord,' she later related, 'and this is what he told me.'

First she went to Peter and the disciples. Then she went away to tell others about her experiences with Jesus. She herself gained disciples. She encountered resistance because she was a woman. Nevertheless, what she had to tell was handed on and written down. Unfortunately we cannot get closer to the content of her teaching than is shown by the Gospel of John and the Gospel of Mary.

This woman is not the perfect initiate nor is she perfect in her love for Jesus. Nor is she is a model of penitence or of femininity. She is a person of flesh and blood who knows what it is to suffer and to arise from suffering. Mary Magdalene had a special experience at the empty tomb through which she began to tell of Jesus' resurrection and what his suffering, death and resurrection meant.

This Mary Magdalene told of the new life, despite death and the constant threat of suffering. She told of being made a true Human Being and of the new lifestyle which belongs to that. She comforted and encouraged and pointed out the right direction, from darkness to light, from death to life. And above all, she bore witness to the joy which accompanies a person on this good way, whatever happens.

Significance for Christian faith

What could it mean for Christian faith if this Mary Magdalene were taken seriously? The fictitious, classical picture of Mary Magdalene as a penitent sinner served the sacrament of confession, the belief in God's mercy and the necessity of penitence. That image confirmed not only the rite and the doctrine of the church but also the traditional notion of sexuality as sin and of woman as a sexual being. Much is gained by dropping this fictitious picture, and nothing important is lost. There are plenty of examples of God's mercy and forgiveness and of people who were in need of confession and penitence. Peter could easily take over this role from Mary Magdalene.

A historically reliable picture of Mary Magdalene does not confirm the traditional doctrine and the existing rite, as the classical picture does, but is in tension with them. Those who take the historical picture seriously accept the extra-biblical Gospel of Mary as a source of faith and thus are critical of the conviction that only the Bible contains the word of God. Those who adhere to the historical picture of Mary Magdalene will also make a clear distinction not only within the Old Testament but also within the New Testament between what is culturally determined and what could really be the gospel. In addition, they will regard a church with an exclusively male hierarchy and a church which exercises power as not in keeping with the gospel. Moreover, they are no longer willing to think in terms of the good and the bad, because according to Mary Magdalene's teaching in the Gospel of Mary the forces which keep a person from God are not only outside (the church or any entity) but also within, within every person.

In a historically reliable picture of Mary Magdalene it is no longer external obedience that is central but inner steadfastness. It is no longer a matter of sitting wordlessly at the Lord's feet but of speaking and acting autonomously. With this Mary Magdalene sin and penitence are not central, but the confusion of the world and the liberation from this confusion that the Saviour makes possible. What is central is not self-castigation but joy, not just the Lord's suffering but also his greatness. What is central is not belief in dogmas but the inner will to seek, to find and to follow the Lord.

Notes

2. Who was Mary Magdalene?

1. The Greek text of the New Testament can be found in *Novum Testamentum Graece*. For the translation I follow the New Revised Standard Version (NRSV) unless otherwise indicated.
2. The NRSV has 'a woman in the city, who was a sinner'.
3. The NRSV has 'and many others'.
4. The NRSV has 'and provided for them out of their resources'.
5. The NRSV has 'welcomed'.
6. The NRSV has 'listened to what he was saying'.
7. The NRSV has 'distracted by her many tasks'. The Greek *polle diakonia* which literally translated would mean 'much ministry' has been rendered by 'her many tasks'. In English the words 'deacon' and 'diaconate' derive from the Greek *diakoneo*.
8. The NRSV has 'to do all the work by myself'. The Greek *diakonein* has been rendered by 'do the work'. I translated instead by 'to perform the ministry'.
9. The NRSV has 'distracted'.
10. The NRSV has 'perfume'. See also verses 12.3, 4.
11. The NRSV has 'he whom you love'.
12. Jerome, Letter 127 5.3; see Chapter 7.
13. The Coptic text may be found in B. Layton 1989. The English translation is by Isenberg 1989; the square brackets indicate where the text is damaged or illegible.
14. See note 3.

3. Disciple and Witness

1. The NRSV has 'among them were Mary Magdalene, and Mary the mother of James the younger and of Joses, and Salome'.
2. The NRSV has 'these used to follow him and provide for him'. The Greek verb I translated with 'serve' is *diakoneo*, from which the English words 'deacon' and 'diaconate' derive. Cf. Luke 8.1-3 and 10.38-42 in Chapter 2.
3. The NRSV has 'the mother of Joses'.
4. The NRSV has 'the mother of James'.
5. The NRSV has 'Many women were also there, looking on from a distance: they had followed Jesus from Galilee and had provided for him.'
6. The NRSV has 'Greetings!'
7. The NRSV has 'innocent'.
8. The NRSV has 'Mary the mother of James'.
9. See e.g. 1.16-20; 8.34; 10.21, 28 and 10.35-45.
10. Mark 4.35; 5.21; 5.37; 6.35; 11.1-6; 14.12-16.
11. Other writings also mention Jesus' women disciples. In the Gospel of Thomas Salome says

to Jesus 'I am your disciple' (GosThom 61). The Gospel of Peter introduces Mary Magdalene as 'the disciple of the Lord' (GosPet 12.50). The Wisdom of Jesus Christ and the Apocalypse of James speak of twelve male and seven female disciples (WJC 90.16-18 and ApocJam 38.16-17 and 42.20-24). The women disciples are also mentioned in literature that belongs to the church tradition: Tertullian, *Against Marcion* 4.19.1 and Instruction of the Apostles 3.6. It is typical of Mark that the Gospel connects no specific names with the word 'disciples'. This could explain why Mark does not call the women mentioned by name disciples. This characteristic of Mark is interpreted as an open invitation to readers to identify themselves with the disciples and through the story to discover precisely what discipleship means.

12. Cephas in Paul and Simon in Luke.
13. For the Coptic text see C. Schmidt 1919. For the translation of the Coptic and Ethiopic into English see C. Detlef G. Müller 1991 (in Hennecke, Schneemelcher, Wilson 1991).
14. Müller has 'the daughter of'.
15. For the Greek text and a translation into French see M. G. Mara 1973. The English translation is from R. E. Brown 1994.
16. For the Coptic text and an English translation see C. R. C. Allberry 1938. The translation here is from M. W. Meyer 2004.
17. For the Greek text and a French translation see M. Borret 1967. The English translation is from H. Chadwick 1953 (reprinted 1980).
18. For the Coptic and Greek texts and a translation into French see A. Pasquir 1983. The English translation is from E. A. de Boer 2005.
19. For the Coptic text see B. Layton 1989. The English translation is from T. O. Lambdin 1989.
20. DialSav 139.11-13. This can also be translated with: 'the woman who knew the All'. The words of Jesus she repeats are about the wickedness of each day (Mt. 6.34), the labourer being worthy of his food (Mt. 10.10; Lk. 10.7; 1 Tim. 5.18) and the disciple resembling his teacher (Mt. 10.25).
21. For the Coptic text see C. Schmidt 1978 and the English translation V. MacDermot 1978.
22. Translation M. W. Meyer 2004.
23. Translation: first part MacDermot 1978, slightly modernized; second part Meyer 2004.
24. E. Mohri 2000, pp. 319–70.
25. 'Pure spirit' in Pistis Sophia 87. There and elsewhere Jesus also calls her *pneumatike*, which can be translated 'focused on the spiritual' (Pistis Sophia 87; 116; 118). 'More focused on the kingdom', Pistis Sophia 17.
26. Pistis Sophia 33, 43, 76, 113, 124, 125.

4. Mary's Teaching

1. Lk. 24.45-49 and Mt. 28.16–20, see Mt. 5-7.
2. Mk 16.7.
3. Mk 1–9.
4. Mk 16.7; cf. Mk 14.28; Mt. 28.7; cf. Mt. 26.32; Lk. 24.6-7 cf. Lk. 9.18-22.
5. The NRSV has 'his mother, and his mother's sister, Mary the wife of Cleopas, and Mary Magdalene'.
6. The NRSV has 'the other disciple, the one whom Jesus loved'.
7. The NRSV has 'my brothers'.
8. See John 13.21-24.
9. To show the difference I translated *agapao* with 'love' and *phileo* with 'befriend' (see also Jn 11.3, 5) although the meaning of both words is closely related.
10. Perhaps Mary Magdalene and Jesus' mother? Is the latter also a disciple from the moment of the crucifixion?
11. See Chapter 9.

12. For the English translation and a commentary see A. A. Long and D. N. Sedley 1987, vol. 1, p. 274. For the Greek text see vol. 2.
13. Ibid., p. 273.
14. Ibid., p. 412.
15. Ibid., p. 418.
16. For the English translation and a commentary see I. G. Kidd 1971, p. 209.
17. For the Greek text and an English translation see W. A. Oldfather 1967. Here the English translation is from F. H. Sandbach 1975, p.167.
18. Ibid., p.168.
19. Translation W. A. Oldfather 1967.
20. For the Greek text and an English translation see F. H. Colson and G. H. Whitaker 1959, VI, pp. 20–1.
21. Colson translates 'man'.
22. Colson translates 'but to the man who is man pre-eminently, who verifies'.
23. For the Greek text and an English translation see Colson and Whitaker 1958, II, pp. 217–18.
24. Colson translates 'man'.
25. For a translation from the Armenian text into English see R. Marcus 1953 II, pp. 33–4.
26. Marcus translates 'wicked man' and 'wise man'.
27. Marcus translates 'foolish men'.
28. See also Gospel of Thomas 57.
29. Gen.1.1–2.4.
30. Rom.13.11-14; Eph. 4.20-32; Col. 3.9-17.
31. Rom. 8.11; Gal. 2.20 and 4.19; Col. 1.27-28.
32. Philo, *Allegorical Interpretation* 1.31-32 and 37-38.
33. Philo, *On Abraham* 32.
34. Eph. 4.21-24 and Col. 3.9-17; cf. Rom.6.1-14, cf. 2 Pet. 1.3-11. According to this letter, through knowledge of Jesus we partake in the divine nature and escape the corruption that prevails in the world through desire. This knowledge leads to a new lifestyle.
35. Philo, *On the Confusion of Tongues* 86, 91, 95–6, 101–3. Compare the formless passion in GosMar 8.2.

5. Apostle

1. For such dissension see also 1 Cor. 1.10-17.
2. The NRSV has 'by a believing wife'.
3. The Gospel of Luke.
4. Lk. 8.2 and Lk. 24.10.
5. Lk. 8.3 and Lk. 24.10. Susanna from 8.3 is omitted in 24.10; she is replaced there by Mary of James.
6. See also Gal. 4.11; Phil. 2.16.
7. The title has been added later.
8. See e.g. ActPhil 8.16, 21 and 13.1-2, 4.
9. Lk. 10.1.
10. From Atheniensis, National Library 346. The Greek text and a French translation can be found in F. Amsler, F. Bovon and B. Bouvier 1999.
11. These are not meant to be the Greeks, but the pagans of the time.
12. The Greek verbs used for Martha are *diakoneo* and *kopiao*. See Lk. 10.40 and cf. Rom. 16.6.
13. Mt. 5.38-48; Luke 6.27-35.
14. In the summaries of the twelve apostles, Philip and Bartholomew are mentioned together in Mt.10.2-4; Mk 3.16-19 and Lk. 6.14-16.
15. This city is identified as Asian Hierapolis in Phrygia. There is an impressive funerary

monument to Philip there, dating from the end of the fourth or beginning of the fifth century.

16. Probably the viper is meant as a reference to the originally Phrygian mother goddess Cybele, who was also called the mother of the gods. As such she was venerated in Rome as well. The popularity in Rome is perhaps the reason why her name is not mentioned here and there is only an allusion to it.

17. Gen. 3.1-19.

18. Gen. 4.1-16.

19. Mt.18.16-20.

20. Lk. 12.22-28.

21. Jn 20.17.

22. From Atheniensis, National Library 346.The Greek text and a French translation can be found in F. Amsler, F. Bovon and B. Bouvier 1999.

23. There is a reference to this in Vaticanus Graecus 808 with this sentence: 'They laid down in the house of Stachys the blind man to whom they had restored sight by spittle and the sorcery that they bore in them' (ActPhilMart 22). In our text the spittle is Mary's. See also Mk 7.31-37; 8.22-26, where Jesus heals a deaf mute and a blind man with his spittle. Matthew and Luke do not take over these stories. Could perhaps the story have displeased the person who tore the page out?

24. From a short version of The Martyrdom, Xenophontes 32.The Greek text and a French translation can be found in F. Amsler, F. Bovon and B. Bouvier 1999.

25. From a somewhat longer version than in Xenophontes, Vaticanus Graecus 824. The Greek texts of the Martyrdom from Vaticanus Graecus 824 and Xenophontes 32 are printed side by side with a French translation in F. Amsler, F. Bovon and B. Bouvier 1999.

26. From a longer version of The Martyrdom, Vaticanus Graecus 808. The Greek text of the Martyrdom from Vaticanus Graecus 808 has not been edited. A French translation can be found in F. Amsler, F. Bovon and B. Bouvier 1996. Part of the Greek text is printed in the introduction to R. A. Lipsius and M. Bonnet 1959 II, 2, pp. xiii–xv.

27. Xenophontes 32 Acts 15.1 relates that her husband Tyrannographus (which means 'tyrant of the darkness') married her for her wealth. She was Syrian by birth and her illness was caused by the poison of the snakes of the city which had bitten her because she was an alien.

28. Other versions say that Mary first addressed her in Syriac.

29. Christ.

30. Manuscript C has another sentence here: 'so that they may note her shamelessness and perceive that she is lying when she says: "I am not a woman, but as a man." She accompanies them and there is no doubt that she has intercourse with them.'

31. Xenophontes 32 has here: 'When they wanted to undress Mary, the outward appearance of her body altered and it changed into a glass shrine glittering with light, and they could not come to her.'

32. F. Bovon 2002.

33. For Lady Wisdom see Proverbs 8.1-36; Jesus Sirach 1.1-21; 6.18-32; 14.20–15.10; 24.18-22; 51.13-22. Wisdom as mother occurs in Jesus Sirach 15.2-5; 24.18-22.

34. This story is in the Berlin codex under the title The Act of Peter. There is a translation into English in J. M. Robinson (ed.) 1988.

35. Brock 2003, pp.127–9.

6. Eve and Apostle of the Apostles

1. For the preserved Georgian text and a translation into Latin see G. Garitte 1965. For a translation into German see G. N. Bonwetsch 1902.

2. Song 3.1-4.

3. Song 3.1.

4. Song 3.1.
5. Lk. 24.1, 22.
6. Song 3.1.
7. Lk. 24.5.
8. Song 3.1, 3.
9. Song 3.3.
10. Song 3.3.
11. Mk 16.6.
12. Song 3.3.
13. Mt. 28.8-9; Jn 20.14.
14. Jn 20.16. Translated, it means 'my Master'.
15. Song 3.4.
16. Jn 20.17. Mary also wants to ascend to the Father.
17. Song 3.3-4.
18. Song 3.4.
19. Jn 20.17.
20. According to tradition, Solomon is the author of the Song of Songs.
21. Song 3.4.
22. Gen. 3.15.
23. Gen. 3.1-6.
24. The meaning is that the old Eve is conquered by the death of Christ on the cross.
25. Gen. 3.16.
26. Gen. 3.7.
27. 2 Cor. 5.25.
28. For the Greek text see I. Hilberg 1910.
29. The other questions are:
    – What are the things that the eye has not seen and the ear has not heard (1 Cor. 2.9)?
    – Isn't it a mistake to see the sheep and the goats in Matthew 25 as the Christians and the pagans? Are they not rather metaphors for the good and the bad?
    – Must we understand the meeting with the Lord in the air in 1 Thessalonians 4.15 and 17 as bodily or spiritual?
    – Was the risen Christ before his ascension only with the disciples or also in heaven and elsewhere?
30. Jn 20.17.
31. Mt. 28.9.
32. Lk. 8.2; Mk 16.9.
33. Rom. 5.20.
34. Jn 20.14-15.
35. Jn 20.17.
36. Those who were crucified with Jesus: Mt. 27.38; Mk 15.27; Lk. 23.33.
37. Mt. 27.44 and 15.32.
38. Lk. 23.39-43.
39. For the Latin text see M. Adrien 1952.
40. Mt. 28.7; Mk 16.5; Jn 20.14.
41. Jn 20.14; Mt. 28.9.
42. Mt. 28.9.
43. Jn 20.17.
44. Matt. 28.2-3; Jn 20.1.
45. Mt. 28.8; Jn 20.2 and 13-15.
46. Mt. 28.8; Jn 20.11.
47. Mt. 28.9; Jn 20.13 15.
48. Mt. 28.9; Jn 20.14-15.

49. Mt. 28.9; Jn 20.14-15.
50. Jn 20.17.
51. Jn 20.17.
52. Jn 20.20.
53. Jn 11.2 and 12.3.
54. Col. 3.12.
55. Jn 20.17.
56. Mt. 12.50; Mk 3.35.
57. 1 Tim. 2.12.
58. 1 Cor. 14.35.
59. Origen, *Commentary on John* 6.287; 10.245; 13.179-80.
60. Jn 20.16, 28.
61 Tertullian, *Against Praxeas* 25.2.
62. Jn 20.17 and Mt. 28.9.
63. Letter 59 in *c.* AD 396 and Letter 65 in AD 397.
64. Acts 18.26.
65. For the quotations see Letsch-Brunner 1998, pp. 202–4.
66. See also Letter 120.5 (*c.* AD 406), where Jerome again goes into the difference between Jn 20.17 and Mt. 28.9.
67. 1 Tim. 2.12.
68. 1 Cor. 14.35.
69. See n. 1 in this chapter.
70. Mk 16.7; Mt. 28.7.
71. Mt. 28.8-9.
72. Some translations read: 'Eve is named apostle.' The Latin translation of the Georgian text that has been preserved reads *Eva fit apostola*. She is not called apostle but is made apostle.
73. See earlier in 25.4, where Martha/Mary as Eve asks to be united with the heavenly body of Christ.
74. Gen. 3.18, 20.
75. Lk. 24.9-11.
76. Jn 20.19.
77. For the Latin text see O. Faller SJ, 1964.
78. Jn 4.23.
79. Ps. 12.2.
80. Jn 14.6.
81. Jn 20.16-18.
82. Gen. 3.1-19.
83. Rom. 5.20.
84. Mt. 28.17-18; Lk. 24.10-11, 34.
85. Ps. 97.7; Heb. 1.6.
86. See n. 28 in this chapter.
87. Mt.18.3 and parallels.
88. Jn 13.5; Mt. 26.48-50; Jn 4.7-29; Lk. 10.39; Mt. 28.9.
89. Isa. 14.12-15; Ezek. 28.14-17.
90. Lk. 11.43; 20.46; Isa. 14.15.
91. 1 Pet. 5.5.
92. Lk. 18.10-14.
93. For the Latin text and a French translation see S. Poque 1966.
94. Mt. 28; Mk 16; Lk. 24.1-32.
95. Rom. 12.3.
96. Lk. 24.11.
97. Gen. 3.6.

98. For the Latin text see Letsch-Brunner 1998, p. 203. She refers to *Corpus Christianorum Series Latina* 76A, p. 655, dated AD 393.

7. Mary Magdalene as an Argument

1. For the Coptic text and a translation into German see S. Petersen 1999, pp. 246, 249.
2. *Didascalia Apostolorum.* For the Syriac text and a translation into English see R. H. Connolly 1929. I have modernized his English in some phrases.
3. *Canones Ecclesiastici Sanctorum Apostolorum.* For the Sahidic text and a translation into English see G. Horner 1904.
4. Peter said earlier that three widows had to be consecrated as deacons, two to persevere in prayer for those who were tormented by tribulations and in order to ask for revelations about what they needed and one to care for women who were sick.
5. *Constitutiones Apostolorum.* For the Greek text and a translation into French see M. Metzger 1986.
6. For the Coptic text and a translation into English see J. Brashler and D. M. Parrott 1979, p. 487.
7. For the Syriac text and a translation into Latin see J. T. Beelen 1856.
8. Lk. 10.1.
9. Jn 4.27.
10. Jn 20.17.
11. 2 Kgs 4.27. Here the woman is called the Shunamite.
12. Lk. 8.1-3.
13. For the Latin text see I. Hilberg 1918. For a translation into German see Letsch-Brunner 1998, pp. 247–56.
14. The Hebrew word *migdal* means 'fortification', 'stronghold' and 'tower'.
15. See Letters 39, 60, 66 and 77.

8. A Woman to Learn From?

1. The other letters are the Second Letter to the Thessalonians and the letters to the Ephesians, to the Colossians, to Timothy and to Titus.
2. Galatians is also dated earlier than 1 Corinthians or at about the same time.
3. Literally the Greek says woman and man, but in this fragment I agree with the NRSV in translating 'wife' and 'husband'.
4. The NRSV has 'husband'.
5. The NRSV has 'his wife'.
6. The NRSV has 'husbands'.
7. The NRSV has 'wives'. In this paragraph where I translate 'woman' and 'man' the NRSV has 'wife' and 'husband'.
8. The NRSV has 'wives'. In this paragraph where I translate 'woman' and 'man' the NRSV has 'wife' and 'husband'.
9. See also Rom. 14.1–15.7.

9. Two Forces

1. For the Latin translation by Origen's contemporary Rufinus of the Greek text, which has not been preserved, see H. J. Frede and H. Stanjek 1998, and for a translation into English see T. P. Scheck 2001.
2. Rom. 16.6.
3. Tit. 2.3-4.
4. 1 Tim. 5.10.
5. For the Greek text see *Patrologia Graeca* 39.
6. Acts 21.9; Judg. 4.1; Ex. 15.20; Lk. 1.48.
7. 1 Tim. 2.12; 1 Cor. 11.5.

8. 1 Cor. 11.3.
9. 1 Tim. 2.14.
10. For the Greek text see G. Ficker 1905, pp. 456–8.
11. Acts 21.9; Judg. 4.1.
12. 1 Cor. 11.5.
13. Lk. 1.48.
14. Ex. 15.20.
15. 1 Cor. 14.34-35; 1 Tim. 2.12.
16. 1 Cor. 11.4.
17. Lk. 1.48.
18. Here the Montanist is dealing mockingly with the exegesis of the orthodox that the covering of the head must be interpreted allegorically as women not being allowed to write books under their own name. You cannot make a dogma out of an allegory.
19. Gal. 4.22-24.
20. 1 Thess. 5.17.
21. For the Greek text and an English translation see R. E. Heine 1989, pp.132–5.
22. All the names are explained except for the name Cataphrygians. Literally the text reads 'those (named) after Phrygia' in Greek: *kata Phrygias.*
23. Gen. 3.6.
24. Ex. 15.20.
25. Acts 21.9.
26. Gal. 3.28.
27. Gen. 3.26.
28. 1 Tim. 2.12.
29. 1 Cor. 11.8.
30. 1 Tim. 2.14.
31. Gen. 3.16; 1 Tim. 2.12, 14.
32. For the Greek text see C. Jenkins 1909, pp. 41–2.
33. 1 Cor. 14.34.
34. Acts 21.9.
35. For Deborah see Judg. 4.1-14; 5.1-31. For Miriam see Exodus 20–21.
36. For Huldah see 2 Kings 22.14-20 and 2 Chron. 34.22-38.
37. Lk. 2.36.
38. 1 Tim. 2.12.
39. Tit. 2.3.
40. 1 Cor.14.35.
41. 1 Cor. 14.34-35.
42. For the Latin text see J. G. P. Borleffs 1957. The English text here is based on E. Evans 1964; however, I have felt it necessary to make changes on a number of important points.
43. *Ichtus* is Greek for fish and at the same time is the abbreviation of the confession 'Jesus Christ, the son of God, is our Saviour'.
44. 1 Cor. 6.12; 10.23.
45. 1 Cor. 14.34-35.
46. According to the Stoa the basic elements of matter are earth, water, air and fire.
47. See Misset-van de Weg 2000.
48. *On the Veiling of Virgins* 9.1.
49. For the Greek text and a Latin translation see *Patrologia Graeca* 132, Theophanes Kerameus, pp. 641–8. The relevant fragment is on pp. 643–6.
50. Lk. 24.8.
51. Paul compares life as a believer with a race: 1 Cor. 9.24-25 and Phil. 2.16.
52. Theophanes probably refers to Simon the Compilator (Symeon Metaphrastes; instead of the Greek word for 'Compilations', *metaphrases*, the Latin translation of Theophanes'

sermon in Greek has 'Metaphrastes') who in the tenth century compiled an extensive work on the lives of saints which became authoritative in the Byzantine tradition. Symeon Metaphrastes' account of Thecla can be found in J. P. Migne, *Patrologia Graeca* 115, pp. 821–46.

53. Lk. 24.11.
54. For the Latin text see I. Hilberg 1918. For a translation into German see Letsch-Brunner 1998, pp. 247–56.
55. 1 Tim. 4.2.
56. 1 Tim. 2.12.
57. *Summa Theologiae* 3, The resurrection of the Lord, 3a:53–59. See Jansen 2000, p. 55.

10. The East and the West
1. For the Greek text see *Patrologia Graeca* 88, 1947, 1847–66.
2. 1 Thess. 4.26.
3. Mt. 27.51.
4. Mt. 27.51.
5. Mt. 27.51.
6. Jn 19.34.
7. Jn 20.6.
8. Mt. 9.20-21.
9. Mt. 27.63-64.
10. Jn 11.1-44.
11. Mt. 27.65.
12. Jn 2.19.
13. Jon. 1.17–2.10 and Mt. 12.40.
14. Mt. 28.1.
15. Mt. 26.69-75.
16. Mt. 27.45.
17. Mt. 28.2.
18. Mt. 28.3.
19. Mt. 28.3.
20. Mt. 28.4.
21. Mt. 28.5.
22. Mt. 28.5.
23. Mt. 28.6.
24. The lion of Judah (Gen. 29.9).
25. Mt. 28.6.
26. Hos. 13.14 and 1 Cor. 15.59.
27. Mt. 28.9.
28. Isa. 27.11.
29. Mt. 28.8.
30. Mt. 28.9.
31. Mt. 28.10.
32. Mt. 28.10.
33. Mt. 4.18-20.
34. Lk. 7.36-50.
35. Acts 9.3-4, 15.
36. For the Latin text of the two sermons and a translation into German see M. Fiedrowicz 1998.
37. 2 Cor. 2.15.
38. Lk. 7.47.
39. Jn 20.10.

40. Jn 20.11.
41. Mt. 10.22.
42. Lev. 3.9.
43. Gen. 37.3.
44. Song 3.1.
45. Song 3.2.
46. Song 3.3.
47. Ps. 42.3.
48. Ps. 27.8; 105.4.
49. Isa. 26.9.
50. Song 2.5.
51. Song 5.6.
52. Jn 20.12.
53. Jn 1.3.
54. Jn 1.14.
55. Ex. 25.17-20.
56. 1 Jn 2.2.
57. Jn 20.13.
58. Gen. 46.27.
59. Jn 20.14.
60. Jn 20.15.
61. Jn 20.15.
62. Jn 20.16.
63. Ex. 33.12.
64. Jn 20.17.
65. Mt. 28.9.
66. Jn 20.17.
67. Phil. 2.6.
68. Jn 1.1-3.
69. 1 Cor. 1.24.
70. Jn 10.30.
71. Jn 14.28.
72. Lk. 2.51.
73. Jn 20.17.
74. Jn 20.18.
75. Gen. 3.6.
76. Ps. 110.7.
77. Job 40.20 (Vulgate).
78. Job 40.26.
79. Mt. 26.70.
80. 2 Sam. 4.1-27.
81. Lk. 7.39.
82. Lk. 10.38-42.
83. Mt. 25.75.
84. Lk. 23.43.
85. Lk. 19.8.
86. 1 Pet. 2.2.

Translated Texts in Chronological Order

First century

First half of first century

Philo, *On Abraham*
Philo, *That the Worse is Wont to Attack the Better*
Philo, *Questions and Answers on Genesis*
Philo, *Questions and Answers on Exodus*
Aetius, *Teachings*

Middle of first century

Paul, First Letter to the Corinthians (*c.* 53)
Paul, Letter to the Galatians (*c.* 55)
Paul, Letter to the Romans (*c.* 55–57)

Second half of first century

Letter to the Colossians (*c.* 70–100)
Letter to the Ephesians (*c.* 70–100)
Gospel of Mark (*c.* 70)
Gospel of Matthew (*c.* 80)
Gospel of Luke (*c.* 80–90)
Acts of the Apostles (*c.* 80–90)
Gospel of John (*c.* 90)
First Letter to Timothy (*c.* 100–125)

Second century

First half of second century

Epictetus, *Discourses*
Mark 16.9-20
Gospel of Mary
Gospel of Peter
Gospel of Thomas

Middle and second half of second century

Letter of the Apostles
Claudius Galen, *On the Teaching of Hippocrates and Plato*
Celsus, *On the True Doctrine* (*c.* 178)
First Revelation of James
Alexander of Aphrodisias, *On mixing and multiplying* (end of second century)

Third century

Hippolytus, *Commentary on the Song of Songs* (*c.* 200)
Tertullian, *On Baptism* (*c.* 200–206)
Instructions of the Apostles (beginning of third century)
Gospel of Philip
Origen, *Commentary on the Letter to the Romans*
Origen, *Commentary on 1 Corinthians*
Pseudo-Clement of Rome, *Two Letters on Virginity*
Psalms of Heraclides
Pistis Sophia

Fourth century

Apostolic Church Order (beginning of fourth century)
Dialogue between a Montanist and an Orthodox (middle of fourth century)
Jerome, *To Antony,* Letter 12 (*c.* 374)
Epiphanius of Salamis, *Medicine Chest* (*c.* 374–377)
Constitutions of the Apostles (*c.* 375)
Didymus the Blind, *On the Trinity* (*c.* 379)
Ambrose, *On the Holy Spirit* (*c.* 381)
Ambrose, *Commentary on the Gospel of Luke* (*c.* 390)
Jerome, *To Marcella,* Letter 59 (*c.* 396)
Acts of Philip (end of fourth or beginning of fifth century)

Fifth century

Jerome, *To Principia,* Letter 127 (412)
Augustine, Sermon 232
Joannes Stobaeus, *Anthology* (second half of fifth century)

Sixth century

Gregory of Antioch, *Sermon on the Bearers of Ointment* (middle of sixth century)
Gregory the Great, Sermon 25 (591)
Gregory the Great, Sermon 33 (592)

Twelfth century

Theophanes Kerameus, Sermon 31

Bibliography

Texts and translations

Adriaen, M., *Sancti Ambrosii Mediolanensis Opera IV: Expositio Evangelii secundum Lucam, Fragmenta in Esaiam*, Corpus Christianorum Series Latina 14, Turnhout: Brepols 1957.

Aland, K. and Nestle, E. (eds), *Novum Testamentum Graece* XXVII, Stuttgart: Deutsche Bibelstiftung 1993.

Allberry, C. R. C., *A Manichaean Psalm-Book. Part II*, Manichaean Manuscripts in the Chester Beatty Collection Vol. II, Stuttgart: W. Kohlhammer 1938.

Amsler, F., Bovon, F. and Bouvier, B, *Actes de l'apôtre Philippe. Introduction, traduction et notes*, Apocryphes 8, Turnhout: Brepols 1996.

—, *Acta Philippi: Commentarius*, Corpus Christianorum Series Apocrypha 12, Turnhout: Brepols 1999.

Bammel, C. P., Frede, H. J. and Stanjek, H., *Der Römerkommentar des Origenes. Kritische Ausgabe der Übersetzung Rufins, Buch 7–10*, Vetus Latina 34, Freiburg: Herder 1998.

Beelen, J. T., *Sancti Patris Nostri Clementis Romani: Epistulae binae de Virginitate*, Leuven: C. J. Fonteyn, Vanlinthout 1856.

Boer, E. A. de, 'Translation of the Coptic Manuscript', in Boer, E. A. de, *The Gospel of Mary: Listening to the Beloved Disciple*, New York and London: Continuum International 2005, pp.18–21. See also *The Gospel of Mary. Beyond a Gnostic and a Biblical Mary Magdalene*, Journal for the Study of the New Testament Supplement Series 260, London and New York: T&T Clark 2004.

Bonwetsch, G. N., *Hippolyts Kommentar zum Hohenlied*, Leipzig 1902.

Borleffs, J. G. P., *Q.S.Fl. Tertulliani: De Baptismo*, Corpus Christianorum Series Latina 1, Turnhout: Brepols 1957, pp. 275–95.

Borret, M. (SJ), *Origène, Contre Celse. Introduction, texte critique, traduction et notes*, Sources Chrétiennes 132, Paris: Editions du Cerf 1967.

Brashler, J. and Parrott, D. M., 'The Act of Peter. BG 4:128,1–141,7', in Parrott, D. M., *Nag Hammadi Codices V, 2–5 and VI with Papyrus Berolinensis 8502, 1 and 4*, Nag Hammadi Studies 11, Leiden: E. J. Brill 1979, pp.473–93.

Brown, R. E., 'A Literal Translation of GPet', in Brown, R. E. *The Death of the Messiah. From Gethsemane to the Grave: a Commentary on the Passion Narratives in the Four Gospels*, New York: Doubleday 1994 (two vols), pp.1318–21.

Chadwick, H., *Origen: Contra Celsum* Cambridge: Cambridge University Press, New Impression edition 1980.

Colson, F. H. and Whitaker, G. H., *Philo in Ten Volumes*, The Loeb Classical Library, London: William Heinemann 1929–62.

Connolly, R. H., *Didascalia Apostolorum: the Syriac version translated and accompanied by the Verona Latin fragments*, Oxford: Clarendon Press 1929.

Evans, C. E. (ed.), *Tertullian's Homily on Baptism*, London: SPCK 1964.

Étaix, R., *Gregorius Magnus. Homiliae in Evangelia*, Corpus Christianorum Series Latina 141, Turnhout: Brepols 1999.

Faller, O. (SJ), *Sancti Ambrosii Opera. De Spiritu Sanctu, libri tres; De incarnatione Dominicae Sacramento*, Corpus Scriptorum Ecclesiasticorum Latinorum 79, Vienna: Hoelder-Pichler-Tenpsky 1964.

Ficker, G., 'Widerlegung eines Montanisten', *Zeitschrift für Kirchengeschichte* XXVI (1905), 447–63.

Garitte, G., *Traités d'Hippolyte sur David et Goliath, sur le Cantiques des cantiques et sur l'Antéchrist. Version Géorgienne éditée*, Corpus Scriptorum Christianorum Orientalium 263, Leuven 1965.

—, *Traités d'Hippolyte sur David et Goliath, sur le Cantiques des cantiques et sur l'Antéchrist. Version Géorgienne traduite*, Corpus Scriptorum Christianorum Orientalium 264, Leuven 1965.

Heine, R. E., *The Montanist Oracles and Testimonia*, North American Patristic Society, Patristic Monograph Series 14, Leuven: Peeters and Macon; GA: Mercer University Press 1989.

Hilberg, I., *Sancti Eusebii Hieronymi Epistulae. Pars 1: Epistulae I-LXX*, Corpus Scriptorum Ecclesiasticorum Latinorum 54, Leipzig: F. Tempsky and Vienna: G. Freytag 1910.

—, *Sancti Eusebii Hieronymi Epistulae. Pars III: Epistulae CXXI-CLIV*, Corpus Scriptorum Ecclesiasticorum Latinorum 56, Leipzig: F. Tempsky and Vienna: G. Freytag 1918.

Holy Bible, The. New Revised Standard Version, New York and Oxford: Oxford University Press 1989.

Horner, G., *The Statutes of the Apostles or Canones Ecclesiastici*, London: Williams & Norgate 1904.

Isenberg, W. W., 'The Gospel according to Philip. Translated', in Layton, B. (ed.), *Nag Hammadi Codex I1,2–7 together with XIII, 2* Brit. Lib. Or. 4926(1) and P. Oxy.1, 654, 655. Vol. I. Gospel according to Thomas, Gospel according to Philip, Hypostasis of the Archons, Indexes; Vol. II. On the Origin of the World, Expository Treatise on the Soul, Book of Thomas the Contender*, Nag Hammadi and Manichaean Studies 20–21, Leiden, New York and Cologne: E. J. Brill 1989, 143–215.

Jenkins, C., 'Origen on I Corinthians', *Journal of Theological Studies* 9 (1909), 231–47, 253–372, 500–14; 10, 270–5.

Lambdin, T. O., 'The Gospel according to Thomas. Translated', in, Layton, B. (ed.), *Nag Hammadi Codex I1,2–7 together with XIII, 2* Brit. Lib. Or. 4926(1) and P. Oxy.1, 654, 655. Vol. I. Gospel according to Thomas, Gospel according to Philip, Hypostasis of the Archons, Indexes; Vol. II. On the Origin of the World, Expository Treatise on the Soul, Book of Thomas the Contender*, Nag Hammadi and Manichaean Studies 20–21, Leiden, New York and Cologne: E. J. Brill 1989, pp. 53–93.

Layton, B., 'The Gospel according to Thomas. Edited,' in Layton, B. (ed.), *Nag Hammadi Codex I1,2–7 together with XIII, 2* Brit. Lib. Or. 4926(1) and P. Oxy.1, 654, 655. Vol. I. Gospel according to Thomas, Gospel according to Philip, Hypostasis of the Archons, Indexes; Vol. II. On the Origin of the World, Expository Treatise on the Soul, Book of Thomas the Contender*, Nag Hammadi and Manichaean Studies 20–21, Leiden, New York and Cologne: E. J. Brill 1989, pp. 52–92.

Layton B., 'The Gospel according to Philip. Edited', in Layton, B. (ed.), *Nag Hammadi Codex I1,2–7 together with XIII, 2* Brit. Lib. Or. 4926(1) and P. Oxy.1, 654, 655. Vol. I. Gospel according to Thomas, Gospel according to Philip, Hypostasis of the Archons, Indexes; Vol. II.*

On the Origin of the World, Expository Treatise on the Soul, Book of Thomas the Contender, Nag Hammadi and Manichaean Studies 20–21, Leiden, New York and Cologne: E. J. Brill, pp. 142–214.

Letsch-Brunner, S., 'Anhang: Übersetzung von Epistula 127', in Letsch-Brunner, S., *Marcella, Discipula et Magistra. Auf den Spuren einer Römischen Christin des 4. Jahrhunderts*, Beihefte zur Zeitschrift für die Neutestamentliche Wissenschaft und die Kunde der älteren Kirche 91, Berlin and New York: Walter de Gruyter 1998, pp. 247–56.

Lipsius, R. A. and Bonnet, M., *Acta Apostolorum Apokrypha*, Darmstadt: Wissenschaftliche Buchgesellschaft 1959.

Long, A. A. and Sedley, D. N., *The Hellenistic Philosophers. Vol. 1: Translations of the Principal Sources with Philosophical Commentary; Vol. II: Greek and Latin Texts with Notes and Bibliography*, Cambridge: Cambridge University Press 1987.

Mara, M. G., *Évangile de Pierre. Introduction, texte critique, traduction, commentaire*, Sources Chrétiennes 202, Paris: Editions du Cerf 1973.

Marcus, R., *Philo: Supplement. Vols 1–2*, The Loeb Classical Library, London: William Heinemann 1953.

Metzger, M., *Les Constitutions Apostoliques*, Sources Chrétiennes 329, Paris: Editions du Cerf 1986.

Meyer, M. and Boer, E. A. de, *The Gospels of Mary. The secret tradition of Mary Magdalene the companion of Jesus*, New York: HarperSanFrancisco 2004.

Migne, J. P., *Patrologia Graeca 39, Didymus Alexandrinus*, Paris 1863.

Migne, J. P., *Patrologia Graeca 88, Gregorii Episcopi Antiocheni*, Paris 1864.

Migne, J. P., *Patrologia Graeca 132, Theophanes Kerameus* (translated into Latin by Francesco Scorso, SJ, 1644), Paris 1864.

Mohrmann, C., *Monumenta Christiana. Eerste reeks, geschriften van de kerkvaders*, Utrecht and Brussels: Het Spectrum 1948.

Muller, C. Detlef G., 'Epistulae Apostolorum', in Hennecke, E., Schneemelcher, W. and Wilson, R. McL., *New Testament Apocrypha. Volume 1 Gospels and Related Writings, Revised Edition*, Cambridge: James Clarke and Louisville, Kentucky: Westminster/John Knox Press 1991, pp. 249–84.

Oldfather, W. A., *Epictetus: The Discourses as reported by Arrian, the Manual, and Fragments*, The Loeb Classical Library, London: William Heinemann (two vols) 1967.

Pasquier, A., *L'Évangile selon Marie (BG 1): texte établi et présenté*, Bibliothèque Copte de Nag Hammadi, section 'Textes' 10, Quebec: Les Presses de l'Université Laval 1983.

Poque, S., *Augustin d'Hippone: Sermons pour la Pâque. Introduction, texte critique, traduction et notes*, Sources Chrétiennes 116, Paris: Éditions du Cerf 1966.

Robinson, J. M. (ed.), *The Nag Hammadi Library in English*, Leiden: E. J. Brill, 1988.

Scheck, T. P., *Origen: Commentary on the Epistle to the Romans Books 6–10*, Washington: The Catholic University of America Press 2001.

Schmidt, C. and Wajnberg, I., *Gespräche Jesu mit seinen Jüngern nach der Auferstehung*, Texte und Untersuchungen 43, Leipzig 1919.

Schmidt, C. (ed.), *Pistis Sofia. Translation and notes by V. MacDermot*, Nag Hammadi Studies 9, Leiden: E. J. Brill 1978.

Schoedel, W. R., 'The (First) Apocalypse of James', in Parrott, D. M. (ed.), *Nag Hammadi Codices V,2–5 and VI with Papyrus Berolinensis 8502,1 and 4*, Nag Hammadi Studies 11, Leiden: E. J. Brill, 1979, pp. 65–103.

.

.

.

Commentary on the texts.

Boer, E. A. de, *Mary Magdalene – Beyond the Myth,* London: SCM Press 1997.

—, *The Gospel of Mary: Listening to the Beloved Disciple,* New York and London: Continuum International 2005. See also *The Gospel of Mary. Beyond a Gnostic and a Biblical Mary Magdalene,* Journal for the Study of the New Testament Supplement Series 260, London and New York: T&T Clark 2004.

Bovon, F., 'Le privilège Pascal de Marie Madeleine', *New Testament Studies* 30 (1984), 50–62.

—, 'Mary Magdalene in the Acts of Philip', in F. Stanley Jones (ed.), *Which Mary? The Marys of Early Christian Tradition (Symposium Series 19),* Atlanta: Society of Biblical Literature 2002, pp. 75–90.

Brock, A., 'Setting the Record Straight – The Politics of Identification', in F. Stanley Jones (ed.), *Which Mary? The Marys of Early Christian Tradition (Symposium Series 19),* Atlanta: Society of Biblical Literature 2002, pp. 43–52.

—, *The First Apostle. The Struggle for Authority,* Harvard Theological Studies 51, Cambridge, MA: Harvard University Press 2003.

Dopp, S., and Geerlings, W., *Lexikon der antiken christlichen Literatur,* Freiburg, Basel and Vienna: Herder Verlag 2002 (revised third impression).

Duperray, E., *Marie Madeleine dans la mystique, les arts et les lettres (Actes du Colloque International, Avignon 20–21–22 juillet 1988),* Paris: Beauchesne 1989.

Gryson, R., *Le ministère des femmes dans l'Église ancienne,* Recherches et syntheses, section d'histoire IV, Gembloux: Editions J. Duculot, SA 1972, English translation *The Ministry of Women in the Early Church,* Collegeville, MN: Liturgical Press 1976.

Jantzen, G. M., *Power, Gender and Christian Mysticism,* Cambridge Studies in Ideology and Religion 8, Cambridge: Cambridge University Press 1997.

Jensen, A., *Gottes selbstbewusste Tochter. Frauenemanzipation im frühen Christentum,* Freiburg, Basle and Vienna: Herder Verlag 1992, English translation *God's Self Confident Daughters: Early Christianity and the Liberation of Women,* Louisville, KY: Westminster/John Knox Press 1996.

Kidd, I. G., 'Posidonius on Emotions', in A. A. Long, *Problems in Stoicism.* London: Athlone Press 1971, pp. 200–15.

King, K. L., *Gospel of Mary of Magdala. Jesus and the First Woman Apostle,* Sonoma, CA: Polebridge Press 2003.

—, 'Why All the Controversy? Mary in the Gospel of Mary', in F. Stanley Jones (ed.), *Which Mary? The Marys of Early Christian Tradition,* Symposium Series 19, Atlanta: Society of Biblical Literature 2002, pp. 53–74.

Letsch-Brunner, S., *Marcella, Discipula et Magistra. Auf den Spuren einer Römischen Christin des 4. Jahrhunderts,* Beihefte zur Zeitschrift für die Neutestamentliche Wissenschaft und die Kunde der älteren Kirche 91, Berlin and New York: Walter de Gruyter 1998.

Long, A. A., 'The Stoic Concept of Evil', *The Philosophical Quarterly* 18, 1968, pp.329–43.

MacDonald, M. Y., *Early Christian Women and Pagan Opinion. The power of the hysterical woman,* Cambridge: Cambridge University Press 1996.

Marjanen, A., *The Woman Jesus Loved. Mary Magdalene in the Nag Hammadi Library & Related Documents,* Nag Hammadi and Manichaean Studies 40, Leiden, New York and Cologne: E. J. Brill 1996.

—, 'The Mother of Jesus or the Magdalene? The Identity of Mary in the So-Called Gnostic Christian Texts', in F. Stanley Jones (ed.) *Which Mary? The Marys of Early Christian Tradition,* Symposium Series 19, Atlanta: Society of Biblical Literature 2002, pp.31–42.

Misset-van de Weg, M., 'Een toevlucht voor de zijnen: een beeld van God in de Handelingen van Thecla', in R. Roukema (ed.), *Het andere christendom: de gnosis en haar geestverwan-*

ten, Zoetermeer: Meinema 2000, pp. 115–36.

Mohri, E., *Maria Magdalena. Frauenbilder in Evangelientexten des 1. bis 3. Jahrhundert*, Marburger Theologische Studien 63, Marburg: N. G. Elwert Verlag 2000.

Newsom, C. A. and Ringe, S. H. (eds), *The Women's Bible Commentary*, Louisville, KY: Westminster/John Knox Press 1992.

Petersen, S., *'Zerstört die Werke der Weiblichkeit!': Maria Magdalena, Salome & andere Jüngerinnen Jesu in christlich-gnostischen Schriften*, Nag Hammadi and Manichaean Studies 48, Leiden, New York and Cologne: E. J. Brill 1999.

Pinto-Mathieu, E., *Marie-Madeleine dans la Littérature du Moyen Age*, Paris: Beauchesne 1997.

Roukema, R., *De uitleg van Paulus' eerste brief aan de Corinthiers in de tweede en derde eeuw*, Kampen: Kok 1996.

—, *Gnosis en geloof in het vroege christendom. Een inleiding tot de gnostiek*, Zoetermeer: Meinema, 1998, English translation: *Gnosis and Faith in Early Christianity: An Introduction to Gnosticism*, London: SCM Press 1999.

—, (ed.), *Het andere christendom: de gnosis en haar geestverwanten*, Zoetermeer: Meinema 2000.

Sandbach, F. H., *The Stoics*, London: Chatto & Windus 1975.

Schaberg, J. D., *The Resurrection of Mary Magdalene. Legends, Apocrypha, and the Christian Testament*, London and New York: Continuum 2002.

Schüssler, Fiorenza, E. (ed.), *Searching the Scriptures, Volume 2: A Feminist Commentary*, New York: Continuum and London: SCM Press 1995.

Synek, E. M., 'Die andere Maria. Zum Bild der Maria von Magdala in den östlichen Kirchentraditionen', in *Oriens Christianus* 79,1994, pp. 181–96.

Vander Stichele, C., 'Het Petrusevangelie: docetisch of polemisch?', in R. Roukema (ed.), *Het andere christendom: de gnosis en haar geestverwanten*, Zoetermeer: Meinema 2000, pp. 47–64.

General books on Mary Magdalene.

Bellevie, L., *The Complete Idiot's Guide to Mary Magdalene*, New York: Alpha Books 2005.

Burnet, R., *Marie-Madeleine (I-XXI siècle): De la pécheresse repenti à l'épouse de Jésus. Histoire de la réception d'une figure biblique*, Paris: Editions du Cerf 2004.

Haskins, S., *Mary Magdalen. Myth and Metaphor*, London: HarperCollins 1993.

Jansen, K. L., *The Making of the Magdalen. Preaching and Popular Devotion in the Later Middle Ages*, Princeton, NJ: Princeton University Press 2000.

Jones, F. Stanley (ed.), *Which Mary? The Marys of Early Christian Tradition*, Symposium Series 19, Atlanta: Society of Biblical Literature 2002.

Novels, poetic and esoteric literature.

Brown, D., *The Da Vinci Code*, New York and London: Bantam Press 2003.

Fredriksson, M., *According to Mary Magdalene*, London: Orion Books 1997.

Leloup, J.-Y., *L'Évangile de Marie: Myriam de Magdala*. Paris: Albin Michel, 1997, English translation: *The Gospel of Mary Magdalene*, Rochester, VT: Inner Traditions 2002.

Oyen, P. G. van, *Evangelie van Maria Magdalena: een vertolking met commentaar*, Deventer: Conversion Productions 1998.

Slavenburg, J., *Het evangelie van Maria Magdalena*, Deventer: Ank-Hermes 1994.

Starbird, M., *The Woman with the Alabaster Jar: Mary Magdalen and the Holy Grail*, Santa Fe, NM: Bear & Co 1993.

Stolp, H., *Maria Magdalena of het lot van de vrouw*, Baarn: Ten Have 2000.

Index